INGE K BROU
DON M BROV
FRANK E CLARKSON
PAUL S R

SUSAN R VOGEL

Psychological Androgyny
(PGPS-133)

Pergamon Titles of Related Interest

Bleier SCIENCE AND GENDER:
A Critique of Biology and Its Theories on Women
Bornstein/Bornstein MARITAL THERAPY:
A Behavioral-Communications Approach
Heilbrun HUMAN SEX-ROLE BEHAVIOR

Related Journals*

CLINICAL PSYCHOLOGY REVIEW
WOMEN'S STUDIES INTERNATIONAL FORUM

*Free sample copies available upon request

Psychological Androgyny

Ellen Piel Cook
University of Cincinnati

PERGAMON PRESS
New York   Oxford   Toronto   Sydney   Paris   Frankfurt

Pergamon Press Offices:

U.S.A.   Pergamon Press Inc., Maxwell House, Fairview Park,
Elmsford, New York 10523, U.S.A.

U.K.   Pergamon Press Ltd., Headington Hill Hall,
Oxford OX3 0BW, England

CANADA   Pergamon Press Canada Ltd., Suite 104, 150 Consumers Road,
Willowdale, Ontario M2J 1P9, Canada

AUSTRALIA   Pergamon Press (Aust.) Pty. Ltd., P.O. Box 544,
Potts Point, NSW 2011, Australia

FRANCE   Pergamon Press SARL, 24 rue des Ecoles,
75240 Paris, Cedex 05, France

FEDERAL REPUBLIC   Pergamon Press GmbH, Hammerweg 6,
OF GERMANY   D-6242 Kronberg-Taunus, Federal Republic of Germany

Copyright © 1985 Pergamon Press Inc.

Library of Congress Cataloging in Publication Data

Cook, Ellen Piel, 1952-
    Psychological androgyny

    (Pergamon general psychology series ; 133)
    Bibliography: p.
    Includes index.
    1. Androgyny (Psychology) 2. Sex differences
(Psychology) I. Title. II. Series. [DNLM:
1. Identification (Psychology). 2. Sex
Characteristics. BF 692.2 C771p]
BF692.2.C66 1985   155.3'3   84-26620
ISBN 0-08-031613-1
ISBN 0-08-031612-3 (pbk.)

Printed in the United States of America

ju
4-4-86

CONTENTS

PREFACE

Psychological androgyny is an idea whose time has come. Most simply defined, psychological androgyny refers to the balanced blending of both masculine and feminine characteristics in a given person. The idea itself is an old one. Since androgyny was "rediscovered" in the early 1970s, hundreds of articles have been published on its meaning, correlates, and consequences. Unfortunately, the rapid proliferation of conceptual articles and research reports resulted in more confusion than illumination. A sense of integration is lacking. The psychological androgyny literature is replete with conflicting definitions of basic terms; unique assessment methods and scoring procedures; contradictory research hypotheses; fragmented and often puzzling data and interpretations; and values statements variously asserted, denied, or disguised. The purpose of this book is to provide a critical review and synthesis of current theory and research and psychological practice concerning psychological androgyny for students, researchers, and practitioners. My goal was to stimulate readers to think about androgyny in a way which recognizes its complexity and encourages them to explore these ideas further for themselves.

This book on psychological androgyny differs from other books discussing the topic in several important respects. First, this book provides a unique overview of varied perspectives concerning androgyny rather than an in-depth presentation of one line of conceptualization and research (for an example, see Spence & Helmreich, 1978). I have attempted to compare and integrate these varied theoretical assumptions and lines of research. Second, I have also attempted to be as objective as possible in my analysis. Although some authors have scrupulously avoided a particular slant in their writings, still other authors appear to have accepted androgyny's virtues at the outset. The purpose of this particular book is *not* to argue that androgyny is either good or bad, but to explore its current conceptualization and implications. I hope that my own sex-role values have not unduly colored my discussion. Finally, this book is intended to provide an unusually broad (although not necessarily comprehensive) review of the androgyny concept's appearance in sex-role theory, research, and practice. Topics include the concept's foundations in earlier sex-role theory and research; definitions and assumptions about androgyny; measurement issues; results of androgyny research; suggestions for future research on androgyny; and its applications in psychological practice.

As discussed in this book, the topic of psychological androgyny is firmly rooted in a rich theoretical and empirical literature on sex roles. Two decisions were made early to maintain the focus of the book on androgyny per se, and to facilitate review of the voluminous literature. First, the literature included in the book generally addresses psychological androgyny directly. Other literature which may have implications for the study of androgyny but does not specifically discuss it is not included (for example, the extensive literature on female/male differences of various types). However, brief overviews of relevant topics in other sex-role literature (see first and last chapters) are included at various points to provide a framework for discussion of psychological androgyny.

Second, this review was intended to be extensive although not necessarily exhaustive. With a few exceptions, the references chosen for inclusion in the book are articles published in professional journals or books and book chapters. In particular, doctoral dissertations were not surveyed. Although published work certainly is not uniform in quality, this decision narrowed down the references to those which had passed some level of external professional review. These references are also more likely to be accessible to the reader. This decision should thus encourage interested readers to check out my conclusions for themselves by consulting the original references.

I am indebted to a number of individuals for their contributions to this book. Jerry Frank and Lynn Rosen of Pergamon Press provided guidance, expert handling of the manuscript, and enthusiastic support at a time when it was especially appreciated. An anonymous reviewer supplied a new focus and incisive commentary. A number of experts left their mark upon this book at various stages of development through their critiques and invaluable suggestions, most notably Pat Doherty, Nancy Downing, Beverly Prosser Gelwick, Puncky Heppner, Jim O'Neil, and Murray Scher. Liz Grimm labored cheerfully over numerous drafts and bravely tackled new challenges of the word processor. My stepdaughter Rebecca patiently respected my working habits over several summers. Finally, my husband David contributed in ways too numerous and personal to mention. This book is also his.

Psychological Androgyny
(PGPS-133)

Chapter 1
ANDROGYNY:
BACKGROUND AND CONCEPT

Thought processes of human beings inevitably involve making discriminations and contrasts: between light and dark, good and evil, you and me. Humans are unique from other living beings in their ability to confer symbolic meanings upon these perceptual distinctions. As famed anthropologist Claude Levi-Strauss stated,

> Passage from the state of Nature to the state of Culture is marked by man's (sic) ability to view biological relations as a series of contrasts; duality, alternation, opposition, and symmetry, whether under definite or vague forms, constitute not so much phenomena to be explained as fundamental and immediately given data of social reality (DeBeauvoir, 1952/1977, pp. 73–74)

Sex (gender) is a duality central to our social reality. Human beings have long known that only females menstruate, gestate, and lactate. Males' role in the magical process was far less clear until rather recently. It was known, at least, that they were "not female." What else being female/not female (or correspondingly, male/not male) meant was open for speculation. The content of this speculation has formed the history of sex roles.

Men and women have appeared to differ from one another, on the average, in ways that are as enduring, predictable, and pervasive as the physical differences to which these nonphysical differences corresponded. These reliable nonphysical differences were consistent with a social system which dichotomized family, work, and social interaction roles along sex-linked lines. Traditional assumptions about differences between men and women have inevitably colored social scientists' attempts to interpret the differences that they saw in the society in which the scientists themselves were embedded. Today, social scientists and mental health practitioners are re-examining past formulations about sex differences with a newly-critical eye, opened by the adoption of new values about how the sexes could and ought to behave. The result is a rapidly growing new body of literature on the sexes' behavior, emphasizing similarities rather than differences and individual rather than male/female differences.

1

This reformulation of the nature of the characteristics shared by, as well as contrasting, the sexes has been spurred by a new way of looking at the psychological underpinnings of sex roles. This reconceptualization greatly expanded the realm of possible variations in the sexes' behavior which could be highlighted, synthesized, and dissected. The concept underlying this new view is simple in essence but revolutionary in its implications. The concept is psychological androgyny: the blending of positive masculine and feminine characteristics within a given person. The concept permitted delineation of complex configurations of femininity and masculinity in both men and women. Most significantly, the concept of androgyny and its related assumptions challenged traditional mental health ideals for the sexes. These traditional ideals had fundamentally accepted sex role standards which, in light of recent social changes, no longer appeared desirable, enforceable, or workable. What does androgyny mean to researchers, mental health practitioners, and the public they serve in a time of rapid sex-role change? How is it related to past work on sex roles in conception if not in spirit? What have researchers learned about the correlates and consequences of sex roles, now that the range of options for theorizing about, measuring, and analyzing masculinity and femininity has opened to them? How can androgyny be useful to mental health practitioners trying to help confused clients who are sorting out the multiplicity of options suddenly exhorted for men and women, or who are struggling to overcome the consequences of conforming to a sex-role system that stunts their growth as individuals? And, what are the values about sex roles that underlie androgyny? Are they truly more growth-affirming and consistent with the realities of human behavior and/or what we believe to be true about sex roles than the more traditional values that they replace? These questions form the focus of this book.

The concept of androgyny is rooted in previous conceptions about the nature of the psychological differences between the sexes. As will be seen in the next section, traditional views of sex roles portrayed the sexes to be as psychologically different as they were physically different. New views about masculinity and femininity, which androgyny represents, utilize the same terminology as more traditional views, but reframe the concepts to acknowledge a much broader range of sex-role possibilities for members of both sexes.

THE TRADITIONAL VIEW OF SEX ROLES

Sex Roles, Masculinity, and Femininity

Differences in the behavior of men and women are linked to but not determined by physical sex. *Sex* or *gender* is the physical structure determined by chromosomes, gonads, and hormones and is for most practical purposes unalterable. The labeling of "male" versus "female" occurs at birth. *Gender identity* is the basic sense an individual develops of being female or male, which usually follows smoothly from labeling of sex at birth. Psychologists generally agree that a clear sense of physical maleness or femaleness is essential to psychological health, because there are fundamental differences in sexual functioning in adulthood (e.g., men can impregnate and women bear children as a result) (cf. Bem, 1976).

The early labeling of physical sex has a marked impact on the child's psychological development. This labeling begins the *sex-typing* process, whereby a person acquires and values the particular characteristics considered appropriate for her or his sex in that culture (cf. Mischel, 1970). These sex-linked constellations of personality traits, attitudes, preferences, and behaviors that a person learns through the sex-typing process are *sex roles*.[1] Sex role is a multidimensional concept. A wide range of diverse personality traits, values, activity preferences, styles of adornment and social interaction, and so on is socially defined and expected as a consequence of sex labeling. *Masculinity* refers to those characteristics that have traditionally been associated with men; *femininity* with women.

Sex is innate, but sex role for a person is learned. As Jaggar (1977) crisply stated, sex roles are not determined by those concerned or assumed voluntarily; they must be learned. The result of the sex-typing process is an individual's *sex-role identity*, the pattern and level of masculine and feminine characteristics adopted and exhibited in some manner by a person. Various combinations of feminine and masculine characteristics could presumably be learned by a person, but not all combinations have been traditionally considered to be equally acceptable for men and women. A high level of masculine characteristics for men and feminine characteristics for women with the relative exclusion of the other dimension represents the traditional sex-role identities. Men and women who display these traditional sex-role identities are sometimes labeled *sex-typed*.

The characteristics typically associated with each sex are generally well known by members of a particular society. *Sex-role stereotypes* are these widely held conceptions about the sexes that attribute certain sets of characteristics uniquely to one sex. By their nature, stereotypes function to assign common characteristics to members of a given group and may or may not be accurate descriptions of the actual characteristics of any one member of the group. Stereotypes tend to exaggerate or distort the actual degree of differences between the sexes (see Basow, 1980, for a discussion of the consequences of sex-role stereotypes). Individuals' self-descriptions do not appear to be strongly related to the stereotypes they hold about the sexes (Spence,

---

[1]Some authors would prefer the use of the term gender role, to distinguish clearly these sociocultural components from biological sex (cf. Gould & Kern-Daniels, 1977; Rosen & Rekers, 1980; Unger, 1979). "Sex role" will be used to be consistent with most current terminology. For similar reasons, "sex" and "gender" will be used synonymously. A connotation of sexual behavior is not intended unless explicitly stated.

Helmreich, & Stapp, 1975). In general, though, men tend to view the characteristics typically associated with men as more descriptive of themselves than do women. The same pattern is true for women and feminine characteristics (cf. Bem, 1974; Spence et al., 1975).

The nature of the characteristics widely associated with each sex in our society has been well documented. Classic research by Broverman and associates (Broverman, Broverman, Clarkson, Rosenkrantz, & Vogel, 1970; Rosenkrantz, Vogel, Bee, Broverman, & Broverman, 1968) on sex-role stereotypes pointed out the existence of these "highly consensual norms and beliefs about the differing characteristics of men and women" (Broverman et al., 1970, p. 1). Characteristics stereotypically associated with each sex's traditional role are compiled below, and are available in a number of sources (cf. Broverman et al., 1970; Broverman, Vogel, Broverman, Clarkson, & Rosenkrantz, 1972; Forisha, 1978; Foxley, 1979).

> Men (Masculinity)—aggressive, independent, unemotional, objective, dominant, competitive, logical/rational, adventurous, decisive, self-confident, ambitious, worldly, act as a leader, assertive, analytical, strong, sexual, knowledgeable, physical, successful, good in mathematics and science, and the reverse of the feminine characteristics listed below.
>
> Women (Femininity)—emotional, sensitive, expressive, aware of others' feelings, tactful, gentle, security-oriented, quiet, nurturing, tender, cooperative, interested in pleasing others, interdependent, sympathetic, helpful, warm, interested in personal appearance and beauty in general, intuitive, focused on home and family, sensual, good in art and literature, and the reverse of the masculine characteristics above.

Despite the apparent diversity of the characteristics within each grouping above, there are some common threads linking them to one another. Two classic conceptualizations have been convenient in distilling major themes underlying femininity/masculinity distinctions. One conceptualization of masculinity and femininity that originates in familial roles is the distinction of *instrumentality* versus *expressiveness*. Instrumentality is defined as the coordination and adaptation of the family system's needs with the outside world. Expressiveness involves maintenance and regulation of the family's emotional needs and interactions within itself. Instrumentality connotes a goal orientation and a general insensitivity to the responses that others have to the person's behavior. Expressiveness connotes a sensitivity to others' responses and a concern with interpersonal relationships (Parsons & Bales, 1953). Men were assumed to have a predominantly instrumental orientation, whereas women were expressive. Skills necessary for expressive functions include nurturance and emotional expressiveness, whereas instrumental tasks require characteristics such as independence and self-reliance (cf. Spence & Helmreich, 1978).

A second framework for viewing masculinity and femininity was based on the work of Bakan (1966), who proposed the existence of two fundamental modalities of all living organisms. *Agency* is concerned with the maintenance of the organism as an individual. It involves assertive activity, differentiation, self-protection, self-expansion, an urge toward mastery, and forming separations from others. *Communion* is aimed toward integrated participation of the organism with a larger whole. It involves selflessness, relationships, contact, cooperation, union with others, and openness. Bakan argued that communion is characteristic of femininity (and women), and agency of masculinity (and men).

In sex-role literature, a blending of the instrumental and agentic commonly characterizes the core of masculinity, and of the expressive and communal for femininity. Not all of the stereotypic characteristics listed previously fit neatly into this hybrid distinction. Yet social scientists have widely accepted this abstract description of femininity and masculinity. This description has formed the basis for newly developed measures of masculinity and femininity, and has facilitated generation of research hypotheses about possible correlates and consequences of masculinity and femininity. Most importantly, however, this conceptualization of the psychological cores of these dimensions encourages expanded discussion of sex roles beyond the biological sex differentiation to which they are linked.

To summarize briefly, two sets of characteristics have been stereotypically associated with each sex in our society. Masculine characteristics have been described as involving goal orientation, assertive activity, self-development, and separations from others (instrumental/agentic). Femininity involves sensitivity, emotionality, selflessness, and interrelationships (expressive/communal). The pattern and level of feminine and masculine characteristics adopted and exhibited by a person is the sex-role identity, and is learned through the sex-typing process. A feminine sex-role identity for women and masculine identity for men was the traditional sex-role ideal, although other identity variations are possible. The nature and consequences of the masculine/feminine distinctions have been a major focus in sex-role research.

Traditional conceptualizations of femininity and masculinity maintained an emphasis upon the distinctions between the sexes. A clear differentiation between the sexes in a wide range of characteristics was viewed as typical and desirable. To some extent, the psychological differences that appeared in early childhood were believed to be linked to physical sex differences present from birth (or before). Theorists who emphasized the learned rather than innate nature of psychological sex differences still tended to view these differences as desirable.

More recent perspectives on sex roles grew from these traditional views. These new perspectives were intended to remedy some conceptual and values issues concerning sex roles that became obvious during the past two decades. One of the more influential insights in recent years has been that psychological sex differences are probably not based upon physiological differences to the extent previously thought.

The Origins of Sex Differences

In the traditional view of masculinity and femininity, the psychological attributes that presumably distinguished the sexes flowed smoothly from easily observed physiological differences. The assumption was that the sexes must be as dichotomous psychologically as they appear to be physically. This *linear model of sex differentiation* presumes that genetic differences, physiological differences, and ultimately psychological differences somehow form a logical progression (Kaplan & Bean, 1976). In this model, masculinity is not only typical in men but *expected* and healthy. Variations from the norm in an individual man's characteristics are viewed as deviant. The same reasoning applies to femininity and women. Traditionally, the sexes have indeed differed overall in clothing style, life plans and career choices, color and reading preferences—in many highly visible and more subtle ways that seemed to correspond regularly to essential physical differences. But why *do* the sexes differ psychologically from one another?

Shape, size, and reproductive differences are easily attributable to genetics. Beyond these, current research indicates that the majority of the observed modal psychological differences between the sexes are probably socioculturally determined rather than the natural consequence of biologically based differences. In a landmark book Maccoby and Jacklin (1974) sought to synthesize hundreds of single, and often singular, studies to arrive at a comprehensive picture of how the sexes differ from early childhood to adulthood. They concluded that the only "sex differences that are fairly well established" are in the areas of verbal, visual-spatial, and mathematical abilities (differences that are not present until late childhood) and aggression (present from very early childhood on). They conclude that "there are many popular beliefs about the psychological characteristics of the two sexes that have proved to have little or no basis in fact" (p. 355). In accounting for their results, they propose the interaction of biological with sociocultural processes, where one sex may have a "greater readiness to learn" (p. 363) certain types of behaviors. (See also Kaplan & Sedney, 1980, for a brief review of biological influences.)

Although Maccoby and Jacklin's procedures for synthesizing and analyzing the literature have been questioned (J. H. Block, 1976), their emphasis on the interaction of the biological with sociocultural determinants of sex differences has been echoed in other sources (cf. Parsons, 1980; Petersen, 1980). Weitz (1977) emphasized the value of distinguishing between issues of biological origins of behavior, which may produce differing predispositions for behavior, and contemporary maintenance systems, in which sociocultural institutions can have a tremendous impact on how the fundamental predisposition is elaborated.

Generally, sociocultural determinants have been given greater weight than biological factors in causing psychological sex differences. On the individual level, studies of hermaphrodites—individuals whose biological sex variables of chromosomes, hormones, and internal/external genitalia are not in agreement—provide a unique perspective on the interaction of biological and sociocultural determinants of sex roles. Because hormonal anomalies often cause hermaphrodites' genitalia to be ambiguous, the sex assigned at birth may be concordant or discordant with genetic sex. The subjects' later behavior suggested that sex-socialization processes overrode physiological factors in determining their sex-role identity. Money and Ehrhardt (1972) labeled sex of assignment and rearing as the most important determinant of sex-role identity and behavior.

On the broader social level, the sociocultural mechanisms perpetuating the roles, expectations, and sanctions governing the behavior of the sexes appear so powerful that alternatives are difficult to conceive (Laws & Schwartz, 1977). The power of these mechanisms probably accounts for why men's and women's roles are so enduring across societies and over time (Weitz, 1977). (For a brief sampling of anthropological literature, see Lee & Stewart, 1976.) In fact, alternatives *are* possible, as evolutionary changes in sex-role patterns over time illustrate. For example, the well established roles of man as breadwinner, woman as homemaker and primary parent within the nuclear family in Western society may date back only to the Industrial Revolution and the growth of the middle class (cf. Bardwick, 1979; Kaplan & Sedney, 1980; Scanzoni, 1975; Shorter, in Weitz, 1977; Spence & Helmreich, 1978).

Even though biological differences apparently do not predestine psychological differences, biological factors probably do still play a part in differentiating the behavior of women and men. As noted above, sociocultural processes may interact with some biological predispositions and influences. The relative impact of each set of influences is virtually impossible to discriminate, as the biological and the sociocultural are intermingled at the moment of sex labeling at birth. What the interaction does suggest, however, is that the impact of the biological is less direct or significant than the linear model of sex differentiation proposes. Biological factors do not appear to be necessary and sufficient determinants of observed sex differences.

The biological basis for sex differences posited in the linear model of sex differentiation has not been supported in research. Over the years, social scientists have generally recognized that learning begun after birth is primarily responsible for enduring psychological differences. Traditional theories in sex-role development have still emphasized, however, that the ideal sex roles for men and women are quite different.

THEORETICAL PERSPECTIVES ON SEX ROLES

Theoretical perspectives on sex roles have focused upon how children acquire a sex-role identity during their early years of life. Although some theorists have conceded that some changes in sex-role identity are possible, it has been generally assumed that once formed, the sex-role identity is stable and persists into adulthood. Thus, adult patterns and problems of sex roles can presumably be linked to what was developed in those early formative years. It has also been generally assumed that men do and should usually develop a strong masculine sex-role identity, and women a feminine sex-role identity.

The primary theories can be distinguished in terms of what types of variables and processes are considered most crucial in the sex-typing process. The most influential theories have been the identification, social learning, and cognitive-developmental theories. Another theory that attempted to present a synthesis of the other theories has also been influential.

Identification Theory

Mussen (1969) defined identification as "a particular kind of imitation: the spontaneous duplication of a model's complex, integrated pattern of behavior (rather than simple discrete responses), without specific training or direct reward but based on an intimate relationship between the identifier and the model" (p. 718). Identification with the same sex parent (or caretaker) presumably permits the child to learn elaborate yet subtle sex-typed patterns of characteristics without direct training, as the child attempts to become more similar to the parent in ideals, attitudes, behaviors, and feelings. This process may appear to occur naturally, without any deliberate attempt to learn on the part of the child.

Original conceptions of identification were based in Freud's psychoanalytic theory of child personality development (cf. Bronfenbrenner, 1960). Freud proposed two types of identification. For both sexes, anaclitic identification with the mother occurs in early childhood, and is founded upon the intense dependency relationship children have with their mothers. As mothers begin to withdraw some of the intense nurturance characteristic of early infancy, the young child identifies with the mother in response to this threatened loss. Girls maintain this identification with their mothers over time, and thus acquire traditional feminine characteristics. For boys, anaclitic identification is replaced by identification with the aggressor (or defensive identification), or identification with the father. Boys resolve their feelings of competition and fears of reprisal from their fathers because of the boys' desire for their mothers by becoming instead like the father. In both types of identification, the child has a strong relationship with the parent before identification occurs (see Bandura, 1969 and Mischel, 1970 for a review of early research on identification).

Although the psychoanalytic conceptions of identification have been modified somewhat over the years, the importance of children's efforts to become like a same-sex model (especially a parent) in the sex-typing process has been emphasized by many theorists. Maccoby and Jacklin (1974) summarize some common themes concerning identification and imitation in sex typing found in major sex-typing theories: (a) The rate and extensiveness of the sex-role acquisition process suggests that more than simple reinforcement occurs. Imitation must be involved; (b) parents are the most likely models in the sex-typing process, because they are highly available, powerful, and nurturant; (c) children are more frequently exposed to same-sex than other-sex models. Thus, they are likely to acquire more sex-appropriate characteristics; (d) because children are likely to imitate models whom they perceive to be similar to themselves, they will imitate same-sex models more than other-sex models.

There has been some difference of opinion about whether identification and imitation are the same thing. Maccoby and Jacklin's discussion suggests that they view the concepts to be essentially interchangeable. Bandura (1969) used the terms as synonyms to refer to learning that occurs from modeling. He noted that although other theorists make distinctions between the terms for a variety of reasons, research indicates that the same learning process appears to be involved. In contrast, Mussen's (1969) definition of identification emphasized the essential presence of an intimate relationship between the parent and child not necessarily required for imitation, and the acquisition of complex behavioral patterns in contrast to simple responses often emphasized in imitation learning. Despite these differences of opinion, both identification and imitation indicate that the child can learn sex-appropriate behavior through observation of others, without specific training.

In summary, proponents of identification assume that children acquire an extensive range of characteristics through an intimate relationship with their same-sex parent. In the child's efforts to become more like the parent, sex-appropriate characteristics are obtained.

Social Learning Theory

A classic statement of the social learning approach is provided by Mischel (1970). He defined sex typing as a process by which individuals learn to acquire, value, and adopt for themselves behavior patterns considered to be most appropriate when expressed by their sex. Sex typing is an example of the general processes by which children become socialized, and should thus be characterized by the same variables used to describe socialization in general.

The most important variables in socialization (and sex typing in particular) relate to social learning and its associated cognitive processes. Sex-role behavior is learned through a child's interaction with others in the environment. Early in life children learn to recognize gender (sex) by observing others and interpreting these differences through their own cognitive processes. Their conceptions of their own sex identity as male or female and their knowledge about their society's sex-role stereotypes are thus initially acquired by observing sex differences in behavior around them. These conceptions are likely to be highly similar but not identical to others' sex-role stereotypes and behavior, because the child forms a unique synthesis of what he or she has observed.

Observational learning and reinforcement by others are essential in developing the child's sex typing. Mischel viewed identification and imitation as essentially equivalent, because both terms describe the tendency for individuals to reproduce the characteristics exhibited by others. Mischel suggested that a child may be more likely to imitate same-sex models because (a) they perceive these models as similar to themselves, (b) these models have attributes and resources desired by the child, and (c) the child is reinforced more for learning sex-typed behavior.

Mischel argued that observational learning and cognitive processes are especially important for acquisition of sex-typed behaviors, but actual performance of behaviors that the child has already learned is strongly affected by reinforcement. Individuals learn of the different consequences for sex-typed behavior through observation of these consequences following from others' behavior as well as being directly rewarded or punished for certain behaviors themselves. The sexes rapidly learn sex-linked expectations for behavior by perceiving their parents' and others' attitudes and attributes. Gradually, sex-typed behaviors acquire different value and meaning for the sexes, and individuals learn to regulate their own behavior by their self-evaluations. Subtle discriminations and generalizations across situations and among types of behavior refine sex-typed behavior patterns.

Mischel emphasized that sex typing is a complex process resulting in many fine gradations of behavior. Because of individuals' cognitive processing of the differences they observe and the complex factors affecting what is learned by observing others, children may exhibit sex-typed behavior somewhat different from their parents', and behavior that differs across situations.

In summary, social learning theory emphasizes how the sexes develop different meaning, valuing, and frequency of behavior through observation of others, direct or indirect reinforcement of their own or others' behavior, and their own cognitive processing of these differences. Reinforcement is primarily important in determining an individual's choice among possible behaviors in a situation. Later, personal self-evaluation in terms of an individual's personal standards and rules becomes more important.

Kagan's Theory

Kagan (1964) emphasized the role of identification and social learning processes in the development of sex-role identity. He assumed that all children have a need to acquire a sex-role label for themselves typical for their sex, and will strive to make their own characteristics congruent with those recognized as desirable for their sex.

In early childhood, children learn to dichotomize the world into male versus female classes, and learn also which attributes and behaviors are considered desirable for their sex to possess. This publicly shared belief about sex-typed characteristics that the child learns is the sex-role standard. The sex-role standard is essentially a condensation of characteristics perceived in a child's parents and more generally in society. Kagan asserted that "all children have a need to acquire a self-label that matches their biological sex" (p. 145), that is, masculine for males, feminine for females, and thus matching the sex-role standard. This motivation impels the sex-typing process.

Same-sex identification forms the foundation of the sex-role identity, and is the consequence of a desire for a strong sex-role identity. In identification, children attempt to strengthen their belief that they possess the desirable psychological characteristics of their same-sex parent/parental surrogate by becoming more similar to him or her in more easily observable ways (e.g., interests and habits). In addition to the identification process, sex-role identity is affected by the actual degree to which the child acquires desirable sex-typed responses, and the child's perception that others perceive the child as possessing their characteristics. Parents' and others' rewards and punishments can facilitate the adoption of sex-typed behavior. Finally, the degree to which children perceive themselves as possessing the desired sex-typed attributes affects the strength of their sex-role identity. As they learn and perform sex-typed behaviors, the label of self as masculine or feminine should also change. The more children perceive themselves to possess sex-typed characteristics, and the more children believe that others recognize these characteristics in themselves, the stronger the children's sex-role identity will be.

Kagan thus described a process whereby a child's early dichotomization of the world as male/female coupled with a strong desire to match personal characteristics with the sex-role standard leads to different sex-role identities for the sexes. Kagan assumed that all children want to develop a sex-typed identity, and variations from the sex-traditional ideal represent failure to do so to some extent. However, he did recognize that certain aspects of the sex-role standard may cause unnecessary anxiety and restrictions for individuals, and that perhaps these aspects should be changed.

Cognitive-Developmental Theory

Kohlberg's (1966) cognitive-developmental theory links the progressive acquisition of sex typing to more general maturation in children's thinking processes. Kohlberg speculated that changes in sex typing are the "product of general motives to structure, and adapt oneself to, physical-social reality, and to preserve a stable and positive self-image" (p. 166). Children actively create their gender (sex) identity and associated sex stereotypes and values through their efforts to understand the world around them.

In cognitive-developmental theory, the content the child learns about sex roles is determined by the environment, but the child's cognitive maturation affects the *structure* of thought about sex roles (Huston, 1983). The sex-typing process is rooted in more general changes in the child's cognitive understanding of physical objects, which occurs with age. Kohlberg proposed that this common developmental process occurs because children define their sex-role concepts fundamentally in terms of physical sex differences. Sex typing thus represents a child's increasingly sophisticated cognitive organization of the world around him or her in sex-linked terms.

Self-categorization as male or female happens early in life. This self-categorization or gender identity is the foundation for organizing future information and attitudes about the sexes. At first, the gender identity is not stable. Children appear to be confused about whether their own and others' sex can be easily changed and what characteristics truly determine sex assignment. A sense of *gender constancy* depends upon attaining a certain level of conceptual growth which permits the child to understand that certain characteristics of physical objects (including sex of humans) can remain constant even though they might *seem* to change (as when women wear men's clothing).

A stable gender identity serves as the basis for stable sex-role stereotypes. The sex stereotypes that the child develops are not simple reflections of adults' behaviors or explicit lessons about sex differences from adults. Instead, stereotypes appear to arise from children's observations and interpretations of physical and role-related sex differences in our society that widely support sex distinctions. These sex stereotypes become increasingly refined over time.

Once basic sex-role concepts are formed, the child develops personal sex-typed preferences and values. Kohlberg proposed that children have a basic need to value things that are consistent with or similar to themselves, so would be positively drawn toward characteristics associated with their sex. This valuing process occurs spontaneously rather than from deliberate efforts by adults to teach these values.

Finally, after the development of a basic gender identity, sex stereotypes, and sex-typed values, the child tends to identify with a same-sex model, often a parent. This modeling process occurs because children find a same-sex person to be more similar to them, and they desire to master the attractive characteristics of that person. A deeper emotional attachment is generally the result of the identification. Kohlberg deemphasized the importance of the parents in the sex-typing process, noting that parents' attitudes may actually interfere with developing "appropriate" sex typing.

Kohlberg's theory was unique in its proposal that sex stereotypes do not necessarily become more rigid and dichotomous over time. Instead, he proposed that development of stereotypes follows a curvilinear pattern. The stereotypes are quite rigid in early childhood before a sense of gender constancy is attained. Then, children realize that not all sex-typed characteristics are crucial to maintain a gender identity, and they learn that some variations in these nonessential characteristics (e.g., hair style) can occur without changing physical sex. They should then become more flexible in their sex stereotypes with their increasing cognitive maturity.

In summary, Kohlberg proposed that qualitative changes in children's thinking processes lead to changes in children's perceptions of themselves and others. These changes are reflected in their sex-related classifications, stereotypes, and values. The role of specific learning processes and identification are secondary to the child's independent, age-related attempts to understand the nature of the sex differentiation observed within the broader society. In cognitive-developmental theory, sex stereotypes, sex-typed values, and same-sex identification are the *consequences* of a sex-typed identity rather than the cause.

Mussen's Theoretical Synthesis

Mussen (1969) attempted to provide a synthesis of ideas presented in the other theories. He suggested that learning, identification, and cognitive processes are all involved in sex typing, and emphasized the early years as crucial. Labeling by others as male or female occurs early. The sex label must be regarded by the child as positive and rewarding, and should be applied to the child with signs of love and acceptance. This label and its positive connotations motivate the child to perform sex-typed behavior.

Parents play several important roles. After sex labeling, parents promote sex typing by providing models and rewards/punishments for sex-typed behavior. Parents also actively guide children's interest in sex-appropriate activities. Reinforcement processes gradually increase a child's sex-appropriate characteristics and behaviors. Identification with same-sex parents and others is essential to deepen and refine sex-typed behavior. Although Mussen recognized identification, learning, and cognitive processes as influential, he appeared to emphasize identification as most crucial in promoting acceptance and self-confidence about adoption of same-sex characteristics.

The final set of processes Mussen described in sex typing is the cognitive processes. Over time a child's cognitive abilities increase so that the child's conceptions about sex roles also become more extensive and accurate. The child gradually comes to distinguish between invariant and less important aspects of sex roles. The final result is a sex-role identity which, once established, is fixed and stable.

Commentary

Huston (1983) provides a good summary of the social learning and cognitive developmental theories. Social learning theory defines sex typing as sex differences in behavior. A person's role in the sex-typing process is more passive or reactive in that the mechanisms for change largely originate in the environment. Observational learning and reinforcement processes generally account for the sex-typing process, although individuals' cognitive processes are given a somewhat secondary role. Sex-typed behavior is likely to be situation-specific. Changes in sex-typed behavior can occur if observational learning or reinforcement patterns are altered.

In contrast, Huston states that cognitive-developmental theory emphasizes that concepts rather than behaviors are central in the sex-typing process. The child has an active role in perceiving and organizing input from the environment. Acquisition of and changes in sex roles are to some extent limited by the child's level of cognitive and personality development.

Huston provides a detailed review of research on sex typing within the past decade. Recent research documents the importance of cognitive processing in the acquisition of sex roles, and the role of the environment in determining the content of masculinity and femininity, how they are viewed, and the actual performance of related behaviors. Same-sex parental identification has been deemphasized as a crucial source of sex-role acquisition (for an earlier review of these issues, see Maccoby & Jacklin, 1974).

More central to the discussion here are the views about sex roles, which these classic theories have perpetuated over the years. First, it was generally assumed that children of one sex develop very similar sex-role identities: masculine for boys, feminine for girls. Although the potential diversity of sex-role identities is occasionally acknowledged (cf. Mischel, 1970), the possibility of diversity is not given serious attention. Second, the traditional sex-role identities are considered to be desirable and even ideal for the sexes. Any divergence from these identities was typically labeled to be deviant (cf. Kagan, 1964). Third, the sex-role development, identity, and behavior of children are the primary focus. The early years of childhood are assumed to be critical in the sex-typing process (cf. Mussen, 1969). The theories appear to suggest that adult sex-role characteristics are the direct consequence of this early development. Social learning theory suggests that changes in learning conditions may prompt changes in sex-typed behavior (Mischel, 1970), where cognitive-developmental theory points to changes in the nature of sex stereotypes that continue into adolescence (Kohlberg, 1966; see also Huston, 1983). The implications of these ideas for the nature of sex roles in adulthood were not elaborated.

Huston's (1983) research review indicates that the variables and processes outlined in the social learning and cognitive-developmental theories continue to be influential in studies on the sex-typing process in children. Researchers are now more likely to recognize that traditional sex-role identities are not the only or necessarily the most desirable outcomes of sex-role development in childhood. It has also become clear to researchers that sex roles continue to be important in adulthood, that a range of sex-role related characteristics can be easily observed in adults, and that some of these characteristics may indeed change over time. These observations required a new theoretical framework to encompass them.

The reconceptualization of masculinity and femininity underlying androgyny opened the range of possibilities for analysis of sex roles through accepting complex patternings of feminine and masculine characteristics within and across both sexes. This new view emerged with social scientists' growing awareness of the inadequacies of the traditional model of masculinity and femininity.

THE NEED FOR CHANGE

The model of masculinity/femininity as denoting two dichotomous, sex-linked dimensions served quite well for many years. In recent years, however, a growing dissatisfaction with the traditional methods of conceptualizing sex differences has been expressed. In the early 1970s social scientists rediscovered androgyny and embraced it as providing a logical and workable alternative to the then-current but unsatisfactory model of sex roles. This was a classic case of an idea whose time had come. Part of the dissatisfaction with the existing model is traceable to ongoing social changes that highlighted the inadequacies of current views of male/female roles. A second source of dissatisfaction was social scientists' growing awareness of psychology's deficiencies in analyzing the sexes' behavior.

The Importance of Social Changes

The upsurge of the feminist movement in the past two decades underscored the outworn utility of traditional women's and men's roles and the assumptions that had perpetuated them. With industrialization and the rise of the middle class, traditional arguments for "women's proper role" became less convincing, because newly emerging occupations demanded less of men's superior physical capacities and more of the training and education that both sexes were capable of mastering. This is especially true of higher paid, powerful, high status jobs (cf. Skovholt, 1978). Occupations also increasingly required "feminine" traits such as an ability to cooperate with others, as well as "masculine" characteristics such as dominance. Labor demands accompanying World War II taught men that they could perform domestic chores, and taught women that collecting paychecks was not necessarily unfeminine. Despite the "orgy of exaggerated domesticity" that resulted after the war when adults returned to the patterns of their childhood, the old stereotypes were effectively jarred (Money & Tucker, 1975; Spence & Helmreich, 1978).

Along with the changes in the nature of work have come significant developments on the home front, which to some extent lessened the viability of traditional role distinctions, especially for women. Women's labor force participation has increased as has the divorce rate. Family size has decreased, and there is more time before and after the birth of children (cf. Hoffman, 1977; Marecek, 1979). Many women have recognized that home and family life is an important source of satisfaction in life, but that it is not the *only* source of satisfaction that they need (cf. Baruch, Barnett, & Rivers, 1983). The primary emphasis in the socialization of women upon preparation for motherhood may no longer be appropriate, for a variety of reasons.

Thus, widespread concern about sex roles is a response to a shifting social climate as well as a cause of further changes. As Spence and Helmreich (1978) stated, "the current recodification of normative expectations for the two sexes may be less a blueprint for the future than a belated recognition of contemporary societal realities" (p. 10).

Problems with Psychology's Views of Sex Roles

At the same time, and perhaps predictably so, social scientists became increasingly aware of the need to develop a new framework for discussing sex roles. Part of the problem was a simple lack of literature to address sex-role related issues, especially after childhood. Few studies of sex differences in adolescents and adults have been reported until recently. When sex differences were found in research, they were casually reported, dismissed as inconsequential, and seldom explained (cf. Kaplan & Sedney, 1980; Maccoby & Jacklin, 1974; Wesley & Wesley, 1977).

A more subtle problem with psychological research on sex differences was the manner in which these studies were conceptualized and conducted. Despite the fact that researchers tend to view themselves as objective and value-free, traditional approaches to the study of sex roles incorporated the biases of the larger society in which the scientists lived (Rebecca, Hefner, & Oleshansky, 1976). (See Kaplan & Sedney, 1980 for an extensive analysis of the effects of cultural values upon the study of sex roles.) The linear model of sex differentiation perpetuated powerful conceptions about how the sexes do and should behave.

Social scientists implicitly adopted this linear model in their study of sex differences by dividing the sexes into two nonoverlapping groups as the focus of comparison. In Spence and Helmreich's (1978) words, "the categorical variable of biological gender has been widely regarded as being so intimately associated with masculine and feminine role behaviors and with the presumed psychological differences between men and women that the distribution of the sexes on the latter variables has implicitly been assumed to be strongly bimodal—that is, sexual differentiation of modal females and males is marked and the sexes exhibit relatively little overlap" (p. 10). A focus on male versus female differences in sex-role research obscured how women and men can be similar to one another, and how individual men (or women) may differ from others of their sex on characteristics targeted as sex-role relevant.

Kaplan and Bean (1976) argued that as a result of the linear model of sex differentiation, researchers looked for and found sex differences, while similarities between the sexes were relabeled, overlooked, or dismissed. The cost of treating "similarities as inconsequential findings or, at best, unexplainable results" was a "female-male dichotomy that failed to represent the diversity of personal qualities and the complexity of the culture" (p. 2). The prevalence of between-sex studies with mixed findings and of borderline significance (cf. Maccoby & Jacklin, 1974) clearly indicates that these between-sex differences are not as robust as once assumed.

Whether or not there were significant female/male differences in studies, there have always been individuals whose responses diverged to some extent from the typical responses of their sex. Researchers considered such individual variability to be a nuisance and dismissed it, or labeled it as an indication of deviance in the respondent. Conformity in sex-appropriate characteristics was assumed to be an index of an individual's normality, with deviation implying maladjustment of some sort (Spence & Helmreich, 1978). Thus, the many individuals whose responses did not fit the dichotomous model of sex roles were labeled as deviant themselves.

An area of sex-role research that social scientists began to view as particularly problematic was masculinity-femininity (m-f) trait research, which will be discussed in more detail in the next chapter. In brief, researchers had believed that a single trait described the psychological differences between the sexes. Over time, research documented how measures based on this single trait idea were inadequate in representing how the sexes were different and similar to one another psychologically. Measurement of femininity and masculinity would continue but with different assumptions, formats, and hypotheses.

The linear model of sex differentiation that posed the sexes to be actually or ideally as psychologically different as they were physically different shaped the way social scientists explored sex roles. Gradually it was recognized that these preconceptions about the sexes did not account for the presence of between-sex similarities and within-sex differences. Awareness of broader sex-role changes in society highlighted how inadequate the practice was of labeling as deviant any behavior that countered traditional sex-role standards. A more sophisticated model of sex roles was needed, one which could conceptualize similarities *between* the sexes and differences *within* each sex as well as the reverse. Such a model was available—one which posited masculinity and femininity as positive traits existing in everyone regardless of sex and which had favorable implications for all. The coexistence of positive masculine and feminine dimensions is androgyny.

THE CONCEPT OF ANDROGYNY

As a newly discovered old concept, androgyny has filled a troublesome void in sex-role theory and research: how to discuss masculinity and femininity conjointly without the prescriptive, sex-specific values of more traditional views. As Laws and Schwartz (1977) discussed in reference to sexual behavior norms, the process of naming can suddenly make an option outside of the prevailing social realities imaginable and real in itself, and thus open for consideration. With the naming of androgyny, new options for the sexes' self-descriptions and behaviors could suddenly be universally discussed. Androgyny as an alternative conceptualization in theory and research has received widespread attention. Definitions and assumptions pertinent to androgyny will be discussed in this section.

The Historical Androgynous Perspective

The idea of androgyny is an ancient one, as C. Heilbrun's (1973) essay on its roots in classical mythology and literature well illustrates. Kaplan and Sedney (1980) review the recurrence of androgynous themes in literature and religion over centuries. Whether used as a metaphor for personal wholeness or a celebration of the masculine and feminine tendencies in life itself, androgyny as a blending of the two sets of masculine and feminine characteristics has most often been seen as representing an ideal, which provides a unique set of capabilities and sensibilities.

In the psychological literature, discussion of the benefits of androgyny is more recent. Years ago Carl Jung spoke of masculinity and femininity as inherent in everyone, with both striving for recognition and integration within the functioning of each individual. Jung emphasized the need for all individuals to recognize and integrate within themselves those cross-sex characteristics that are inconsistent with dominant sex-role traits. This integration is essential to personal wholeness (Olds, 1981). Bakan (1966) associated personal maturity with the integration of agency (masculinity) and communion (femininity) in a person. Bakan's two modalities represented qualitative differences in the sexes' personalities for Carlson (1971, 1972), who spoke of the need for a model of sex differences that could accommodate psychological and social processes as well as genetic differences. J. H. Block (1973) used these two dimensions to describe sex-role behaviors beyond the typical male-female differences. Androgyny, as defined by Block, represents a successful balancing of agency and communion, a process that involves coping with the demands of each dimension. With Bem's (1974) pioneering work came a method for measuring masculinity and femininity as newly conceptualized—a research method that was the prototype for extensive research in recent years. The new trend was under way.

It is generally agreed that androgyny refers to a blending of masculinity and femininity. Beyond this, there are marked differences in what aspects of sex-role phenomena are denoted. A brief discussion of what is *not* meant by the term androgyny in this book may help clarify the topics of interest here.

What Androgyny Is Not

Although a realization of androgyny may carry with it changes in many aspects of sex roles, as used here androgyny is *not* synonymous with: (a) economic or sexual emancipation, (b) the absence of any sex-role differentiation, or (c) physical hermaphroditism or bisexuality.

First of all, androgyny in popular usage is frequently viewed as a goal of the Women's Liberation Movement, in that men and women would be viewed as complete equals in potential and worth. In speaking of the Women's Liberation Movement, Safilios-Rothschild (1972) labeled the goal as permitting individuals to develop their potentialities and inclinations without sex-related restrictions. Kaplan and Bean (1976) similarly advocated an acceptance of individual diversity in a pluralist society.

The individual fulfillment advocated by Safilios-Rothschild and Kaplan and Bean implies changes on two very different levels: in the acceptance of both feminine and masculine qualities by individuals, and in significant political and social changes in attitudes, customs, and laws. These two types of changes do not automatically follow from one another, and cannot be addressed as synonymous. The successful unification of personal masculine and feminine characteristics will not guarantee that any person will receive fair and equal treatment under the law or in the labor market. Conversely, passage and enforcement of an Equal Rights Amendment would not make any particular man or woman psychologically different. It is important to distinguish descriptions of individual functioning (androgyny) from projected social changes that involve the removal of traditional sex-role prescriptions. Kaplan and Bean (1976) also simply defined individual androgyny not as building toward certain specific roles or personalities, but helping each person to overcome personal sex-role related constraints imposed on his or her own temperament and potential. As will be seen, androgyny usually connotes something more specific.

Second, androgyny is sometimes equated as the absence of any sex-role differentiation. For Wesley and Wesley (1977), it implied a zero difference between sex stereotypes. Osofsky and Osofsky's (1972) androgynous society would have no stereotyped behavior differences in roles because of sex alone. Such a view of androgyny fails to distinguish between major role differences that have significant implications for the sexes' behavior and secondary sex-role differences that have minor impact, if any. For example, convergences in the sexes' dress styles, use of colognes, and manners may occur with no corresponding shifts in how men and women expect themselves and others to behave. These secondary differences may have no discernible relationship to the psychological dimensions of masculinity and femininity, and, even if changed, may result in little modification of the sexes' traditional modes of behavior. A truly "androgynous world" may well have many fewer basically inconsequential differences between the sexes, but limiting the definition of androgyny to such a lack of differences seems to be unnecessarily restrictive.

Third, androgyny is sometimes used as a label for physical sex ambiguity or bisexuality. The possession of both masculine and feminine physical sex characteristics (chromosomes, hormones, genitalia, etc.) or the failure to develop clearly into those of one sex is termed hermaphroditism. This physical ambiguity does not often lead to an undifferentiated sex-role identity. Such individuals typically exhibit a decidedly unambiguous masculine or feminine sex-role identity (cf. Money & Ehrhardt, 1972). Bisexuality typically refers to having sexual attraction for, and engaging in, sexual behavior with both women and men. Sexual preference is now generally viewed as separate from sex-role identity (cf. Rosen & Rekers, 1980).

What is androgyny, then? On one level, the term simply denotes the possession of masculine and feminine characteristics simultaneously by a given person. More generally, it refers to the body of psychological theory, assessment, research, and counseling/therapy approaches that recognize masculinity and femininity as independent psychological domains desirable for both sexes. A number of unique views of androgyny can be distinguished. In all of these views, a series of assumptions are generally accepted. These assumptions address the nature of the dimensions of masculinity and femininity, and their implications for behavior.

Assumptions About Androgyny

An obvious assumption about androgyny is that masculinity and femininity are discriminable dimensions that have important consequences for human behavior. This is the most universal assumption. However, there is no universal consensus of opinion on what types of variables constitute these dimensions and what exactly their implications for behavior are. This lack of consensus makes various views of androgyny very different, as will be seen in the next section. A corollary of this assumption is that the dimensions are independent but not mutually exclusive, which makes it possible to describe persons by the degree to which they simultaneously endorse each set of characteristics (cf. Kelly & Worell, 1977).

Second, positive aspects of masculinity and femininity are generally referenced in discussions of androgyny. Androgynous persons are thus described in terms such as independent and affectionate, assertive and understanding (cf. Bem, 1974), although conceivably they could also be defined as domineering and nagging, harsh and weak—negative aspects of traditional concepts of masculinity and femininity.

Third, the *combination* of both masculine and feminine characteristics is deemed to have desirable implications for an individual's behavior regardless of sex. Under this assumption, the negative consequences of traditional sex roles accrue from the elimination of one set of characteristics from a person's personality or behavioral repertoire (cf. Bem, 1974, 1975). The blending of positive masculine and feminine characteristics afforded by androgyny is supposedly superior in promoting healthy adjustment in a variety of settings.

For this proposition to work, two other assumptions must also be made. First, there should be a close correspondence between a person's possession of masculine and feminine *traits* (or underlying predispositions for behavior), and other more easily observable sex-role characteristics such as attitudes and performance of certain behaviors. Second, the two dimensions of masculinity and femininity should be about equal in desirability for both sexes. Masculinity and femininity are expected to contribute equally to the superior personal functioning of androgynous persons. The magnitude of the combination is also believed to make a difference: the more of both masculinity and femininity you possess, the better off you are.

Finally, androgyny is seen as a highly desirable, even ideal, state of being. Spence and Helmreich (1979b) noted that a basic proposition underlying androgyny theory is that perpetuation of traditional sex-role distinctions is dysfunctional. Androgyny can be the sex-role model of well-being (Kaplan, 1979). Kaplan and Sedney (1980) based their extensive analysis of sex-role literature upon this model. As Bem (1974) stated, "perhaps the androgynous person will come to define a more human standard of psychological health" (p. 162). Counselors and therapists frequently view androgynous behavior as the goal of their interventions (Baker, 1980).

Professionals quickly recognized that these assumptions provide a conceptualization of sex-role behavior that avoids traditional assumptions about sex-appropriate behavior. Variations from the old standards for the sexes could be seen as classifiable, normal, and even desirable. Counseling interventions could be more readily designed to encourage such variations, while identification of persons who could benefit from counseling around sex-role issues would be easier to accomplish. Researchers could utilize a more sophisticated approach to understanding differences between and within the sexes.

These assumptions have been generally accepted by professionals endorsing the concept of androgyny. Various definitions of androgyny to be discussed below have distinctive implications for what sex-role characteristics should be addressed in consideration of androgyny, and how these characteristics are believed to interact. Because of their powerful impact upon the androgyny literature, the conceptualizations developed by Bem (1974, 1979, 1981a) and Spence and Helmreich (1978, 1979b) will be discussed in greater detail.

What Androgyny Is

A number of formulations of psychological androgyny can be readily distinguished according to how the dimensions of masculinity and femininity are viewed.

Conjoint models. Three *conjoint* models depict the way in which masculinity and femininity together produce personal characteristics and styles unique from those of traditional sex roles. The conjoint models have been associated with specific scoring procedures recommended for use with the androgyny measures (see Chapter 2).

Perhaps the most commonly recognized view of androgyny is that of *modulation* or *balance*. In the balance view, masculinity and femininity are extreme tendencies when appearing individually without the presence of the other. When present jointly, however, each dimension tends to moderate the influence of the other, or in Bakan's (1966) terms, mitigates the other. Thus extreme aggressive, dominating characteristics of masculinity are tempered with femininity's sensitivity to others, just as femininity's possible oversubmissiveness and compliance are balanced with masculinity's independence and assertiveness. This balance notion was the basis of Bem's (1974) first conceptualization and scoring of androgyny.

The two other conjoint models address the absolute as well as the relative levels of masculine and feminine characteristics possessed by an individual. Of the three conjoint models, the *additive* model enjoys the widest acceptance at present. Androgyny in the additive model represents a summation of the independent influences of masculinity and femininity. This is essentially a "more is better" view, in that high levels of both sets of characteristics earn a person the label of androgynous, and are seen to provide more advantages than low levels (cf. Spence, Helmreich, & Stapp, 1975).

The more recent *multiplicative* or *interactive* model focuses upon the unique consequences stemming from the combination of masculinity and femininity in that androgyny would indicate "emergent properties" (Spence, 1983) that could not be predicted from levels of masculinity or femininity alone. Androgynous persons could presumably display special characteristics resulting from the potentiating interaction of the dimensions. For example, as Harrington and Andersen (1981) speculated, "increments of psychological femininity would yield larger increments of creativity among high-masculine individuals than among people with low masculinity" (p. 746). (For reviews of these models, see Harrington & Andersen, 1981; Lubinski, Tellegen, & Butcher, 1983; Spence & Helmreich, 1979c; Taylor & Hall, 1982.) The nature of the characteristics emerging from a multiplicative interaction has not been extensively described. Kaplan's (1979) proposal of hybrid characteristics as described below may appropriately fit here.

Developmental models. Two other models adopt a *developmental* perspective, where androgyny represents surpassing the known and familiar masculine/feminine dichotomy toward emergence of unique characteristics. In Kaplan's (1979) *hybrid* stage, the new behavioral patterns represent an end product of synthesis of the dimensions. Presumably, the characteristics resulting from the synthesis include, but go beyond, the original dimensions, for example, assertive-dependency or compassionate-ambition. Elements of the balance model can be noted here as well. The presence and meaning of hybrid androgynous characteristics have not been further documented.

Androgyny as *sex-role transcendence* shares the hybrid model's developmental flavor. Hefner, Rebecca, and Oleshansky (1975) and Rebecca, Hefner, and Oleshansky (1976) have postulated the existence of a final stage in development where sex-role standards become irrelevant in determination of behavior, as masculine and feminine qualities are smoothly blended together into a process orientation to life. It incorporates but extends beyond situational flexibility, because a person eliminates masculinity and femininity as separate dimensions. A distinct value orientation is apparent here; the authors regard androgyny as portrayed in other formulations to be less advanced in that the concept preserves masculinity and femininity as separate domains. Olds (1981) envisions androgyny as surpassing the old dualities of masculinity and femininity toward a fluid, integrated wholeness.

Cognitive schema theory. Androgyny as *cognitive schema* (Bem, 1981a, 1981b) shares the sex-role transcendence view's emphasis upon the elimination of traditional sex-appropriate distinctions as criteria in perceptions and decisions. In this view, androgyny represents a particular way of processing information. In contrast to sex-typed persons, androgynous persons do not use sex-related connotations as guides in their information processing, and may in fact be unaware of sex-appropriate distinctions in a given situation. In addition to the unique focus upon cognitive processing, this perspective differs from sex-role transcendence in that androgynous persons' freedom from using sex-based distinctions is not by definition developmentally superior but merely different from the processing of people who do rely upon these distinctions.

Personality trait model. In the two remaining views of androgyny, certain categories of masculine/feminine characteristics are specified to be of primary interest. In Spence and Helmreich's (1979b) *personality trait* view, androgyny denotes a certain naturally occurring high level of masculine and feminine traits in one person. Traits are defined as "internally located response predispositions or capacities that have considerable transituational significance for behavior but are neither conceptually equivalent to behavior nor its sole determinant" (p. 1037). Spence and Helmreich consider the nature of masculine and feminine traits to be a variant of the instrumental/agentic and expressive/communal distinctions. Characteristics attributable to persons labeled as androgynous are directly traced to the properties of the masculinity and femininity scales used to define them. These ideas will be discussed more fully later in the chapter.

Behavioral model. Behavioral androgyny was described in Kelly and Worell's (1977) review as representing high social competencies, in that an individual has a wide repertoire of socially approved behaviors to draw from in a variety of situations. A person may simply be skilled in selecting and performing behaviors that successfully solve problems or obtain positive social reinforcement. Androgyny as behavior flexibility should produce healthier, more adaptable persons in this complex, changeable society (Yager & Baker, 1979). Orlofsky (1981b) extended the definition of sex-role related behaviors to incorporate leisure and recreational activities and interests, vocational preferences, social and dating behaviors, and marital behaviors.

The array of definitions of androgyny described here illustrates that what the term androgyny denotes is by no means uniform in the literature. Some professionals have defined androgynous persons as those who possess both masculine and feminine traits (personality trait) where others have emphasized socially appropriate behaviors (behavioral) or a particular type of cognitive processing (cognitive schema). Others look past familiar masculine/feminine characteristics to the birth of new hybrid characteristics (hybrid view). Androgyny has connoted the balancing or moderating of masculinity and femininity by each other (modulation), the beneficial summation of both dimensions' positive qualities (additive), the potentiating interaction of the two dimensions (multiplicative), or elimination of sex-stereotypic standards in perceptions and decisions, effectively rendering the masculinity/femininity dichotomy irrelevant (sex-role transcendence or cognitive schema). These definitions are not mutually exclusive, however. Frequently, acceptance of more than one definition is implicit in a single article. Few professionals would dismiss all but one definition as untenable, preferring instead to consider the relative merits of each perspective within the group. All of the definitions do share a common judgment about the power of masculinity and femininity and the value of moving beyond a prescription based upon sex for whoever should possess and express them. With several notable exceptions, these definitions of androgyny have not been developed into theories about how and why sex-role related differences occur.

ANDROGYNY THEORY

The theoretical statements by Bem (balance, cognitive schema) and by Spence and Helmreich (personality trait, additive) are unique in their extensiveness and their demonstrated heuristic value. As perspectives on androgyny these statements stand out from the others in another important respect.

Rather than being the major focus of attention, androgyny per se simply represents part of a more comprehensive model about the interrelationships and consequences of masculinity and femininity.

Bem's Original View

Bem (1974) was originally interested in exploring how possession of masculine and feminine characteristics may have an impact on a person's flexibility of behavior across situations. Masculinity and femininity were viewed by Bem as complementary groups of positive traits and behaviors. Society labels these mutually exclusive, heterogeneous categories of attributes as more characteristic of, and desirable for, one or the other sex. Through measuring the degree to which each category is descriptive of an individual, it is possible to determine to what extent respondents are sex-typed. In other words, sex-typed individuals would have internalized society's sex-appropriate standards for desirable behavior to the relative exclusion of the other sex-appropriate characteristics.

Internalization of these stringent standards by sex-typed persons would have a marked impact on their behavior. Sex-typed persons will be more motivated to correspond to society's definitions of desirable male and female behaviors in their behavioral expectations, self-descriptions, and actual behaviors. As a result, their limited range of behaviors may cause them problems in adjusting to certain situations. In contrast, the androgynous person is one who is much less sensitive to these definitions of desirable behavior and thus is freed from the need to conform to them. He or she is able to adapt flexibly to a variety of situations, rather than using these sex-typed standards as the only guides for personally desirable behavior (Bem, 1974, 1979).

These ideas are similar to those earlier proposed by Kagan (1964). In both theories, sex-typed individuals internalize society's sex-appropriate standards for behavior, and are motivated to match their own characteristics to these standards. This process is believed to have a major impact on a range of characteristics. There is an essential difference between these theories, however. Kagan assumed that the end-product of this process, traditional sex-typing, is healthy and desirable. Acquisition of a sex-typed self-label is positive in that it facilitates learning and expression of socially desirable sex-typed characteristics. Individuals whose sex-role identities diverge from this sex-typed ideal are not given much attention in his theory, beyond being considered deviant.

For Bem, this sex-typing process has a negative result. The desire to conform to these standards can prevent individuals from engaging in adaptive behaviors that are less sex-typical. The "deviants" from this process are likely to be healthier, and have been given considerable attention in her research (cf. Bem, 1976). The difference in sex-role values inherent in these theories is clear.

Bem (1974) designed the Bem Sex Role Inventory to distinguish between people whose self-descriptions include both feminine and masculine characteristics from those whose self-descriptions are limited to one dimension alone. These differences in self-descriptions are presumably linked to pervasive differences in other sex-role related behaviors.

Gender Schema Theory

Bem's (1981a, 1981b) recent theoretical interests have shifted to cognitive processing differences between sex-typed and nonsex-typed persons. As in her original view, individuals presumably differ in the extent to which they use culturally based definitions for appropriate female and male behaviors as guides for evaluating their own and others' behaviors. The gender schema theory is more specific about how these differences occur, and what their implications for behavior are.

Recent information-processing perspectives on personality state that individuals are routinely exposed to more incoming information than they can reasonably handle. Consequently, everyone selects from this information a portion to assimilate and understand, and whenever possible, attempts to understand new information in light of previously developed concepts and associations. Individuals' information processing is aided by internal cognitive structures that permit them to perceive, interpret, and organize incoming information effectively. These cognitive structures that assist individuals in their ongoing information processing are schemas (cf. Bem, 1981a; Markus, 1977; Markus, Drane, Bernstein, & Siladi, 1982). Bem's (1981a) gender schema theory focuses upon how cognitive schema linked to society's standards for sex-appropriate behavior affect individuals' self-concepts and behavior.

Bem proposed that the process of sex-typing by which children become psychologically masculine or feminine occurs in several steps. First, children learn of the existence of sex-based distinction. throughout society, and which attributes are most appropriate to their own sex. This learning process teaches children the network of sex-linked associations, which is the content of the gender schema. Once learned, the gender schema will predispose the child to perceive the world in gender (sex)-linked terms.

Second, the gender schema functions to shape individuals' evaluations of themselves. Children learn that certain aspects of the personality are appropriate for their sex alone and thus for themselves. As a result, they begin to evaluate their own adequacy as individuals in terms of the gender schema they have recently developed. The gender schema serves as a standard for evaluating personal characteristics and behavior in line with society's definitions for the sexes. Individuals are motivated to conform to these definitions. When individuals observe their own conformity to these standards, the sex-based differentiation of the self-concept is strengthened. A traditional sex-role identity is the result. Bem does not explicitly discuss how and why certain individuals later identified as androgynous avoid this sex-typing process.

Bem's theory proposes two interesting new perspectives within androgyny theory. First, sex-typed individuals can be distinguished from nonsex-typed individuals in terms of their gender-schematic processing. Sex-typed individuals are those who, because of an "internalized motivational factor," (Bem, 1981a) organize incoming information in terms of culturally based definitions of masculinity and femininity, and whose self-concepts and behavior are shaped as a result. In contrast, sex-related connotations of attributes or behavior are not similarly salient for nonsex-typed persons. Thus in Bem's latest theoretical statements, the *content* of what constitutes the classes of masculinity/femininity is not emphasized, but rather the type of cognitive *processes*: whether a person has a generalized readiness to classify perceptions into one of the two classes and then act advisedly based upon this processing. In Bem's (1981a) words, "sex-typed individuals are seen as differing from other individuals not primarily in terms of how much masculinity or femininity they possess, but in terms of whether or not their self-concepts and behaviors are organized on the basis of gender" (p. 356).

Second, Bem (1979) proposed that androgyny measures[2] can be used to identify people who engage in gender-schematic processing. For schematic individuals, the feminine versus masculine connotations of the items should be salient to them. Their sex-typed self-descriptions in terms of these items presumably reveal their recognition of these groupings and their (cognitively based) efforts to organize their self-concepts in a manner consistent with society's distinctions between the sexes. In contrast, nonsex-typed persons would be free to respond to the individual items' content rather than their masculine/feminine connotations so central to gender-schematic processing.

Gender schema theory is unique in the androgyny literature for its emphasis upon explaining how and why sex typing and androgyny occur. Broad social values pertaining to the sexes' desirable attributes and behaviors are explicitly linked to an individual's psychological functioning. Bem's theory also addresses how the sex-related associations learned early in life continue to affect self-concepts and behavior into adulthood. Finally, her theory explicitly recognizes the presence of individual differences in sex roles. Everyone is exposed to society's lessons about sex-related dichotomies and the importance these dichotomies presumably have in many aspects of life. However, individual differences in degree of sex typing can occur depending upon "the extent in which one's particular socialization history has stressed the functional importance of the gender dichotomy" (Bem, 1981a, p. 362).

---

[2]The term "androgyny measures" will be used to denote masculinity and femininity measures that incorporate the assumptions listed here and that permit classification of androgynous types.

Gender schema theory has its roots in cognitive-developmental and social learning theory. Huston (1983) pointed out that gender schema theory and cognitive-developmental theories share a focus upon individuals' "active, constructive cognitive process" (p. 400). Huston also noted a difference in the theories' views of the origins of gender-based schemas. Cognitive-developmental theory states that physical sex differences make gender salient to individuals. The development of gender schema would thus be inevitable. In contrast, Bem (1981a) emphasized that gender salience occurs because society itself differentiates between the sexes so extensively. In gender schema theory, then, gender schema are the result of socially determined, and in Bem's view, artificial and largely unnecessary distinctions among individuals.

Gender schema theory and cognitive developmental theories also emphasize that acquisition and maintenance of sex-typed behavior patterns are rooted in individuals' conceptions of themselves. Once individuals classify themselves by sex, a motivational factor comes into play. To paraphrase Bem (1981a), an individual's self-esteem becomes the hostage of the gender schema, and individuals attempt to maintain a stable self-image consistent with the sex-differentiated world that they see around them (Kohlberg, 1966). In both theories, sex-typed patterns of interests, attitudes, behavioral preferences, and so on are the consequence of this early categorization of the self and the world in sex-differentiated terms.

Gender schema theory shares with social learning theory an emphasis upon a person's acquisition of sex-based distinctions present in the environment. Mischel (1970) stressed how individuals' sex-role related behaviors are likely to be influenced in complex ways by their learning histories and situational factors. Despite the implication of individual differences, social learning theory generally assumes that individuals become traditionally sex-typed. Variations from this pattern are not explicitly recognized. In contrast, gender schema theory speaks less of individual variability, instead focusing upon the two main categories of sex-typed versus nonsex-typed persons. Gender schema theory does recognize that traditional sex typing frequently does not occur, and thus encourages discussion of how and why these variations occur.

Spence and Helmreich's Views

Spence and Helmreich's approach is an example of psychological trait research reviewed by Mischel (1970). Mischel described a trait as "an abstraction invoked to explain enduring behavioral consistencies and differences among individuals" (p. 11). Trait approaches generally assume that the trait in question is a behavioral predisposition common to many individuals that is stable, enduring, varying in amount across individuals, and that can be inferred through various indicators. A favorite way to infer the presence of the dispositions or traits is through administration of a questionnaire. The questionnaire presumably elicits signs of the underlying disposition in the form of a person's responses. Generally, these trait indicators are believed to be related additively to the underlying disposition (e.g., the more feminine-keyed items you endorse on the questionnaire, the more of the underlying trait of femininity you are believed to possess).

Spence and Helmreich (1978, 1979b) described their interests as examining two underlying, stable trait dimensions at the core of the personality. Masculinity and femininity are characterized as internally located response predispositions or behavioral tendencies corresponding to these distinctions. Masculinity is instrumental/agentic and femininity is expressive/communal in nature (Spence & Helmreich, 1978). The terms "femininity" and "masculinity" were chosen as labels for these traits because the expressive/communal and instrumental/agentic trait dimensions have typically been associated with women and men respectively. For research purposes, Spence and Helmreich use responses on the Personal Attributes Questionnaire (PAQ) to infer the degree to which a person possesses the masculinity and femininity traits.

Spence and Helmreich are cautious in their expectations about what variables will be related to trait masculinity and femininity. Behavior in any given situation is likely to be determined by many factors other than internal response predispositions. They are interested in examining general behavioral tendencies believed to be associated with masculinity and femininity as broad trait dimensions rather than predicting a particular behavior in a particular situation. They have also cogently argued that relationships of these traits to other variables such as preferences for sex-typed activities and sex-role attitudes is low. To account for sex-role preferences and behaviors, other variables in addition to expressive and instrumental traits must be considered (see Spence & Helmreich, 1980, for a complete discussion of this issue). Finally, they have warned that it may not be correct to assume a relationship between masculinity and femininity trait scores and variables not directly related to the content of the trait measures. They predict relationships only with behavior directly related to instrumental/agentic (e.g., achievement) and expressive/communal (e.g., empathy) traits (cf. Spence & Helmreich, 1978).

Spence and Helmreich (1979b) have explicitly stated that the PAQ and their research using it are not intended to address broader concepts in the sex-role literature such as sex-role identity or sex-role stereotypes. In their research they typically compare individuals who report varying degrees of the two trait dimensions. For this purpose, they have frequently distinguished individuals with varying levels of femininity and masculinity as a way of highlighting the unique and additive effects of these trait dimensions. They warn, however, that this convention should not be interpreted as delineating sex-role (identity) categories, and that, in fact, research purposes at times might be better served by *not* grouping individuals into categories (Spence & Helmreich, 1979c).

Consistent with this focus, Spence and Helmreich employ the term "androgyny" to refer only to the possession of high levels of feminine and masculine traits. Any characteristics commonly reported by androgynous persons should be directly traceable to the instrumental/agentic and expressive/communal traits possessed by them (Spence, 1983; Spence & Helmreich, 1979b). Spence and Helmreich have generally been concerned with exploring the correlates of the total range of degrees of trait masculinity/femininity rather than focusing upon the consequences of one particular combination of levels (e.g., the high/high level combination of androgyny) (Spence & Helmreich, 1978).

Spence and Helmreich (1978) have also recognized the importance of self-definitions or self-concepts. Personal definitions about what it means to be a man or woman in the present culture are incorporated into a personal self-concept, influenced by the extent to which individuals see themselves as fitting (or see it as important to fit) their own concept of "appropriate" men or women. Spence and Helmreich are characteristically conservative in their speculations about this process. The culturally based belief systems are likely to be complexly determined, and vary among individuals and situations to some extent. The interplay between personal characteristics and eventual self-concepts is also complex. As Spence and Helmreich (1978) stated, "if, as we suspect, there is substantial variability among men and women in the constellations of sex-typed characteristics they possess, differences among individuals in the nature of their self-definitions of masculinity or femininity are the inevitable consequence" (pp. 116–117). Their research to date has centered around implications of the trait distinctions rather than exploration of correspondence between the attributes and self-concept. The former emphasis is of primary interest in this text.

Spence (1983) acknowledged that her thinking about femininity and masculinity has changed over the years. Spence and Helmreich's earliest research (Spence, Helmreich, & Stapp, 1975) used sex-stereotyped adjectives to study the nature of self-descriptions in characteristics that stereotypically differentiated between the sexes, and the relationship between these self-descriptions and broader sex stereotypes. It was assumed that trait items representing consistent stereotypes about sex differences would also be items that could indicate actual differences between the sexes (Spence & Helmreich, 1979b). These trait items could then to used to study the nature of masculinity and femininity. The instrumental/expressive content of the original items was determined after the items had been selected.

In subsequent research Spence and Helmreich shortened their list of adjectives to those items specifically describing expressive and instrumental qualities. They then argued that the instrumental/expressive distinction appears to be the foundation of the socially expected and actual differences in the personalities of men and women (Spence & Helmreich, 1979b). Their attention in later research was focused explicitly upon these trait distinctions. Recently

Spence (1983) asserted that the PAQ is a conventional personality test, the masculinity and femininity labels for their PAQ scales are misleading, and masculinity, femininity, and androgyny are "murky, unanalyzed concepts" (p. 442). Thus, their conceptualizations have become far more focused and less linked to broader conceptualizations about masculinity and femininity.

In my view, Spence and Helmreich's work is especially notable in the androgyny literature for its careful distinctions among related terms, its explicit discussion of the theoretical and statistical implications of different ways to measure androgyny, masculinity, and femininity, and its coherent program of research. Spence and Helmreich's research program is unique in how it has systematically explored facets of the same perspective. Finally, their analysis and commentary about various perspectives within the androgyny literature have helped to clarify fundamental conceptual and empirical issues in the area.

Comparison of Bem's and Spence and Helmreich's Views

In their theory and research, Bem, and Spence and Helmreich have attempted to expand conceptions of masculinity and femininity beyond the dichotomous, sex-appropriate prescriptions of earlier work on sex roles. Their theoretical ideas are also intended to explain primarily sex-role related differences in adulthood rather than sex-role acquisition in childhood. There are some important differences in how Bem in her gender schema theory (which largely incorporates her earlier work) and Spence and Helmreich in their trait approach present their focus and view of masculinity, femininity, and androgyny.

The most fundamental difference between Bem's and Spence and Helmreich's work is one of *focus.* The purpose of Bem's work appears to be to outline pervasive sex-role related processes among individuals who produce extensive sex-role differences in self-concepts, attitudes, preferences, and behavior in our society today. In Bem's view, gender schema may be expected to have a significant impact on a range of behaviors for two reasons. First, society teaches children that "the dichotomy between men and women has extensive and intensive relevance to virtually every aspect of life" (Bem, 1981a, p. 362). This dichotomy is, of course, the basis of gender schema. Second, the presence or absence of gender schema presumably shapes how individuals perceive and then react to a wide range of information. As a result, Bem has predicted that gender schema's effects should be discernible in numerous ways: through self-descriptions, memory patterns, reactions to others, and so on (recent research on gender schema is discussed in Chapter 3).

Spence and Helmreich's work appears to be far more focused in contrast: to determine the specific correlates and consequences of two personality trait dimensions that have been linked to sex differences. Spence and Helmreich

(1979b) have readily acknowledged that many aspects of sex roles as broadly defined cannot be accounted for by their trait dimensions, and that such aspects probably require different conceptualizations and measurement. However, Spence and Helmreich have also repeatedly stressed that they do not expect any significant relationships with variables that are not directly tied to their definitions of the masculinity/femininity dimensions. These differences in focus can be easily seen in how Bem, and Spence and Helmreich have justified and designed their research.

A second distinction between Bem's and Spence and Helmreich's approaches lies in how they regard femininity and masculinity as currently measured. This distinction is one of *process* versus *content.* Bem (1981a) has emphasized that her gender schema theory is one of process concerning how some individuals divide the world into male/female classes. Bem uses androgyny measures to distinguish among persons who do and do not utilize gender schematic processing. Presumably, any set of items that can evoke use of the gender schema would be appropriate for use. Not surprisingly, she favors her own Bem Sex Role Inventory, but she has stated that other androgyny measures could work equally well (Bem, 1981a). The actual content of the masculinity and femininity dimensions is irrelevant, as long as items representing these dimensions have the power to evoke the gender schema in some individuals.

In contrast, the content of femininity and masculinity dimensions is precisely the focus of Spence and Helmreich's work. Spence and Helmreich use the PAQ to assess a specific type of content associated with masculine and feminine distinctions: the instrumental and expressive trait domains. Measures in the sex-role literature that do not show a similar focus may assess other types of masculine and feminine phenomena (cf. Spence & Helmreich, 1980) and are not appropriate for Spence and Helmreich's purposes. Thus, in Bem's perspective, diverse definitions of femininity and masculinity may work well in testing the implications of her theory, where Spence and Helmreich would assert that how the dimensions are defined does indeed make a difference.

Finally, these researchers view androgyny itself quite differently: as *type* versus *label.* To Bem, androgyny represents a very specific way of looking at the world, freed of sex-based connotations that can restrict behavior. Her earlier work emphasized the superior adaptability of androgynous persons. In research, Bem is likely to compare androgynous and nonandrogynous persons to validate the existence of differences in behavior which distinguish them so clearly (Bem, 1975, 1981a). In this way, androgyny represents a type of person in Bem's theory.

Spence and Helmreich view androgyny as representing one possible combination of levels of masculinity and femininity, and in their research androgyny is accompanied by other categories representing different combinations of the traits. The term androgyny is used as a descriptive label to aid in data analysis. Spence (1983) has emphasized that they do not regard androgyny (or the other masculinity/femininity combinations) to signify a unique concept or type of person, and that characteristics of androgynous persons are phrased specifically in terms of the instrumental and expressive characteristics that they endorse.

These comparisons can be summarized in terms of *expansiveness* versus *precision*. Bem's theory and related research have been expansive in the breadth of variables involved, types of research hypotheses, and presumed implications for understanding sex roles in general. Spence and Helmreich's work has been more precise, focusing upon a well-defined type of sex-role variable, and limiting their expectations to those derived from their trait dimensions.

Spence and Helmreich's and Bem's views of masculinity, femininity, and androgyny are the best developed in the androgyny literature. Spence and Helmreich's work has provided insights into the multiple determinants of sex roles, the importance of precise definitions of variables under study, and the need for careful data analysis. However, Bem's expansive focus is more characteristic of the androgyny literature in general. Researchers have typically assumed that differences in masculinity/femininity self-descriptions point to more pervasive, underlying sex-role differences and that a wide range of variables should correspond meaningfully to masculinity/femininity differences. Except for Bem's and Spence and Helmreich's theoretical statements, androgyny theory has not progressed beyond certain central assumptions described earlier in the chapter. The androgyny measures, the foundation for androgyny research, are discussed in the next chapter. How well each of the central assumptions has been supported in research will be discussed in Chapter 3. Research pertaining to Bem's and Spence and Helmreich's theoretical statements will also be discussed in Chapter 3.

SUMMARY

Psychological androgyny refers to the blending of positive masculine and feminine characteristics within a person. This concept is rooted in previous conceptualizations about the nature of psychological differences between the sexes, but reframes the conceptualizations to acknowledge a much broader range of sex-role options for men and women alike.

Certain sets of psychological characteristics have been typically associated with each sex in our society. The pattern and level of those characteristics adopted and exhibited by an individual is the sex-role identity, which is developed by the sex-typing process. Feminine characteristics involve emotionality, selflessness, interrelationships with others, and sensitivity (expressive/communal). Masculine characteristics have been described as involving assertive activity, self-development, separation from others, and goal orientation (instrumental/agentic). Traditionally, a feminine sex-role identity for women and a masculine sex-role identity for men (with expression of few characteristics of the other dimension) have been considered ideal.

In this traditional view of masculinity and femininity, it was generally assumed that the sexes must be as psychologically different as they were physically different from each other. In this linear model of sex differentiation, the association of masculine characteristics exclusively with men and femininity with women is typical, expected, and healthy. However, research on sex differences has suggested that these associations are probably socioculturally rather than biologically determined as the traditional view of sex differences presupposes. Biological factors may interact with sociocultural processes in some undetermined manner, but the influence of biology is probably less direct than the linear model states.

Sex-role theorists over the years have generally assumed that learning after birth is primarily responsible for sex differences. These theories assumed that the typical and ideal sex-role identity for men and women resulting from the learning process was quite different, although the factors emphasized in this differentiation process were not identical for each theory. Identification theory stressed the child's efforts to become like the same-sex parent through a unique, intense emotional relationship. In social learning theory, a combination of observational learning and reinforcement processes lead to sex differences in the meaning, valuing, and frequencies of behavior. Kagan proposed the blending of identification with social learning processes. In cognitive-developmental theory, maturational changes in thinking processes are linked with children's cognitive attempts to understand the pervasive sex differences in the world around them. Mussen's theoretical synthesis tied together learning, identification, and cognitive processes. In general, these theories perpetuated similar views about the typical and desirable sex-role identities for women and men, and a focus upon how sex roles are determined by early childhood experiences. Variations in sex-role characteristics, the possibility of changes in sex roles over time, and the nature of sex roles in adulthood were given little attention.

In recent years, social scientists have found the traditional view of sex roles to be unsatisfactory. Part of this dissatisfaction stems from ongoing social changes affecting sex roles of both sexes. Social scientists also became increasingly aware of how traditional views about sex roles colored related theory and research. These views labeled prevalent between-sex similarities and within-sex differences as deviant rather than common and normal. The concept of androgyny provided a way to discuss femininity and masculinity without the prescriptive, sex-specific values of more traditional views.

As discussed here, androgyny does not connote economic or sexual emancipation, the absence of any sex-role differentiation, or physical hermaphroditism or bisexuality. In its simplest form, androgyny denotes the possession of masculine and feminine characteristics simultaneously by a person. Proponents of androgyny generally accept a series of assumptions about the nature of femininity and masculinity. Masculinity and femininity are assumed to be unique dimensions that have important consequences for behavior. These dimensions are independent but not mutually exclusive. Positive aspects of femininity and masculinity are generally addressed in discussions of androgyny. The combination of both dimensions is assumed to have desirable implications for an individual's behavior regardless of sex, so that the blending represented by androgyny is superior. It is also generally assumed that there is a close correspondence between a person's masculine and feminine self-descriptions and possession of other sex-role characteristics. The dimensions of femininity and masculinity should contribute equally to the superior functioning of androgynous persons, and possession of high levels of both dimensions is believed to be better than lower levels. Finally, androgyny is assumed to be a highly desirable, even ideal, state of being.

Although these assumptions have been widely accepted by professionals, definitions of androgyny focus upon various types of sex-role characteristics and propose different ways in which these characteristics interact in androgyny. Three conjoint models describe how masculinity and femininity together produce personal characteristics and styles unique from those of traditional sex roles. Two developmental models point to androgyny's surpassing of the feminine/masculine dichotomization in traditional sex roles. Bem's cognitive schema view discusses cognitive processing differences between androgynous and nonandrogynous persons. The final two views of androgyny relate to certain categories of masculine and feminine characteristics: personality traits or sex-role behaviors. The diversity of these definitions suggests that the term "androgyny" may encompass a range of ideas. These definitions may be compatible with one another, and more than one view may be adopted by a researcher.

Bem, and Spence and Helmreich have developed theoretical statements in which androgyny represents part of a more comprehensive model of the interrelationships and consequences of masculinity and femininity. Bem originally proposed that androgynous persons are freed from the need to conform to sex-appropriate standards for desirable behavior, and are thus able to respond flexibly in a variety of situations. Androgynous persons' freedom from sex-typed standards is considered desirable rather than deviant, as has been the case in traditional sex-role theories. In her recent gender schema theory, sex-typed persons are distinguished from nonsex-typed persons in terms of their cognitive processing rather than simply the amount of feminine or masculine attributes they possess. Sex-typed persons utilize gender schemas by which they are prone to perceive themselves and others in terms of male versus female distinctions. In contrast, nonsex-typed (or androgynous) persons do not tend to rely upon the sex-linked connotations implicit in gender schema in their cognitive processing. Gender schema theory provides a unique description for how and why differences between sex-typed and androgynous persons occur.

Spence and Helmreich conceptualize masculinity and femininity as two stable trait dimensions at the core of the personality. In their research, they have stressed that the relationships between femininity and masculinity trait scores and sex-typed behaviors should be expected only for those behaviors directly related to the instrumental/agentic and expressive/communal content of the trait dimensions. Androgyny refers to the possession of high levels of these two traits. In their view, androgyny is a label used to facilitate data analysis rather than denoting a particular type of person. Characteristics reported by androgynous persons should be predictable from the traits represented by their femininity and masculinity scores. Their research over the years has become more focused upon these trait distinctions and less related to more general conceptualizations concerning sex roles. Their work has been invaluable in highlighting the complexities of sex-role behavior, and related theory and research.

Bem and Spence and Helmreich share a focus upon sex-role related differences in adulthood, and an interest in expanding discussion of femininity and masculinity beyond assumptions of traditional theory and research on sex roles. However, there are significant differences between their work in terms of focus, how they view femininity and masculinity as currently measured (a process versus content distinction), and their conceptualization of androgyny (a type versus label distinction). In general, Bem's work has been more expansive in the range of variables encompassed, hypotheses, and implications for sex roles. Spence and Helmreich have focused more precisely upon a well-defined type of sex-role variable, personality traits, and have limited their expectations to those following directly from their definitions of these trait dimensions.

Bem, and Spence and Helmreich have had a significant impact upon theory and research on sex roles. The androgyny measures they have developed have been adopted as standards, and their conceptualizations have provided a starting point for hundreds of studies. Professionals have particularly adopted Bem's more expansive focus, assuming the presence of pervasive sex-role differences underlying differences in masculinity and femininity self-descriptions, and the correspondence of a wide range of variables to these masculinity/femininity differences.

Chapter 2
PRESENT METHODS OF
MEASUREMENT

To some extent, how social scientists measure what they observe determines how they eventually understand human behavior. And, how social scientists develop their measures in some ways reflects their present conceptions of the behavior of interest. This is especially evident in the study of sex roles. Early measures of masculinity-femininity (m-f) incorporated certain specific notions about men's and women's behavior. Recently developed measures of androgyny[1] are founded on new and quite different assumptions about sex roles. The ways in which the measures are truly different from earlier measures can be ascertained by reviewing assumptions underlying traditional measures of m-f.

MASCULINITY AND FEMININITY MEASURES: THE OLD AND THE NEW

Psychological research on sex differences has frequently utilized a trait approach, where trait is defined as "an abstraction invoked to explain enduring behavioral consistencies and differences among individuals" (Mischel, 1970, p. 11). Researchers assumed that there is one unique trait relevant to sex-role phenomena. This m-f trait is present in everyone in varying degrees, stable and powerful in its effects on a variety of behaviors, and capable of being inferred by measuring certain verbal responses or behaviors believed to be related to the trait. In this trait approach, overt behavioral differences between the sexes could be attributable to this trait. The challenges in implementing the trait approach are in defining the underlying traits, deciding what test responses can be considered to be signs of the trait, and determining whether or not the test responses do indeed tap the psychological construct as desired.

In a classic article Constantinople (1973) reviewed two major assumptions common to early m-f measures: *Unidimensionality* and *polarity*. Dimension-

[1] The term androgyny measures will be used to denote masculinity and femininity measures that incorporate the assumptions listed here and that permit classification of androgynous types.

ality refers to whether the topic under scrutiny is a singular trait or a set of presumably related but distinct subtraits. M-f was considered to be unidimensional: one general trait present in both sexes that could be accurately portrayed by one score on a measure. Bipolarity refers to how masculinity and femininity were assumed to be opposites within this single dimension. Constantinople distinguished three aspects of bipolarity in m-f measurement: (a) m-f was viewed as a continuum with extreme masculinity at one end-point, through a zero or neutral point, with extreme femininity at the other end. Responses on an m-f measure would be totaled to give the individual a score placing him or her somewhere on this continuum. Any deviation of a person's score from the pole deemed appropriate for his or her sex was viewed as undesirable; (b) masculinity and femininity were defined as logical reversals: high masculinity meant low femininity, and vice versa. It was impossible to be both simultaneously; and (c) biological sex was used as the primary criterion for item selection in development of the measures. The measure was viewed as successful if it clustered men's and women's responses into two different groups. Items were chosen that yielded significant sex differences, regardless of their content. Items could be diverse, tapping into differences of opinions, interests, attitudes, and so on. The end result was often a hodgepodge of items related only by their ability to separate the sexes statistically.

Subsequent research summarized by Constantinople indicated that these measures, and the assumptions they were designed to reflect, were problematic. As might be expected from the measures' diverse item content, correlations among individuals' scores on various measures were modest at best. Factor analyses supported Lunneborg's (1972) lament that there might be no end to the number of possible factors tapped by these measures (cf. also Engel, 1966). Constantinople (1973) concluded that m-f is probably composed of a number of subfactors rather than a single dimension, that is, it is probably more heterogeneous than homogeneous in nature. M-f as represented by the m-f measures thus appeared to be multidimensional rather than unidimensional, as had been assumed.

The issue of bipolarity was more difficult to test. Social scientists could deliberately construct the m-f measures to be either bipolar or unipolar. The nature of m-f as defined by the measures reflected their choice of bipolarity. Whether the trait itself presumed to underlie the measures is *best* portrayed as unipolar or bipolar is an issue of validity. Constantinople recommended that separation of m-f into unique dimensions may be a valuable idea to consider further.

Finally, the practice of using sex differences as the sole criterion for item selection hampered the formulation of any clear definition of m-f. As Constantinople stated, "While it is clear that something is being measured by the tests of m-f, namely, sex differences in response, the theoretical explication that would tie sex differences, regardless of content, to masculinity and femininity is absent" (p. 405). The question of just what these sex-differentiating items might mean was echoed by Pleck (1975). He noted that items that do differentiate between the sexes may represent traits that are of secondary rather than central importance in the personality. If so, the demonstrated differences between the sexes would not be so important after all.

Despite these shortcomings of measurement, masculinity and femininity remained attractive concepts in explaining behavior. Growing questions on the part of researchers and practitioners about the validity of their long-accepted notions about sex roles prompted the need for new measures to recognize the complex nature of masculinity and femininity, the independent coexistence of these characteristics in everyone, and the variability of these dimensions across and within both sexes.

The androgyny measures to be described in this chapter *are* different from traditional m-f measures in several important respects. First, usage of two separate scales to represent masculinity and femininity can permit a person's score on one scale to be independent of the score on the other scale. That is, a high score on the Masculinity scale would not automatically result in a low score on the Femininity scale, and vice versa. The scores are left free to vary independently of each other. The ability to score individuals for their degree of masculinity and femininity separately provides a much broader spectrum of classification for men and women, both within and between the sexes.

Second, masculinity and femininity are viewed as more complex dimensions than in the past. As will be seen later, several androgyny measures have scales that are each composed of a number of distinguishable factors. Some commonalities of factors have begun to emerge among the measures, which have helped to clarify what the androgyny measures are measuring as a group. Researchers have an active interest in exploring the nature of the constructs being measured and the validity of the measures supposedly assessing them.

Third, and most significant from a theoretical point of view, the notions of sex-linked typicality and desirability are reconceptualized. Previously, what was most typical for one sex (e.g., high femininity for women) was also viewed as most desirable. Now, masculinity and femininity may be more typical for one or the other sex, and more desirable by traditional social standards, but what is ultimately desirable for both sexes is possession of *both* sets of characteristics. By implication, androgyny would be most advantageous for members of both sexes. At present the sex-differentiated status quo is seen as the way it is but not necessarily the best way to be.

To summarize, the androgyny measures differ from traditional m-f measures in the usage of two separate masculinity and femininity scales, recognition of the complexity of the femininity/masculinity dimensions, and the assumption that possession of both dimensions is ultimately most desirable for everyone. Five measures incorporating these perspectives have been most frequently used in research and practice: The Bem Sex Role Inventory, The Personal Attributes Questionnaire, The ANDRO scale, and new Masculinity and Femininity scales drawn from the Adjective Check List and from the California Psychological Inventory. Each of these will be discussed in turn, along with a promising new measure of masculine and feminine role behaviors and interests.

REVIEW OF INDIVIDUAL ANDROGYNY MEASURES

The Bem Sex Role Inventory

The Bem Sex Role Inventory (BSRI)[2] was the first to be widely disseminated and is perhaps the most popular androgyny measure. The purpose of the BSRI, in Bem's words, is to "assess the extent to which the culture's definitions of desirable female and male attributes are reflected in an individual's self-description" (Bem, 1979, p. 1048). Consistent with her conceptualization of masculinity and femininity, the primary criterion for item selection was sex-based social desirability. A list of approximately 200 personality characteristics was first drawn up, which appeared to be positive in value and masculine or feminine in tone. From these preliminary items, two 20-item, logically independent Masculinity and Femininity scales were developed by selecting items that were independently judged by undergraduate women and men to be significantly more desirable in American society for men (Masculinity scale) or for women (Femininity scale). A 20-item Social Desirability scale was composed of items either positive and negative in tone (ten each) but rated as similarly desirable for both sexes. This scale is not used in classifying individuals, but during the BSRI's development helped to insure that the instrument overall was not simply encouraging a general tendency to describe oneself in a favorable light.

The instrument in its final form presents the 60 items in a list format. Directions request respondents to rate themselves on each characteristic using a 7-point scale ("never or almost never" to "always or almost always true"). Mean self-ratings on each scale are computed separately, and are used together as an index of androgyny, or a characterization of the person's total degree of sex-role identification. Recommended scoring procedures will be discussed in a later section. Bem (1979) has recently developed a 30-item form of the BSRI, omitting items that correlated highly with sex and some feminine items low in social desirability.

Bem's early research focused on examining relationships between sex-role classification and performance of sex-typical and sex-atypical behaviors in a

[2]The BSRI was originally published as a research instrument. It is now available for use from Consulting Psychologists Press, 1978.

variety of situations. Correlations between masculinity/femininity and self-esteem have also been explored. In addition, the BSRI has been widely used in a number of other sex-role studies, including statistically based critiques of the instrument itself. The impact of her work on sex-role research was recognized through the granting of one of the American Psychological Association's annual Early Career awards for 1976.

Bem's recent orientation toward gender schematic processes necessitated some reinterpretation of the use of the BSRI. Bem (1981b) asserted that the BSRI does not directly assess gender schematic processing itself, but merely labels those persons (sex-typed) who are theoretically likely to engage in it. Sex-typed persons taking the BSRI are expected to respond to the masculine/feminine connotations of the items as a consequence of their gender schematic processing. For nonsex-typed persons, the BSRI may assess their instrumentality/expressiveness as portrayed by the BSRI items' content.

Spence and Helmreich (1981) viewed the dual purpose implied in Bem's discussion as posing a theoretical dilemma: How can masculine/feminine self-images *and* gender-schematic processing be measured simultaneously? The two possibilities apparently present scoring difficulties as well, simultaneously requiring scoring of two independent continua (masculinity/femininity) and a single unitary dimension (schemata). Spence and Helmreich expressed some interest in the potential utility of the gender schema concept, but suggested that the BSRI is a measure of socially desirable instrumental and expressive traits instead.

Personal Attributes Questionnaire

In contrast to the BSRI, which reflects differential social desirability for the sexes, the Personal Attributes Questionnaire (PAQ) (Spence, Helmreich, & Stapp, 1974, 1975) is composed of scales of characteristics considered socially desirable for both sexes but more *typical* of one sex than the other. In their research Spence and her associates have explicitly defined androgyny as possessing a high degree of masculinity and femininity as the dimensions are represented on the PAQ.

The PAQ was first developed as a modification of a popular instrument to measure sex-role stereotypes, or individuals' beliefs of how men and women differ on a specified set of characteristics (cf. Rosenkrantz, Vogel, Bee, Broverman, & Broverman, 1968). The full-length PAQ is composed of those items that describe "characteristics that are not only commonly believed to differentiate the sexes but on which men and women tend to report themselves as differing" (Spence & Helmreich, 1978, p. 32). Items chosen for the Femininity and Masculinity scales were rated by undergraduate men and women to be ideal for both sexes but significantly more typical for one sex than the other. Thus, Masculinity scale items were rated as socially desirable for both sexes but more typical for men than women. Men were also more likely than women to rate these adjectives as self-descriptive. The same pattern in terms of women holds true for the Femininity scale items. A third scale (Masculinity-Femininity) contains a set of unique items judged to be both typical of and ideal for only one or the other sex. This third scale was retained because it appears to add useful information in empirical analyses, even though the items do not fit into the researchers' definitions of masculinity and femininity.

Inspection of item content indicated that the Masculinity and Femininity scales conformed to the researchers' expectations. The Masculinity scale items referred mainly to instrumental and agentic characteristics, while the Femininity scale items reflected expressive and communal attributes. The Masculinity-Femininity scale has a mixed content, with items relating to aggression and dominance (instrumental-agentic) as well as items relating to susceptibility to emotional hurt and need for emotional support (expressive-communal). These latter items are scored in a reverse direction. The masculinity-femininity items are positively correlated with agentic characteristics on the Masculinity scale and with self-esteem, and to a lesser extent are also negatively related to femininity (Spence & Helmreich, 1978).

Originally, instructions for the PAQ requested respondents to do two sets of ratings: of themselves, and of the typical male and female (usually college students). In the instrument's current use, self-ratings alone are required. The full-length scale has 23 masculine items, 18 feminine items, and 13 masculinity-femininity items (with one item unclassifiable). The shortened version of eight items per scale is usually preferred by researchers. The items are presented on a 5-point bipolar scale (example: "not at all aggressive . . . very aggressive"). Respondents are asked to choose a point on the scale that describes what kind of person they think they are. In scoring, the extreme pole of the item reflecting the scale to which it belongs ("aggressive" is masculine) is weighted 4 points, with more moderate responses scored from 3 points down to 0, the item's bipolar opposite ("not at all aggressive" = 0). It is important to note that for the Masculinity and Femininity scales, the items' bipolar opposites are not labeled as belonging to the other scale; that is, "not at all aggressive" does not belong to the Femininity scale. Although the items are presented in a bipolar fashion, they are not bipolar in Constantinople's sense, described earlier. For the Masculinity-Femininity scale items, the end point reflecting the extreme masculine response is scored 4. Respondents' scale scores are summations of their self-ratings on each item, thus ranging from a possible 0–32 points for the short form.

Typically the Femininity and Masculinity scale scores alone are used in classification of persons and in research. Androgyny is simply and operationally defined as receipt of scores on both the PAQ Masculinity and Femininity scales that exceed the combined-sex median. Spence and Helmreich have emphasized that (a) the median split method was intended to be a handy but by no means the sole method for describing the joint influence of masculinity and femininity; and (b) other types of "androgyny" beyond that of personality traits, for example, attitudinal or behavioral, may be usefully discussed and must be independently assessed (cf. Spence & Helmreich, 1978, 1979b). It is worthwhile to emphasize that Spence and Helmreich might regard the term androgyny as a convenient label for referring to certain degrees of measured masculinity and femininity rather than as a construct in and of itself. The use of the Masculinity-Femininity scale to refine analysis is under investigation (cf. Spence & Helmreich, 1978).

Spence and Helmreich's research to date has focused on three basic areas: (1) the validation of the PAQ, including populations of varying ages and socioeconomic backgrounds; (b) the relation to achievement motivation, hypothesized in previous research as related to sex (gender), self-esteem, and sex-role attitudes; and (c) familial antecedents of masculinity and femininity (Spence & Helmreich, 1978). They express interest in studying relationships between the personality traits of masculinity and femininity, and related phenomena (sex-role attitudes, behavior, and the like) as long as the measures of the latter are conceptualized and developed independently (Spence & Helmreich, 1979b).

The ANDRO Scale

The ANDRO scale (Berzins, Welling, & Wetter, 1978) is a "second-generation" androgyny measure: the rationale was explicitly patterned after that of the BSRI. The purpose was to develop a measure with separate Femininity and Masculinity scales, composed of items positive in tone but selected for their sex-typed desirability. In addition to this obvious similarity to Bem's rationale, items were selected if they were judged to be consistent with "rationally derived abstract definitions of the main content themes of Bem's Masculinity and Femininity scales" (Berzins et al., 1978, p. 128). The BSRI Masculinity scale was interpreted as composed of "a dominant-instrumental dimension comprised of themes of social-intellectual ascendancy, autonomy, and orientation toward risk," with the Femininity scale as "a nurturant-expressive dimension, containing themes of nurturance, affiliative-expressive concerns, and self-subordination" (p. 128). The nature of masculinity and femininity has not been discussed by the authors beyond assertions concerning the scales' congruence with Bem's definitions. Androgyny was conceived as emphasizing high social competence, or the openness to interpersonal and intellectual experiences. Presumably this positive characteristic can be traced back to interacting elements of both dimensions.

The ANDRO scale was developed by keying items from the Personality Research Form (PRF) (Jackson, 1967). The 56 items on the scales (29 masculinity and 27 femininity) were selected from the PRF item pool if they were seen by the authors as fulfilling the criteria listed above (i.e., were consistent with either the BSRI masculinity or femininity themes and were more desirable for the corresponding sex than the other). Ratings performed by samples of undergraduate men and women corroborated the authors' own judgments of the items' sex-typed desirability. Since the PRF had already been extensively used by the authors in previous research, this procedure permitted them to reanalyze earlier data in terms of masculinity and femininity.

In contrast to the BSRI and PAQ, which utilize mainly adjectives, the ANDRO scale items are sentences describing behaviors to which respondents answer "True" or "False." Both true and false-keyed items were included to help control for acquiescent responding. Scores for the Masculinity and Femininity subscales are calculated by summing the number of responses that match the keying for both the true and false items of each subscale. Standardized score equivalents are available. The femininity and masculinity scores can be tabulated from the entire PRF or by administration of the Interpersonal Disposition Inventory, which includes a 20 item PRF Social Desirability scale, four filler items, and five items from the PRF Infrequency scale. A median split procedure is often used as with the BSRI and PAQ, although the "undifferentiated" category (low-low) is renamed "indeterminate."

Research using the ANDRO scale has not been nearly as extensive as with the BSRI and PAQ. Relationships to a number of personality variables assessed by the PRF (such as Dependency and Social Poise) have been examined, and various validation studies have been conducted (Berzins et al., 1978).

The ACL Scales

The Masculinity and Femininity scales keyed from the Adjective Check List (ACL) (Gough & Heilbrun, 1965) were formed by rescoring a previously developed bipolar Masculinity-Femininity (M-F) scale (Heilbrun, 1976). The approach used in developing the original M-F scale utilized a criterion of sex differences in response and a fairly specific definition of psychological masculinity and femininity. Items were chosen to discriminate between men and women, and also "between college males identified with masculine fathers and college females identified with feminine mothers" (Heilbrun, 1976, p. 184). The original criteria of sex and identification were intended to provide more homogeneous or "pure" criterion groups. The method used to measure identification (see Heilbrun, 1981b) was designed to build instrumental/expressive differences into the scales. In the revision Heilbrun simply relabeled the old m-f items representing the polar extremes as either masculine or feminine and developed separate norms by sex for these two subscales. The final item pool included both socially desirable and undesirable characteristics, unlike the other inventories.

Respondents are asked to check adjectives they view as characteristic of their own behavior. Masculinity and femininity items are scored separately by the scale to which they belong. Raw scores reflect the total number of adjectives checked on each scale. The raw scores are transformed into T scores ($M = 50$, $SD = 10$), utilizing separate norm tables for the sexes. The norming procedure controlled for correlations of the scores with the total number of items checked on the ACL.

Heilbrun appears to regard the new scales as a simple modification of the parent M-F scale, as he had quoted research utilizing the single bipolar scale as evidence for the new scale's validity (cf. Heilbrun, 1981b; Heilbrun & Pitman, 1979). Studies with the ACL scales have been performed to investigate parental identification patterns as antecedents of masculinity and femininity, a research interest obvious from the item selection procedure. Topics of other studies include homosexuality, flexibility, sex differences in androgyny, cognitive variables, and miscellaneous personality characteristics (see Heilbrun, 1981b).

The CPI Scales

The Femininity and Masculinity scales keyed from the California Psychological Inventory (CPI) (Gough, 1957) were intended to supplement rather than to replace the CPI Femininity scale, which was seen by Baucom (1976) as having different purposes. Items were chosen for inclusion on the Masculinity scale if at least 70% of a sample of undergraduate men responded in a given direction and the undergraduate women endorsed it at least 10% less frequently than did the men. The same criterion in reverse was applied to select the items for the Femininity scale. Other items were added if they correlated significantly with either scale ($p < .05$) and not with the other scale. The final scales consisted of 54 masculinity items and 42 femininity items. Baucom (1980) also recommended use of a four-way sex-role typology, but preferred labeling high and low scores as those that fell in the upper or lower one third of the respondents' same-sex distributions. Baucom (1980) chose to use within-sex cut-off points rather than those based on the combined-sex score distributions because "combining the two sexes in generating norms and cut-off points for a given scale would have resulted in grouping together two samples who are known to differ on the dimension" (p. 263). Baucom also considered labeling females as masculine or males as feminine to mean that the person is behaving more like the other sex than is typical. His emphasis upon sex-based distinctions is unusual in androgyny research with the exception of the ACL scales.

Research has largely focused on exploring the personality characteristics (Baucom, 1980) and attitudinal correlates (Baucom & Sanders, 1978) of masculinity and femininity. The most recent line of research focuses upon learned helplessness (Baucom, 1983; Baucom & Danker-Brown, 1979). Baucom has emphasized that his scales assess actual behavior of the sexes rather than standards for appropriate behavior, which along with his unique scoring system may lead to lessened convergence with other androgyny measures (Baucom & Sanders, 1978).

Sex Role Behavior Scale

In contrast to these measures that tap personality traits, Orlofsky (1981b; Orlofsky, Ramsden, & Cohen, 1982) developed the Sex Role Behavior Scale (SRBS) to assess sex-role related interests and behaviors. Orlofsky recognized the presence of essential distinctions between sex-typed traits, attitudes, and social roles and behaviors. Other androgyny measures do not assess sex-role related interests and behaviors. The SRBS was designed to assess masculine and feminine behaviors in a manner analogous to other androgyny measures. This similarity permits more comprehensive investigations of the relationships among sex-role traits, attitudes, and role behaviors. Properties of the SRBS as reported here refer to the revision designed to correct problems of subscale length and internal consistency in the original version.

Item selection and scoring procedures were patterned after those used with the PAQ. A large pool of items likely to be more characteristic of one sex was generated, including: (a) leisure and recreational activities and interests; (b) social and dating behaviors; (c) vocational preferences; and (d) marital behaviors. Items were chosen for the Male-valued and Female-valued scales if they were rated by college students as desirable for both sexes but more typical of either men or women respectively. Items on the Sex-specific scale were both more typical of and desirable for one or the other sex. Internal consistency analyses narrowed the scale lengths to 80 items per scale (on the Sex-specific scale, 45 are masculine specific, 35 feminine specific). Respondents are asked to rate each item on a 5-point scale, ranging from "not at all" to "extremely characteristic" of me. Items are simply summed to provide 3 scale scores, with the Sex-specific scale represented by a single bipolar score. Average item scores for each type of item within the 3 scales (12 subscales in all) can also be calculated for more specific sex-role behavior analyses.

Orlofsky designed the SRBS to assess how individuals may exhibit role behaviors and interests stereotypically masculine and feminine yet judged to be appropriate for both sexes. Some bipolar behaviors viewed as appropriate for only one sex were also included. Examination of item content suggested some overlap with other androgyny measures, while the Sex-specific scale items reflected "physical strength, dominance, and aggressiveness" (masculinity) and "accommodation and domesticity" (femininity). Correlations among subscales on the SRBS were modest, showing that individuals are only somewhat consistent in their sex-role behavior (Orlofsky et al., 1982). Larger sex differences were found on the SRBS than on the other androgyny measures, with significant overlap on the male-valued items only (Orlofsky, 1981b). Preliminary analyses have supported the presence of a minimal relationship between the SRBS and other androgyny measures and attitudes about sex roles, indicating general independence rather than close correspondence between these sex-role related phenomena as is often assumed. Orlofsky (1981b) emphasized "the need to stop thinking of sex roles as unitary phenomena" (p. 940) and to begin to assess sex-role behaviors and interests independently from traits and attitudes.

Data pertaining to the SRBS' psychometric properties will be presented at the end of this chapter, as it is a measure unique from other androgyny measures. Except where explicitly noted otherwise, the term "androgyny measures" will refer exclusively to the trait measures discussed first, as these have received the most attention up to the present time.

COMPARISON OF THE MEASURES' CHARACTERISTICS

These relatively new androgyny measures are similar in a number of important respects. They are all based on the assumptions that masculinity and femininity are independent dimensions that are present in members of both sexes, and that operate together to furnish pleasant advantages to individuals who possess high degrees of both dimensions. Each measure requires self-description of some sort from the respondents. With each measure, men as a group score significantly higher than women on the Masculinity scale as women do on the Femininity scale. Within-sex differences form the basis for most research hypotheses. The scores yielded from the respondents' self-descriptions are used to classify a person into one of four sex-role categories. These categories are generally assumed to have distinctive implications for an individual's personality and psychological functioning. It is not surprising that these measures have been regarded by some professionals as providing essentially interchangeable assessments of the same basic ideas: masculinity, femininity, and androgyny.

But are the measures truly interchangeable? Simple inspection of the measures' basic characteristics as summarized in Table 2.1 indicates that there are indeed some obvious differences among the instruments, such as in ranges of possible scores, numbers of items, and so on. Whether these superficial differences actually mean anything in terms of how and what the instruments are measuring is not clear.

The equivalence of the measures can be more thoroughly determined by examining them in the following categories: (a) item selection procedures; (b) internal consistency and test-retest reliabilities; (c) correlations between masculinity and femininity; (d) correlations between measures; (e) scoring procedures; and (f) agreement in classification. Issues related to age and cultural differences and to social desirability will also be discussed.

Table 2.1. A Brief Summary of Scale Characteristics of Androgyny Measures

	BSRI	PAQ	ANDRO	ACL M,F	CPI M,F
Criteria for item selection	Sex-typed desirability	Sex typicality	Congruence with BSRI and sex-typed desirability	Sex-based endorsement; extreme group comparison	Sex-based endorsement
Type of item	Positive adjectives	Positive adjectives	Behavioral statements	Positive and negative adjectives	Behavioral statements
Number of items	20 per scale	8 per scale	29M, 27F	28M, 26F	54M, 42F
Presentation of items	Adjective list	Bipolar adjective	List of statements	Adjective list	List of statements
Range of possible raw scores per scale	20–140	0–32	0–29M, 0–27F	0–28M, 0–26F	0–54M, 0–42F

Note: BSRI = Bem Sex Role Inventory; PAQ = Personal Attributes Questionnaire; ANDRO = Scale from Personality Research Form; ACL M, F = from Adjective Check List; CPI M, F = from California Psychological Inventory. The short form of the PAQ described here is the one preferred by Spence and Helmreich for most research purposes. The BSRI also has a short form with ten items per scale.

Item Selection Procedures

Quite different criteria were used in item selection procedures for the measures. The BSRI incorporated *sex-typed desirability*, in that items generally positive in value were assigned to a scale only if viewed as differentially desirable for the sexes. The PAQ reflects *sex typicality* in that item selection required similar desirability for the sexes but differences in judgments about how typical the item was for each sex. Both the ANDRO scale and the ACL measures were founded in the developers' personal conceptions of what the scales' content should reflect. The ANDRO scale was further based on a criterion of sex-typed desirability. The ACL used an extreme group comparison procedure in an effort to maximize differentiation between the sexes. Items on both the ACL and CPI measures were chosen if there were marked differences in how the sexes responded to them, a *sex-endorsement* criterion.

Certainly there are precedents for utilizing each of these criteria. The BSRI reflects social psychologists' emphasis on the power of attitudes, in this case evaluative expectations for the sexes, to shape behaviors with some cross-situational consistency. The PAQ appears to embody most directly the assumptions underlying current sex-role conceptions: similar desirability of the dimensions for both sexes but "ownership" by one sex because of predominance, for whatever reason. The sex-endorsement criterion might be viewed as a behavioral version of the sex-typicality criterion, in that it reflects how the sexes in reality *do* typically behave rather than simply how individuals judge the sexes to behave.

Item selection procedures were presumably selected to implement the developers' theoretically based conceptions of the dimensions. All of the resulting item pools to some extent yield factors that pertain to the instrumental/agentic and expressive/communal distinction (see Chapter 3). This factor structure was not an explicit purpose of the scale development procedures, however. Questions have arisen about the usefulness of the procedures used in scale development.

Most criticism of selection procedures has been focused upon the BSRI. Orlofsky (1981b) noted that the criterion of sex-based social desirability failed to discriminate between aspects of masculinity and femininity that might be desirable for only one sex, and those that may be differentially desirable for both sexes. Edwards and Ashworth (1977) replicated the item selection procedure twice with male and female judges who were asked to judge how desirable the set of either the masculine or feminine characteristics was in an American female (or male). Only the items *masculine* and *feminine* were rated to be significantly more desirable for a man and woman respectively by both male and female judges. Masculine items as a group were not rated as being significantly more desirable for men; males did rate feminine items as significantly more desirable for women. Correlations between the sexes when rating the same set of items for one sex were significant and stable (above .90). Edwards and Ashworth suggested some of the discrepancies with Bem's original data could be attributable to methodological differences (number of judges used, range of rating scale, sampling and data collection), Type 1 errors in Bem's data, or response bias, although these alternative hypotheses appeared unlikely to them.

In response to Edwards and Ashworth, Bem (1979) indicated that different instructions were used in replication, in that personal ratings rather than judgments of American society's evaluations of these traits were elicited. The methodologies were simply not equivalent. (Bem's rebuttal may also be pertinent to Myers and Gonda's [1982] criticisms of the BSRI, based on data collected with a selected subgroup of BSRI items and a variety of rating targets.) A more recent replication did yield findings congruent with hers for 37 out of the 40 items on the Masculinity and Femininity scales (Walkup & Abbott, 1978).

In a more pointed critique of Bem's item selection procedures, Pedhazur and Tetenbaum (1979) tersely stated that "Bem's effort to construct measures of masculinity and femininity was destined to fail, as it was based solely on an empirical approach in which trait selection was determined by a multitude of nonindependent univariate tests of significance" (p. 1012). Her use of 400 nonindependent *t* tests to obtain a much smaller test of items indicating significant differences in desirability ratings was seen likely to promote misleading findings because of capitalization on chance. They also argued that a strictly empirical, atheoretical approach to scale development is inappropriate when questions of construct validity are likely to arise. In this case, definitions of desirability were not clarified for the initial raters, and traits chosen for inclusion may simply be *less undesirable* for one sex.

In reply, Bem (1979) argued that her scale development procedure was actually quite consistent with her theory: The judges served as "native informants" about their culture's standards for desirable behavior of the sexes. The BSRI was intended to distinguish between persons who use these standards as guides to organizing their behavior and those who do not, so such cultural standards are rightfully reflected in the scales. In addition, the initial list of 200 characteristics was rated by four independent groups of judges, and the selected items were items that all groups judged as being significantly more desirable for one or the other sex. Bem indicated that this concordance for any one item could be expected to occur by chance only 1/160,000, that is, using this criterion would result in .00125 items being chosen by chance rather than the 40 items Pedhazur and Tetenbaum question.

Heilbrun (1981b) compared the set of items chosen by his extreme group comparison to those of alternative masculinity and femininity scales derived from the ACL using variations of the differential sex endorsement procedure. Out of all the items, only about 37% were selected in two out of three studies, whereas about 13% were chosen by all three procedures. By consulting a comprehensive sex-role stereotype listing of ACL adjectives, he concluded that his own items were most consistent with college students' sex-role stereotypes.

To summarize, critiques of item selection procedures have focused mainly upon the BSRI and its criterion of sex-typed desirability, the replicability of the judges' ratings, and the statistical selection procedures. These criticisms have been convincingly countered by Bem. So far there is no evidence to suggest that any one of the item selection procedures used for the five instruments is "superior" in sampling the masculinity and femininity dimensions. The multidimensional nature of sex-role phenomena proposes that a wide range of measures may appropriately assess different aspects of these dimensions.

The various sets of present Masculinity and Femininity scales could measure quite divergent aspects of sex roles. Many researchers have operated on the assumption that the measures are interchangeable, and this assumption may not be true. The validity of this presupposition has decisive implications for how the results of various studies are interpreted singly and as a group. If the measures are truly interchangeable, researchers can integrate results from studies using different measures with confidence. If different aspects of sex roles are tapped by the androgyny measures, however, researchers must be careful to temper their conclusions about any given study in light of just what is measured by the particular instrument chosen for use in the study.

Examination of the statistical properties of the measures—internal consistency, test-retest reliabilities, correlations among scales within and between measures, and results of scoring procedures—can provide concise information about how the measures compare statistically.

Internal Consistency and Test-Retest Reliabilities

Estimates of the internal consistency of scale content, or homogeneity reliabilities, have generally been acceptably high. Wilson and Cook (1984) determined the range of the homogeneity reliabilities across all instruments to be from .62 to .88, with a median of .79. The Masculinity scales yielded somewhat higher coefficients (range = .73 to .88, median = .81) than did the Femininity scales (range = .62 to .80, median = .73). Higher coefficients were obtained for the BSRI (M = .88, F = .78), and for the PAQ (M = .80, F = .80) than for the ANDRO scale (M = .73, F = .62) and the ACL (M = .82, F = .69) (cf. Bem, 1974, Berzins et al., 1978; Helmreich, Spence, & Wilhelm, 1981; Hogan, 1977; Spence & Helmreich, 1978). The results suggest that the content areas within each measure may not be uniform in nature, although the coefficients are acceptably high in most cases.

Test-retest reliability statistics on the measures may generally be considered satisfactory for most purposes. For the ANDRO scales, it has been reported as .81 using a 3-week interval (Berzins et al., 1978); .90 for the BSRI (4 weeks) (Bem, 1974); for the ACL, as .67 (M) and .62 (F) over a 10-week period (Heilbrun, 1976); for the CPI scales, as .80 (F) and .93 (M) using a 3 week interval (Baucom, 1976). For the PAQ test-retest reliability was approximately .60 averaged over the sexes per scale for a 2.5-month period, and over .40 for any two pairs of test administrations periodically occurring over a period of 2 years (Yoder, Rice, Adams, Priest, & Prince, 1982).

Correlations Between Scales

Correlations have been computed between the Masculinity and Femininity scales of a single androgyny measure, and between examples of each type of scale (masculine or feminine) across various measures.

Correlations between masculinity and femininity within measures. One major assumption underlying the concept of androgyny is that masculinity and femininity are independent rather than bipolar in nature. If so, the correlation between the Masculinity and Femininity scales of any one instrument should approach zero. Wilson and Cook (1984) found a range of − .34 to .09. Other studies that computed the intercorrelations separately by sex found comparable results for the BSRI (Bem, 1974) and the ANDRO scale (Berzins et al., 1978). The intercorrelation was found to be higher for men taking the PAQ than for women (.47 and .14, respectively) (Spence, Helmreich, & Stapp, 1975) and for both sexes with the ACL (− .42 for men and − .24 for women) (Heilbrun, 1976). Reasons for these differences have not been clarified. In general, the size of the correlation coefficients suggests that the Femininity and Masculinity scales are imperfectly, but for most practical purposes, sufficiently independent.

Correlations between measures. A major question of interest in comparing the androgyny measures is that of convergent validity: how similar are the scales from different measures that presumably measure the same dimension?

One common method of exploring convergent validities of various measures is to compute the product-moment correlation coefficients between the corresponding scales. The median correlations for all possible pairs of major androgyny measures have been computed as .65 for the Masculinity scales and .53 for the Femininity scales (Wilson & Cook, 1984). Kelly, Furman, and Young (1978) reported mean correlations of .71 and .62 for Masculinity and Femininity scales, respectively. Correlations between the BSRI and ANDRO scales have been replicated with a number of different samples (cf. also Berzins et al., 1978; Gayton, Havu, Ozmon, & Tavormina, 1977). Correlations between the BSRI and either the ACL or the CPI scales appear to be lower but generally statistically significant (Baucom & Sanders, 1978; Small, Erdwins, & Gross, 1979). Correlations for the Femininity scales are generally quite a bit lower than those for the Masculinity scales computed with pairs of scales from the same measures, and in Small et al.'s research neither correlation was significant for women.

The statistics indicate some convergence as expected but not as high as would be desirable for scales presumably measuring the same construct. Some reasons for this modest convergence may be built into the scales. Baucom and Sanders (1978) suggested that the lower intercorrelations between the ACL and BSRI Femininity scales may be attributable in part to the more restricted range of scores on the scales as compared to the Masculinity scales. Differences in androgyny measure construction may also lower the correlations between the BSRI and ACL scales. In accounting for the lower correlations between the BSRI and PAQ, Spence and Helmreich (1978) noted that they would have classified some of the BSRI items to belong instead on the PAQ Masculinity-Femininity subscale using their own selection criteria. Helmreich, Spence, and Holahan (1979) viewed the BSRI as more complex than the PAQ, in that some items are not explicitly related to instrumental and expressive dimensions (e.g., BSRI items of "Masculine" and "Feminine"). These differences in scale composition may affect patterns of intercorrelations.

Correlations have also been computed between androgyny measures and more traditional measures of m-f. Correlations between the ANDRO scales and the M-F scale on the Minnesota Multiphasic Personality Inventory (MMPI) were close to zero; with the M-F scale on the Omnibus Personality Inventory, Masculinity = .04 (men), .08 (women), and .30 (sexes combined), and Femininity = −.22, −.16, and −.42 (Berzins et al., 1978). Correlations between the Fe scales on the California Psychological Inventory (CPI) and the BSRI were −.42 and −.25 (for Masculinity, men and women respectively) and .27 and .25 (Femininity, men and women) (Bem, 1974). Correlations between the Fe scale and the ACL scales showed larger sex differences (Masculinity = −.32 and −.34, men and women; Femininity = .60 and .20) (Baucom, 1976). Correlations between the Fe scale and the PAQ Femininity scale were close to zero, but larger for the Masculinity and Masculinity-Femininity scales in a negative direction (M = −.49 and −.42; M-F = −.64 and −.40, men and women respectively) (Spence & Helmreich, 1978). In this case, significant correlations were obtained because of item content reflecting PAQ personality characteristics as opposed to sex-typed interests. Correlations between the BSRI and the Guilford-Zimmerman Temperament Survey were also close to zero (Bem, 1974). A symbolic measure of m-f using line drawings showed a negligible relationship to BSRI scores (Hogan, 1977).

Betz and Bander (1980) systematically analyzed the relationship between m-f scores on the MMPI, Fe scores on the CPI, and masculinity and femininity scores on the BSRI and PAQ (long form). All correlations were small to moderate in size, and different to some extent by sex. Correlations with the BSRI Femininity scale were positive: MMPI m-f = .49 (men) and .16 (women); Fe scale = .25 (men) and .16 (women). For men, scores on the Fe scale were most strongly related to the PAQ Masculinity-Femininity scale (−.50), whereas for women correlations between the PAQ Masculinity-Femininity and the MMPI M-F and Fe scales were comparatively strongest (−.29 and −.33 respectively). Also using the BSRI, the PAQ, and the MMPI M-F scale, Volentine (1981) found higher correlations between the m-f measure and femininity than with masculinity for both sexes as expected. Analyses of variance by sex-role category showed that androgynous and feminine, and undifferentiated and masculine persons were not differentiated from one another. With the PAQ, no significant differences between the groups were found. Volentine interpreted the results as indicating the m-f measure's better assessment of level of femininity than of masculinity.

Reasons for the differences in magnitude of the correlations are not always apparent. The androgyny measures as a group are minimally and irregularly related to traditional measures of m-f, but in some cases an appreciable portion of the variance is common among the types of measures.

Summary

The androgyny measures share several basic assumptions about the nature of masculinity and femininity. Superficially, they are similar in their purpose and the types of scores they provide. There are also some obvious differences in number and type of items per measure. Quite different criteria were used in item selection procedures.

The meaningfulness of these obvious differences was considered through examining the statistical properties of the measures. Estimates of the measures' internal consistency indicate that the content tapped by each individual Femininity and Masculinity scale is generally uniform in nature. Scores from each scale also tend to be stable over time. As is generally assumed, the Masculinity and Femininity scales within each measure are generally independent from each other. The scales from different measures that assess the same dimension are positively correlated, but not as much as might be hoped. Correlations with traditional m-f measures are small enough to indicate that the androgyny measures are unique from these measures. As a group, these observations suggest that each androgyny measure may be satisfactory according to statistically based standards for such measures, but there are differences among the measures that should not be overlooked.

The impact of these differences on the conclusions that would be drawn from research is not clear. Bassoff and Glass (1982) reported that the average correlations between various measures of mental health and masculinity/femininity were similar regardless of what androgyny measure was used. However, the relationships they report are among the strongest and best validated in the androgyny literature (see p. 116). These relationships may be easy to discern even with less well-constructed measures. For less robust relationships, the measure used may indeed make a difference. Certain measures may be more successful than others in indicating more subtle relationships. In addition to the strength of the relationship, the type of dependent variable may be important to consider. Because the content included on the androgyny measures is not identical, some dependent variables may show a significant association with femininity/masculinity as represented by one androgyny measure, but a nonsignificant association with another measure. The differences among the androgyny measures warrant closer examination.

SCORING PROCEDURES

All of the androgyny measures yield two separate masculinity and femininity scores. From the beginning researchers have been interested in examining how varying combinations of the two dimensions have differential impacts on behavior. Questions have arisen about how the conjoint influence of masculinity and femininity can best be represented in scoring the androgyny measures.

T *Ratio Scoring*

The earliest scoring method, proposed by Bem (1974), utilized a *t* ratio statistic to determine whether the self-description in terms of masculine attributes differed significantly from self-description in feminine attributes. The difference score, Masculinity minus Femininity scale means, was normalized using the standard deviations of an individual's masculinity and femininity scores. An approximation can be computed by multiplying the difference score by a conversion factor of 2.322, which was derived from Bem's original normative samples. Individuals were classified as sex-typed if their masculinity scores were significantly different from their femininity scores (absolute value of $t \geq 2.025$, $df = 38$, $p < .05$). T ratio values that fell between plus and minus one were labeled androgynous. "Near feminine" and "near masculine" categories fell between these cutoffs ($1 < t < 2.025$ and $-2.025 < t < -1$, respectively). As Spence and Helmreich (1979c) pointed out, this method results in a distribution of scores similar to the traditional bipolar M-F scales. With Bem's method, both scores contribute equally to placement of a person's score on the continuum, whereas with the traditional m-f measures the varying proportion of masculine and feminine-keyed items included on a given measure may result in differential weighting of the final score.

The *t* ratio-scoring method was initially preferred because it determined whether a person's self-description using masculine adjectives was meaningfully different, statistically speaking, from that using feminine adjectives. It also permitted ready comparison of distributions of sex-typed persons across various populations. Bem (1979) later stated that the theoretical rationale behind the choice of *t* scores was to distinguish between individuals who tend to cluster the attributes on the inventory into two categories on the basis of sex-typed desirability from those who do not. Whatever the reasons behind the choice, *t* scores in general are statistically respectable and conceptually appealing.

Critiques of the t *ratio method.* Both the conceptualization and statistical soundness of *t* scores have been criticized. Spence and Helmreich (1979c) did not agree that a clear theoretical rationale for use of difference scores was present. In their view, the *t* ratio method implies that masculinity and femininity contribute equally but in opposite directions to their impact on behavior. Individuals high in both instrumental and expressive characteristics (as measured by the BSRI) should exhibit the *same* amount of instrumental/expressive behaviors as those low in both dimensions. They noted that use of the balance method posits a specific, joint relationship among masculinity and femininity and all other criterion variables, which they see as less likely to be valid than models recognizing more complex and varied relationships. Lenney (1979b) viewed the balance model as perhaps more complex than other models, as it requires specific directional hypotheses and constraints in how masculinity and femininity are related to other variables.

In response to Spence and Helmreich, Taylor and Hall (1982) considered the assumption of equal scores for high/high and low/low combinations to be unnecessary for the balance model. Particular patterns of main effects as Spence and Helmreich outline are also not necessary to yield interaction effects. In their view, the balance model continues to deserve empirical attention.

The *t* ratio method was soon found to have certain statistical drawbacks. Strahan (1975) pointed out some problems with its use: (a) The "independence of observations" assumption essential in uses of the *t* test is seriously compromised since the twenty responses comprising each scale may all be influenced by transient factors affecting the respondent at one point of time. The overall scale score may be drastically affected as a result. (b) The critical *t* value of 2.025 is actually quite arbitrary, because it is a function of the total number of items chosen for the scales. (c) A given respondent's *t* score simultaneously reflects mean *differences in levels* of masculinity and femininity, and *variability* in ratings. These aspects should be handled as separate variables. Strahan suggested that use of the simple difference score which is highly correlated with the *t* ratio ($r = .98$), might avoid these problems. Summation instead of subtraction of the scale scores could be used to reflect degree rather than direction of sex typing. Multiple correlation procedures might be more appropriate in relating the scales to other variables, especially with inclusion of the Social Desirability scale to consider response set interpretations. Finally, a factorial analysis of variance using the scale scores as independent variables would help to control for level differences in responding.

Taylor and Hall (1982) argued that the logical statistic for the difference score is the *absolute* rather than the *signed* m-f score. The signed score forms a traditional M-F scale and causes confusion in data interpretation, since it will be correlated positively with femininity and negatively with masculinity. The absolute difference score, however, overlooks the fact that men and women with a high absolute difference score are likely to have different (high-low versus low-high) patterns of scores. This difference score thus obscures important sex by sex-role interactions. The use of the interaction term in two-way analysis of variance to represent balanced versus sex-typed comparisons would, in their view, avoid both sets of problems (see p. 61).

Variations of the t ratio method. Several successors to the androgyny difference score have been proposed. Heilbrun has recently favored a modified difference score incorporating a level as well as a balance distinction: the sum of M and F minus the absolute value of the difference between them (Heilbrun, 1981b). This score incorporates both "extensity" (degree) and balance of endorsement. The use of a continuous score avoids the unreliability of classifications based on cut-off values. He recognized, however, that "low" androgyny confounds a variety of score patterns (low/low, high/low, and low/high). Kalin's (1979) similar procedure (dividing Heilbrun's formula by 2) was reported to result in a diminished correlation between this androgyny score and the Sex-typical scale score (e.g., masculinity and men) for both sexes. Bryan, Coleman, and Ganong (1981) preferred the use of a geometric mean score over Kalin's method. Taylor and Hall (1982) commented that Heilbrun's and Kalin's methods essentially designate either the masculinity or femininity score as the androgyny score, depending upon which score is lower. None of these modifications have attracted much attention to date.

Summary. The *t* ratio method was originally proposed to determine whether a person's masculine self-description differed significantly from the feminine self-description. The method distinguishes persons who report balanced amounts of masculine and feminine characteristics (androgynous) from those whose self-description is not balanced (nonandrogynous). Its use has prompted criticism about its conceptual and statistical soundness. The most serious criticism was that the *t* ratio method fails to consider the absolute strength of an individual's endorsement of feminine and masculine characteristics. Proposals for modifying the procedure have not become popular. A different approach to scoring, the median split method, has been widely adopted as a valuable alternative.

Median Split Scoring

In their early research on the PAQ, Spence, Helmreich, and Stapp (1975) observed the positive correlations between masculinity and femininity, and between each scale and a measure of self-esteem. They suggested that an additive model might well represent androgyny, in which "the absolute strengths of both components (influence) attitudinal and behavioral outcomes for the individual" (p. 35). To operationalize this model, they recommended splitting the total weighted subject population of both sexes at the median of both scales. Respondents are then assigned to one of four categories: high-high (androgynous), low-low (undifferentiated), and two sex-typed categories representing those who had a predominance of one set of characteristics (masculine and feminine).

Bem (1977) reanalyzed results of her previous studies and found significant differences between high-high and low-low scores on some dependent variables. Consequently, she recommended use of the median split procedure and revised the BSRI scoring manual. She stated, however, that the extent and ways in which these high/high and low/low types differ from one another are still unknown. Spence and Helmreich (1979c) have recently recommended the method as especially useful when correlations between masculinity and femininity and the dependent variable of interest are both linear, and the combination of the correlations is basically additive. The research predictions afforded by the median-split method could be as good as those provided by more complex scoring. As Lenney (1979b) emphasized, the method does not require assumptions concerning relationships to dependent variables beyond linearity.

Critiques of the median split method. Although the median split procedure is currently the method of choice, it is by no means uniformly accepted. Pedhazur and Tetenbaum (1979) attacked the median split method as crude, imprecise in classifying individuals whose scores fell close to the median, dependent on samples of convenience (e.g., classrooms) rather than on defined populations, and "unwarranted in view of the factorial complexity of the scales" (p. 1013). Sedney (1981) emphasized that median split scoring does not differentiate primarily between sex-typed and nonsex-typed persons, which was a major purpose in early androgyny research. Use of median splits derived from specific samples to classify individuals discourages generalizing the results of studies to other groups of individuals.

Other researchers have criticized the median split method for its lack of precision. The median split method simply notes whether the femininity and masculinity scores are "high" (above the median) or "low" (below the median). Potentially important information about the actual size of the scores is lost. Multivariate analyses have been proposed as an alternative that avoids this data loss (Bem, 1977; Lubinski, 1983; Richardson, Merrifield, & Jacobson, 1979).

Spence and Helmreich (1979c) recognized that the median split procedure is a simple way to represent the joint influence of masculinity and femininity. They cautioned that the *best* way to represent the dimensions may differ according to the type of data. For example, other methods are preferable if the behavior of an individual subject is to be predicted (Spence & Helmreich, 1979b). Other methods should also be used when the relationships between femininity/masculinity and dependent variables are not linear. A median split procedure can clarify if the balance method or other methods may more precisely fit a given set of data (Spence & Helmreich, 1979c).

Variations of the median-split method. Some variations of the median-split method have been proposed and briefly used in research. Sedney (1981) proposed the use of the scale mid-points or the twenty-fifth percentile to distinguish between high and low levels. DeFronzo and Boudreau (1977) suggested performing a median split with a sample of an approximately equal number of men and women and computing mean values for the dependent variable of interest for each of the four sex-role categories. Main effects and interaction of masculinity and femininity could then be tested with a two-way analysis of variance. In their view, this procedure should be more effective in detecting interaction effects than multiple regression procedures. Motowidlo (1982) proposed deriving the four-way classification using a procedure that calculates the similarity between a person's masculinity/femininity score profile and four sex-role prototype profiles, representing the most extreme examples of each type. Roe and Prange (1982) recommended calculating distances of scale scores from their respective medians, both expressed as standard scores.

Summary. The median split method was developed to represent an additive view of masculinity and femininity in which the absolute levels of both dimensions contribute to the benefits of androgyny. Respondents are assigned to one of four sex-role categories depending on whether their femininity and masculinity scores fall above or below combined-sex score medians. The most pointed criticisms have focused on its lack of precision in representing the individual's levels of the two dimensions. Spence and Helmreich have emphasized that the method should best be viewed as a *convenient* rather than the only way to portray the conjoint influence of femininity and masculinity. The method is not appropriate for all research purposes or with all types of data.

Combinations of T-Ratio and Median Split Methods

Other scoring alternatives represent compromises between the favorite *t* ratio and median-split methods. Orlofsky, Aslin, and Ginsburg (1977) recommended computing *t* scores first in the manner outlined by Bem, but classifying persons whose *t* score fell in the middle range (within $t \pm 1$) as androgynous only if their original mean scores fell above the median as well. This method was designed to capitalize upon the sensitivity of the *t* ratio to detect significant differences between masculinity and femininity, and upon the ability of the median split method to represent differences between high/low and low/low levels of endorsement. Downing (1979) similarly viewed a *t* ratio/median split hybrid as most desirable. She recommended that: (a) the difference between the scales should be $\pm .43$, a value she computed as equivalent to Bem's original *t* ratio cut-off points; and (b) median cut-offs should be sex-specific. Sedney (1981) also preferred a modified *t*-ratio procedure, but recommended use of a universally agreed-upon cut-off point rather than the sample's medians. Spence and Helmreich (1979c) agreed that the hybrid model is more sensitive to differences between masculinity and femininity scores than is the median-split method. They also pointed out that its presumed empirical superiority has not been demonstrated, and as a single model will not be likely to encompass all data.

Comparison of Scoring Methods

Such fine distinctions among scoring methods may appear to be of little practical value. Downing (1979) does conclude that research using the median split or the *t* ratio has been about equally successful in corroborating theoretically based definitions of androgyny. However, most researchers have been interested in comparing various sex-role categories to each other on a range of characteristics. This contrasting across categories requires accurate and reliable classification procedures.

The use of different scoring procedures with the same androgyny measure often results in some individuals being classified in different sex-role categories, as illustrated by Orlofsky et al. (1977). In their study, a simple median split procedure and a difference/median split procedure resulted in different classifications for 30% of the males and 27% of the females. With the difference/median split, more subjects were classified as sex-typed and fewer as undifferentiated. Spence and Helmreich (1979c) compared the classification of 1,766 high students on the PAQ using simple median splits and Orlofsky et al.'s difference/median split procedure. Agreement in classification was also obtained for roughly 75% of the cases. More respondents were classified as androgynous with the difference/median split procedure, where they would be classified as sex-typed or cross-sex typed with the simple median split procedure.

In response to Spence et al.'s (1975) critique of *t* ratio scoring, Bem (1977) compared classifications by *t* ratio and median split methods. There was little difference between the methods in classification of sex-typed persons. About 88% of the women and 80% of the men who were classified as feminine using a median split were classified as feminine or near feminine with a *t* ratio. The comparable statistics for masculine classification were 87% (women) and 96% (men). Over half of the men and two thirds of the women classified as undifferentiated (median split) were classified as androgynous with a *t* ratio. Downing (1979) criticized Bem's (1977) decision to collapse the sex-typed and "near" categories because the "near" categories are statistically more similar to the androgynous categories. Instead, Downing combined the "near" categories into a single residual category. Chi-square analyses with two samples indicated significant differences in classification as provided by Bem's median split and Downing's revised *t*-ratio methods.

To compare the effects of different scoring procedures on data analysis, Bernard (1980) analyzed scores on the 16 PF personality inventory using three procedures with the BSRI: median splits with combined-sex and separate-sex median cut-offs, and Bem's original *t*-ratio method. Discriminant analyses of the 16 PF scores were then performed and compared for the groups classified with each scoring procedure. Bernard concluded that (a) separate-sex median splits resulted in a more even frequency of sex-typed groups than with combined-sex median splits; (b) the *t*-ratio method increased the frequency of androgynous classification for women; (c) the first discriminant function derived from the analysis was very similar for both median split methods; and (d) the *t* ratio scoring produced similar but not identical results. He suggested the combined-sex median split may be the method of choice for most purposes because fewer persons are categorized as cross-sex typed (why this is desirable was not clear). Separate-sex median splits could be preferable when sex-interaction effects are to be explored.

The question of which scoring system to use may not be an issue of deciding which is superior. Taylor and Hall (1982) argued persuasively that Spence and Helmreich's median split method and Bem's *t*-ratio method represent distinct and statistically independent hypotheses about the influence of masculinity and femininity. Using a two-way analysis of variance model as a framework for discussion, they indicated that the median split procedure corresponds to main effect analysis (e.g., comparing high versus low masculinity). The *t*-ratio method suggests analyses of the interaction between masculinity and femininity so that the effects of the diagonal cells (high/high plus low/low versus high/low plus low/high) are examined. The distinction between high-highs and low-lows will be provided if there are significant main effects for masculinity and femininity. The analysis of variance model can simultaneously provide these high-high and low-low distinctions and contrasts between androgynous (balanced) and nonandrogynous (unbalanced) groups through interaction effects. Taylor and Hall view hybrid scoring procedures described earlier as confusing these two types of distinctions.

It has not yet been determined whether different scoring procedures have any appreciable impact on the accuracy of classifying individuals in research or the validity of conclusions drawn about the various sex-role categories. Bassoff and Glass (1982) reported that the average correlations between BSRI femininity/masculinity and numerous measures of psychological health were roughly similar for several scoring methods. The choice of scoring method may slant what conclusions are drawn for single empirical analyses (Spence & Helmreich, 1979c; for other examples, cf. Hoferek, 1982; Marwit, 1981). More research is needed to analyze the effects of using different scoring procedures, so that it can be determined which procedures may be most appropriate for specific purposes. Professionals reviewing studies may be wise to examine the patterns and strengths of relationships among masculinity/femininity and other variables in addition to mean differences among categories. Percentage distributions of sex-role categories between studies should also be compared if the same measure, but different scoring procedures, are used.

It has been shown that different scoring procedures with any single measure may result in somewhat different classifications of individuals. In research this variability due to scoring can interact with another source of variability in classification: that attributable to choice of androgyny measure for use.

AGREEMENT IN CLASSIFICATION ACROSS MEASURES

One question of practical significance to any user of the measure is: Are the measures truly compatible in how they tend to classify individuals into the sex-role categories? How frequently is a person likely to be placed into the same category regardless of instrument used? Usage of the androgyny measures to categorize individuals, whether in research or practice, requires either demonstration of a high degree of agreement across the measures, or prescriptive guidelines for choice of appropriate measure. Lack of agreement when it is assumed to be present may promote misleading conclusions either by researchers drawing conclusions about the behavior of any one type of person, or by practitioners interested in targeting certain types of people for special interventions.

The presence of some differences across instruments can be discerned by examining the distributions of persons across the categories for each of the major measures (see Table 2.2). Some differences according to sex can be expected.[3] For example, it is predictable that more women than men are classified as feminine. The differences in percentages of persons falling in any one category *across* the measures is a more critical issue. For example, the percentage of men classified as masculine may be either 37%, 49%, or 22%, depending on the measure used. Some of the differences are probably attributable to the fact that diverse samples of persons were used. However, the *size* of the discrepancies between the measures suggests that there may be some subtle (or not so subtle) differences among the measures themselves.

Several studies have focused on examining the degree of agreement for various combinations of the instruments. Gayton et al. (1977) determined that only 42% of a combined sample of men and women were classified into the same sex-role category by the BSRI and ANDRO scale, comparable to other results using the BSRI and ACL scales (Small et al., 1979; see also Edwards & Norcross, 1980). Comparisons of the BSRI and PAQ have yielded roughly 50% agreement or less in classification (Hatzenbuehler & Joe, 1981; Lamke, 1982). Another study utilizing all four measures found that about 54% of respondents of both sexes are placed in the same category by any given pair of measures, about 38% by any three, and about 30% in the same category when all four measures are used (Wilson & Cook, 1984). These results are consistent with those reported by Kelly, Furman, and Young (1978).

---

[3]Using a continuous androgyny score derived from the ACL and raw scores rather than standard score transformations, Heilbrun and Schwartz (1982) have concluded men score as more androgynous, presumably because of a greater balance in their endorsement. The general significance of this single study is difficult to ascertain because the androgyny measure and scoring offered in support utilized 25 subject pairs (only 5 male-female) with two 6-point rating scales serving as measures of masculinity and femininity and therefore androgyny. More adequate studies are needed.

Table 2.2. Percentage Distributions of Men and Women
in Sex-Role Categories by Androgyny Measures

Measure		Sex-Role Category			
		Undifferentiated	Feminine	Masculine	Androgynous
BSRI[a]	Men	27%	16%	37%	21%
	Women	20%	34%	16%	29%
PAQ[b]	Men	31%	13%	27%	29%
	Women	21%	39%	11%	30%
ANDRO[c]	Men	22%	10%	49%	19%
	Women	18%	48%	14%	20%
ACL M, F[d]	Men	16%	34%	22%	28%
	Women	14%	36%	22%	28%
CPI M, F[e]	Men	23%	30%	23%	25%
	Women	25%	20%	21%	33%

Note: Percentages are computed by row.

[a]BSRI = Bem Sex Role Inventory. n = 375 men, 290 women. From Bem, 1977.

[b]PAQ = Personal Attributes Questionnaire, long form. n = 234 men, 270 women. From Spence, Helmreich, and Stapp, 1975.

[c]ANDRO Scale from the Personality Research Form. n = 891 men, 1,255 women. From Berzins, Welling, and Wetter, 1978.

[d]ACL M, F from Adjective Check List. n = 90 men, 104 women. From Heilbrun, 1977. The nearly identical distributions by sex are attributable to the use of a median split on normalized distributions (T-score).

[e]CPI M, F from California Psychological Inventory. n = 101 men, 103 women. From Baucom, 1980. Respondents receiving scores in the middle third of their sex's score distributions were omitted from categorization.

It is clear that classification of individuals into the sex-role categories may vary depending upon which androgyny measure is used. Wilson and Cook recommended exploring ways in which the measures should be used depending on specific context or purpose. Until the implications of differences among the measures are better understood, users of the measures should be careful about drawing conclusions about the sex-role categories based on a number of studies when different androgyny measures were used.

GENERALIZABILITY OF THE MEASURES

A pertinent issue in adoption of any personality inventory is its applicability to populations other than those upon which the inventory was based. The androgyny measures were based on the responses of American college students, a rather specialized segment of the total population of men and women. A few studies have explored the possibility of systematic biases within the measures because the original samples were limited.

Age

Most studies have utilized student samples with age left unspecified, usually ranging from 18 to 22 years. The consistency over time of traits and behavior measured by the androgyny measures has not been examined. The possible impact of age has been more indirectly assessed through contrasting different age groups' responses with the university students' response patterns. Cross-sectional comparisons indicate minor differences. High school students' score distributions are highly similar to those of college students (Berzins, Welling, & Wetter, 1976; Spence & Helmreich, 1978). Samples of older men have rated themselves as higher in masculinity than did younger men, although age-related differences were generally insignificant for women (Hoffman & Fidell, 1979; O'Connor, Mann, & Bardwick, 1978; Spence & Helmreich, 1979a). Fischer and Narus (1981a) and Hyde and Phillis (1979) have also found minor variations in scores as a function of age using respondents representing a range of ages.

It is possible, however, that collecting data within a brief time span masks some potentially meaningful differences due to broader sociocultural changes. Heilbrun and Schwartz (1982) reported a substantial increase in continuous ACL androgyny scores when comparing samples drawn from 1958 through 1976. Reasons for the changes remain obscure, but the data suggest the continued need for comparative studies over time.

Socioeconomic Status

Researchers are usually (or should be) aware that personality variables, behaviors, and attitudes may vary as a function of socioeconomic status (SES). Little attention has been given to this factor in androgyny research, perhaps because of the ready availability of largely middle-class college students for sampling purposes. Spence and Helmreich (1978) noted some trend for the PAQ scores of lower than middle-class high school students to be depressed. More students were classified as undifferentiated and fewer classified as androgynous and cross-sex-typed. Comparisons of the SES groups on femininity/masculinity scores were not statistically significant, however. Evanoski and Maher (1979) found minimal differences in the total variance in self-esteem scores accounted for by BSRI scores as a function of SES. The modest size of the differences between SES groups suggests that self-descriptions in masculinity/femininity characteristics do not vary greatly as a function of SES as currently classified.

Geographic and Ethnic Differences

Geographic differences may be inevitable as a consequence of scale construction procedures: the BSRI's original sample was drawn from California, the PAQ's from Texas, and the ANDRO scale's from Kentucky. The measures have been repeatedly used across the country with generally similar score distributions, suggesting that geographical factors do not in themselves slant the data. Two studies specifically looking for geographical contrasts in masculinity and femininity scores found slight differences between Bem's sample and North Dakota students (Vandever, 1977), and no differences with samples drawn from New York and Georgia (Segal & Richman, 1978). On the basis of comparing small numbers of students at the same campus but from different geographic areas, Heilbrun (1981b) suggested that southern females may be more variable than women from the Mid-Atlantic region in their endorsement of masculinity and femininity.

More differences might be expected when non-American samples are utilized. Some differences in classification distributions, correlations between scales, and relationships with other variables have been noted in generally small samples of students from other countries (Hogan, 1979; Maloney, Wilkof, & Dambrot, 1981; Rowland, 1977; Spence & Helmreich, 1978; Whetton & Swindells, 1977). Spence and Helmreich viewed their studies as "crude and tentative explorations," but were encouraged enough by the parallels in the data to recommend continued research in non-U.S. settings.

Tzuriel (1984) suggested that simple translations of androgyny measures developed with American samples might not be appropriate for use with non-American samples, because definitions of masculinity and femininity may differ somewhat across cultures. He proposed development of culture-specific sex-role inventories, such as his Israeli "BSRI." To avoid proliferation of more androgyny measures with limited item overlap, it may be preferable instead to conduct research with items having demonstrated validity for both cultures being compared.

Interestingly, racial differences have not been extensively explored. Heilbrun (1981b) reported an unpublished study by Weller which compared the PAQ scores of samples of black Caribbean and black American students with Spence and Helmreich's (1978) PAQ scores for white students. There were negligible differences on the Femininity and Masculinity scales. On the Masculinity-Femininity scale, black American women scored in a less traditional manner than other women.

SOCIAL DESIRABILITY BIAS

The idea of sex roles necessarily implies some characteristics are differentiated by social desirability, in that some specific set of attributes is labeled to be more appropriate for one sex than the other. The androgyny measures have largely incorporated scale items which are positive in tone, that is, socially desirable to some extent. There is the danger, however, that scores on the androgyny measures may reflect a generalized response tendency to describe oneself in a favorable light rather than masculinity/femininity per se. The research described in this section was carried out to reassure researchers that this is not the case.

Statistical Analyses

The most common research methodology has been to correlate masculinity and femininity scores with some measure designed to detect unusual tendencies to describe oneself in very positive terms. Correlations with the BSRI Social Desirability scale have not exceeded .32, with slightly lower correlations for women and much lower ones when the ANDRO scale rather than the BSRI is used (Berzins et al., 1978). Hogan's (1977) unusually high correlations for samples of high school and college males (.6ʿ for masculinity and .63 for femininity) were obtained from a small Tennessee community and probably reflect factors specific to his study. Correlations obtained for women were more similar (.11 for masculinity and .36 for femininity).

Correlations of roughly .25 or less have been reported with a number of other measures: the BSRI and ANDRO scales, and the PRF Desirability scale (Berzins et al., 1978); and the Marlowe-Crowne Social Desirability scale with the BSRI and ANDRO scales (Berzins et al., 1978). Correlations between the Marlowe-Crowne and Femininity have been somewhat higher with the BSRI (Taylor, 1981) and the PAQ (Spence, Helmreich, & Stapp, 1975).

Analyses by sex-role categories have indicated no significant differences using the BSRI and the Agreement Response scale (Millimet & Votta, 1979). Results have been mixed with the Marlowe-Crowne, indicating lower scores for cross-sex typed persons (Falbo, 1977) or for low-feminine persons (Lee, 1982).

Other Studies

Another method used to study social desirability asks subjects to complete the measures under instructions to respond with a deliberate bias. There is some evidence to suggest that subjects are able to respond to the androgyny measures quite differently under unusual instructions (e.g., "fill it out as the most feminine person imaginable would") (Hinrichsen & Stone, 1978). Hinrichsen and Stone concluded that the BSRI may be highly susceptible to faking. To explore this possibility with the ACL scales, Heilbrun (1976) instructed college students to appear as psychologically healthy (fake good) or as unhealthy (fake bad) as possible on the ACL Masculinity and Femininity scales. Fake good instructions resulted in only modest increases in masculinity and decreases in femininity. Fake bad instructions effected a similarly modest drop in masculinity for men with no real impact on masculinity for women, but a substantial drop in femininity for both sexes. Determination of what femininity items were not checked by respondents under these fake bad instructions could shed some light on what aspects of femininity the students viewed as essential to mental health. Unfortunately, it is not possible to determine how much these scores differ from what the respondents would have received under normal testing procedures.

How differences in social desirability scores may be attributed to the type of items comprising the androgyny measures has recently been considered. Analyses of ACL items indicated a positive correlation between endorsement of positive and negative characteristics of the same dimension for both sexes. As Heilbrun (1981b) concluded, "that is not how a social desirability response is supposed to work" (p. 52). Some of the items on the BSRI have been viewed as relatively undesirable in tone (Pedhazur & Tetenbaum, 1979). In her analysis of the BSRI items, Ruch (1984) noted the existence of a cluster of items negative in tone that refer to susceptibility and immaturity ("childlike," "gullible," "flatterable," "shy"). Puglisi (1980) examined the social desirability of individual items comprising the BSRI scales by asking 80 university students to rate the social desirability of each item to an adult. Mean social desirability ratings for the Masculinity scale items as a group were higher than those for the Femininity scale, a result replicated in a second study. When three offending Femininity scale items were removed ("gullible," "shy," and "childlike"), significant mean differences in social desirability were also removed. He recommended revision of the Femininity scale for use in future research. Richardson, Merrifield, Jacobsen, Evanoski, Hobish, and Goldstein (1980) advocated use of factor scores to eliminate differences in social desirability between Masculinity and Femininity scales.

In summary, although the androgyny measures as a group utilize largely socially desirable items, correlations with measures of social desirability have been modest. The differences in correlations for masculinity and femininity are small enough that they may have little practical consequence. The degree to which subjects may be able to slant their scores deliberately is not clear.

Whitley (1983) has argued that social desirability may be an inherent aspect of sex role theory rather than a confounding factor (as suggested by Auke Tellegen). That is, social desirability is a natural component of how sex-role variables are currently conceptualized and measured. The possibility may help to explain the strong relationship between sex roles and self-esteem (see pp. 94–95). Researchers can consider minimizing the social desirability component of sex-role measures or statistically isolating its effect in order to increase understanding of the relationships between sex role and other constructs related to social desirability.

SRBS CHARACTERISTICS

As mentioned earlier, the psychometric characteristics of the revised SRBS (Orlofsky et al., 1982) are included in a separate section here because the measure differs markedly in intent and item content from the other androgyny measures. Highly significant ($p < .001$) sex differences were obtained on each self-rating scale and on every subscale with the exception of masculine vocational interests. Alpha coefficients for internal consistency were satisfactory for men, women, and combined-sex samples respectively, for the Male-valued (.91, .88, .93), Female-valued (.87, .86, .92) and Sex-specific scales (.84, .83, .97). Combined-sex alpha coefficients were .70 or above.

Combined sex-correlations computed across the four interest/behavior subscales within each major scale ranged from .18–.43 for the Male valued and .37–.50 for the Female-valued subscales. The higher correlations for the Sex-specific subscales (.66–.82) were attributed to the significant sex differences represented by these items. Separate-sex correlational analyses maintained this pattern of results.

Correlations between the PAQ and the original SRBS were small and non-significant except for the Female-valued scales (.24 and .38, men and women). Separate analyses of variance on SRBS scale scores by PAQ group showed a significant main effect with high versus low femininity groups for the female-valued scale only. Analyses performed separately by sex yielded significant differences for these groups on the Male-valued scale as well (Orlofsky, 1981b). Thus there is little correspondence between these contrasting measures of aspects of masculinity and femininity.

SUMMARY

Androgyny measures are based on views about masculinity and femininity quite different from those of traditional m-f measures. Masculinity and femininity are recognized as two separate and independent dimensions, each of which may be multidimensional in nature. Characteristics corresponding to both dimensions are seen as ultimately desirable for members of both sexes to possess, although masculinity and femininity are currently more typical for one or the other sex and more socially desirable for one sex in light of traditional standards for the sexes' behavior.

Each androgyny measure elicits self-descriptions with items keyed for either the Masculinity or Femininity scales. Total scale scores are frequently used to classify a person into one of four sex-role categories. Each category is often assumed to have certain implications for an individual's psychological functioning. Although the measures are often treated as interchangeable, there are differences in basic scale characteristics and item selection procedures, which may or may not differentially color what is being assessed by the various measures. Estimates of the internal consistencies suggest that the content of each measure is somewhat homogeneous. Scores are generally stable over time. The Femininity and Masculinity scales of any one measure are generally independent, as was desired. The measures as a group are not strongly related to traditional measures of m-f, which is also a favorable sign. Studies on age, SES, and geographic differences suggest that the measures can be viewed as appropriate for use with samples other than the undergraduate student populations upon which they were based. Data pertaining to social desirability have also been reassuring overall.

There do appear to be some noteworthy differences among the measures, however. Correlations among matching scales across measures indicate that highly related but not identical aspects of masculinity and femininity are being tapped by the measures. Use of different scoring procedures may classify individuals receiving the same femininity/masculinity scores into different sex-role categories. Not surprisingly, the measures as a group do not show a high degree of agreement in classification.

The effects of these measurement differences on the study and interpretation of sex-role related characteristics and behavior are not yet clarified. More research on the measures and the ideas they represent is necessary. Users of the measures should be aware of the potential problems, cautious in their expectations, and explicit in their own rationales for choice and utilization of the various measures.

Issues of measurement do not, of course, compromise the meaningfulness of the sex-role values upon which the idea of androgyny is based: Enhancing individual potential and self-expression without imposed and internalized standards based on sex alone. However, measurement issues and related critiques have an undeniable importance, if the measures are used to draw conclusions about "real-live" persons. If observation devices are flawed, so will be the conclusions drawn from them.

Chapter 3
RESEARCH ON ANDROGYNY

The concept of androgyny is based upon a number of commonly-held assumptions about the nature of masculinity and femininity, and their conjoint influence upon behavior. The sheer volume of androgyny literature demonstrates the popularity of these ideas in conceptualizing sex-role phenomena. How workable are these assumptions? Do they accurately represent what is now known about masculinity and femininity, or are some revisions in the assumptions necessary? Current research summarized in this chapter may help to provide the answers and some directions for future theory and research about masculinity and femininity.

Most studies of androgyny employ late adolescent and adult samples, although occasionally children are tested instead (e.g., Stericker & Kurdek, 1982). The studies generally explore the correlates and consequences of possessing varying degrees of masculinity and femininity. Some variation of a median-split scoring procedure is often preferred to classify persons into one of four sex-role categories.

The *androgynous* type endorses high levels of feminine and masculine characteristics as self-descriptive, and is often hypothesized to enjoy the psychological benefits of each dimension. For example, such individuals can be independent and capable of leading others (traditionally masculine), yet nurturant and sensitive of others (feminine). Three other sex-role categories are described by varying combinations of masculinity and femininity: *masculine* (high masculine, low feminine), *feminine* (high feminine, low masculine), and *undifferentiated* (low on both). Feminine and masculine or "sex-typed" persons are believed to be disadvantaged to some extent because of their low endorsement of one dimension. Undifferentiated persons presumably suffer the greatest psychological deficits of all (cf. Kelly & Worell, 1977; Piel, 1979).

The discussion of the androgyny research literature will be organized around the following assumptions, in order: (a) Masculinity and femininity are discriminable, meaningful dimensions that are generally independent from each other; (b) these dimensions have important implications for diverse sex-role related characteristics and behaviors; (c) each dimension has a powerful impact upon behavior; (d) specific combinations of femininity and masculinity have a systematic, theoretically consistent effect on behavior;

(e) biological sex interacts with masculinity and femininity to produce variations in behavior; and (f) an androgynous typing, that is, the possession of high levels of masculine and feminine characteristics, is ideal.

First, a word of caution: Summarizing the sprawling body of androgyny research requires much smoothing into shape. Inconsistencies among presumably similar studies are legion. In no small degree, the inconsistencies are attributable to the prevalence of diverse measures, scoring procedures, and statistical analyses. Many studies are single efforts without follow-up, but with results that confirm only a portion of the researcher's expectations. What this "flash of truth" actually signifies is seldom clear. Readers interested in a well-rounded understanding of a given topic area should consult the original sources.

This overview is unique in its focus on fundamental conceptual issues pertinent to androgyny, as first outlined in Chapter 1. Some readers may also be interested in reviewing androgyny research focused upon a particular topic (e.g., androgyny and achievement; femininity/masculinity and its impact on career decisions). The Bibliography provides an extensive, although not necessarily exhaustive, reference list of studies organized by major topic areas.

MASCULINITY AND FEMININITY AS DIMENSIONS

The first major assumption concerning androgyny is that masculinity and femininity are discriminable, meaningful dimensions. The validity of this assumption must be demonstrated before any hypotheses can be made about how these dimensions may shape the behavior of the sexes.

Basically, this validity issue asks whether the current androgyny measures represent masculinity and femininity as these dimensions are currently conceptualized. If theory and its accompanying measures do not support each other, one or both are in need of revision. To answer this question, two types of evidence concerning these dimensions are relevant: (a) factor analyses clarifying the actual content of the various androgyny measures, and (b) analyses of relationships with presumably correlated measures yet distinctive in focus from the androgyny measures.

The nature of masculinity and femininity is further elaborated by an assumption of the dimensions' independence from one another. This assumption is fundamental to hypotheses about each dimensions's unique impact for individuals. Support for this assumption can also be evaluated by a review of relevant statistical analyses.

Factor-analytic Studies

Factor analyses are statistical analyses that attempt to organize a group of variables (or scale items) into a smaller number of dimensions or factors. These factors identify traits or characteristics linking some of the items together (cf. Lindeman, Merenda, & Gold, 1980). Abstract definitions of masculinity and femininity provided in the first chapter would suggest that Femininity scales should show primarily expressive/communal content and Masculinity scales should show content pertaining to instrumentality/agency. Researchers have also been interested in determining how many unique aspects of masculinity and femininity may be included on the androgyny measures.

The number of factors. Extensive explorations of the BSRI's factor structure indicate rather consistent factor structures across studies and multidimensionality of both scales to some extent. Typically, the Masculinity scale has been shown to be composed of two major factors encompassing dominance/leadership/assertiveness/instrumental activity and independence/autonomy, whereas femininity is represented by a single major factor of empathy/nurturance/interpersonal sensitivity. Richardson et al. (1980) and Powell (1979) supported this conclusion using a number of different samples and across sexes. (See also: Berzins et al., 1978; Collins, Waters, & Waters, 1979; Gaudreau, 1977; Gross, Batlis, Small, & Erdwins, 1979; Lorr & Diorio, 1978; Ratliff & Conley, 1981; Ruch, 1984; Sassenrath & Yonge, 1979; Waters, Waters, & Pincus, 1977; Whetton & Swindells, 1977.)

As a group, the other androgyny measures seem to be heterogeneous rather than homogeneous in content. Berzins et al. (1978) determined the factor structure of the ANDRO scale to be similar to that of the BSRI. This conclusion is not surprising because the ANDRO scale's content was modeled directly upon that of the BSRI. The ANDRO scale and ACL scales are more heterogeneous in structure than the BSRI, composed of 10 and 11, and 9 and 7 factors (Masculinity and Femininity scales respectively) (Wilson & Cook, 1984). One exception is the PAQ, for which analyses have yielded single factor solutions per scale. Thus, the PAQ scales appear to be homogeneous in nature (Helmreich, Spence, & Wilhelm, 1981; Wilson & Cook, 1984).

Wilson and Cook also examined the overlap of content of the four measures by examining similarities and differences among their factor structures. The entire sets of masculinity and femininity items were factor analyzed into 25 masculinity factors accounting for 67% of the variance, and 26 femininity factors accounting for 66% of the variance. Fourteen of the masculinity and twelve femininity factors included items originating from one measure. These items were primarily drawn from the ANDRO scale and the ACL scale.

A number of factors jointly labeled as masculine or feminine are apparently incorporated into the androgyny measures. The PAQ appears to be the most simple and focused in content, with the BSRI also showing few factors. Other androgyny measures tap a number of content areas.

Whether this diversity in factor structure represents a fatal flaw in androgyny research is a matter of opinion. Pedhazur and Tetenbaum (1979) questioned whether the BSRI's factor structure permits the use of single summary scores per scale, since the necessary unidimensionality of the scales has yet to be demonstrated (see also Myers & Gonda, 1982). Other researchers have simply recommended that separate scores computed for each masculinity/ femininity factor can increase precision of data analyses (cf. Cano, Solomon, & Holmes, 1984; Feldman, Biringen, & Nash, 1981; Richardson et al., 1980).

Others have argued that androgyny measures need not be simple in factor structure. Bem (1979) did not view the lack of homogeneous, unidimensional scales as "devastating" as did Pedhazur and Tetenbaum. In her view, the BSRI appropriately reflects the heterogeneous collection of attributes arbitrarily clustered into two groups of "masculine" and "feminine" characteristics. The theoretical rationale behind the BSRI does not require the scales to be unidimensional, and to do so is "putting the methodological cart before the theoretical horse" (p. 1049). Ruch (1984) reported that even though the BSRI scales may not be unidimensional, the most important distinction among the items is the subgrouping into masculinity and femininity categories. This primary distinction lends support to the validity of the BSRI, despite some secondary subgroupings within the femininity and masculinity items.

Most androgyny researchers have used single summary scores for the Femininity and Masculinity scales, regardless of the number of distinctive types of content that may be included within the androgyny measure. As noted above, the use of factor scores may provide some information about unique aspects of masculinity/femininity, which is hidden within a summary score. The benefits of using a factor score have not been extensively explored at the present time.

The content of factors. The most important question is whether the content of the androgyny measure factors corresponds to theoretically meaningful definitions of masculinity and femininity. As noted above, the BSRI scales do represent aspects of instrumentality and expressiveness. Berzins et al. (1978) labeled the factors distilled from the ANDRO Masculinity scale as Social-Intellectual Ascendancy, Autonomy, Orientation Toward Risk, and Individualism. The ANDRO Femininity scale was composed of factors labeled as Nurturance and a blend of affiliative concerns and self-subordination. The similarity with factors they obtained from BSRI analyses is predictable: for Masculinity, Social Ascendance, Autonomy, Intellectual Ascendance and Physical Boldness; and for Femininity, Nurturant Affiliation, Self-Subordination, and Introversion.

To highlight major content themes running throughout the measures, Wilson and Cook (1984), performed a factor analysis on factors derived from the analyses of separate Masculinity and Femininity scales. Eight major factors were obtained, with the first two attracting femininity factors ("Expressiveness") and masculinity factors ("Instrumentality") from all four measures. Other factors represented such characteristics as independence, shyness, ambition, fearfulness, and mature autonomy.

Results from the various factor-analytic studies indicate that factors on the androgyny measures correspond well to theoretical definitions of masculinity and femininity. The masculinity factors generally fit descriptions of instrumentality/agency and femininity factors to expressiveness/communion. With the expectation of the PAQ, the androgyny measures are largely multidimensional. The divergences in factor structure among the measures suggests that the measures' scores may be moderately correlated at best. Evidence presented in Chapter 2 indicates that this is the case. Somewhat related but unique definitions of femininity and masculinity are embedded within the androgyny measures as a group.

Relationships with Other Measures

A second statistically based tactic used to clarify the nature of the androgyny measures' femininity and masculinity is to analyze how other personality measures may be related to these measures. The presence or absence of overlapping content can illuminate just how masculinity and femininity are represented on the androgyny measures.

ANDRO analyses. Berzins and associates analyzed which personality factors best discriminate between sex-role categories derived from the ANDRO measure. Such discriminating factors can supply clues about what aspects of masculinity and femininity are represented by the ANDRO scale. Berzins, Welling, and Wetter (1976) determined that measures of the orthogonal dimensions of dominance/submission and affection/hostility correspond in a predictable manner to high versus low levels of masculinity and femininity. Berzins et al.'s (1978) normative analyses for the ANDRO measure included comparisons among the sex-role categories on five principal components yielded from the total PRF. The characteristics of dependency and defensiveness were relevant in uniquely describing differences between sex-typed groups, and social poise and intellectual orientation for the high-high and low-low (androgynous and indeterminate) groups.

BSRI analyses. Wiggins and Holzmuller (1978) proposed that the self-descriptions used in BSRI sex-role classification tap into a variety of content domains. They computed correlations between their "BSRI" scales (using synonymous adjectives) and adjectival scales measuring major interpersonal dimensions. Femininity was most positively correlated with "warm-agreeable" and negatively correlated with its opposite factor of "cold-quarrelsome." Masculinity was most positively correlated with "dominant-ambitious" and "arrogant-calculating" and negatively correlated with "lazy-submissive," the factor opposite to "dominant-ambitious." Data pertaining to the amount of item overlap between these dimensions and the BSRI scales are not provided. Wiggins and Holzmuller (1981) have recommended that the BSRI should be modified to improve assessment of dominance and nurturance. Emphasis upon these dimensions is supported by Lorr and Manning's (1978) study with high school students.

Bernard (1980) used Sixteen Personality Factor Questionnaire (16 PF) scales identified to be expressive or instrumental in nature as possible predictors of BSRI Masculinity and Femininity scale scores. The masculinity scores were found to be rather well predicted by factors E (assertive) and H (venturesome), accounting for 40-44% of the variance for both sexes. The femininity score analyses were less successful, indicating that factors A (outgoing) and I (tenderminded) accounted for less than 10% of the variance. Bernard concluded that expressive dimensions represented in the 16 PF were not strongly related to the Femininity scale.

Mills and Bohannon (1983) computed correlations between the BSRI and subscales of the California Psychological Inventory. Eight scales were significantly correlated with BSRI masculinity, consistent with Bem's conceptualization of masculinity as instrumental/agentic. The small absolute size of these correlations and the absence of significant correlations with femininity indicated the limited overlap of content between the CPI and the BSRI.

Other researchers have attempted to determine content similarity between the BSRI and other personality measures by grouping all items into a common pool and interpreting common factors that link the items from the various measures. BSRI scores appear to be at best moderately related to more traditional m-f measures (Bernard, 1981; Wakefield, Sasek, Friedman, & Bowden, 1976) and may be meaningfully incorporated with dominance and self-constraint measures (Lubinski, Tellegen, & Butcher, 1981).

Statistical analyses with other personality measures support factor analyses that portray BSRI masculinity as representing dominance and assertive activity. BSRI femininity has been less successfully related to some standard personality measures, although correlations were found with scales representing warmth and nurturance.

PAQ analyses. Thomas and Reznikoff (1984) examined relationships between women's scores on the PAQ and the Comrey Personality scales. PAQ masculinity was most related to Activity (vs. Lack of Energy), Extraversion (vs. Introversion), and Emotional Stability (vs. Neuroticism). Femininity was related to Empathy (vs. Egocentrism) and to a lesser degree to Trust (vs. Defensiveness). Modest negative correlations were also reported among Masculinity, Femininity, and Orderliness (vs. Lack of Compulsion) and Social Conformity (vs. Rebelliousness). These relationships are generally consistent with Spence and Helmreich's content definitions of their Masculinity and Femininity scales.

CPI scale analyses. Baucom (1980) explored personality correlates of the CPI Masculinity and Femininity scales by comparing the four sex-role categories per sex on the 18 CPI scales, and according to which ACL items they endorsed or rejected. Mean score profiles per category were similar across the sexes. Correlations with the CPI scales indicated that "masculine persons are comfortable as leaders, understand other people, are accepting and nonjudgmental toward others, and have good intellectual skills . . . feminine individuals are dependable and conscientious, have emotional sensitivity, have good self-regulation, and are achievers" (p. 269). This pattern of correlations was similar to that reported by Harris and Schwab (1979) with the BSRI.

Summary. This admittedly heterogeneous group of studies represents a type of validational research. The structure of present androgyny measures was explored to clarify whether the measures represent current theoretical definitions as intended. The identification of masculinity with instrumental/agentic characteristics (e.g., dominance, autonomy, assertion) and femininity with expressive/communal characteristics (e.g., interpersonal sensitivity, nurturance, warmth) has generally been supported, masculinity somewhat more successfully than femininity.

Suggestions for revisions and use of the measures, particularly the BSRI, have followed these analyses. As noted earlier, use of factor-based rather than total masculinity and femininity scores has been recommended. Second, Gaudreau (1977) advocated dropping the adjectives "feminine" and "masculine," which appeared to be rated highly more as a function of the sex of the respondent rather than in relation to other scale items. Pedhazur and Tetenbaum (1979) also noted the much larger sex differences in response to these items. They viewed the rest of the items rather than these two as troublesome, because they viewed discrimination between the sexes as a primary criterion of validity. This view is not shared by most androgyny researchers. Third, Richardson et al. (1980) noted that the items loading on the femininity factor may not tap the more active components of expressiveness or nurturance. Achievement orientation, a component of agency by definition, is also not directly assessed. For some uses of the androgyny measures, revisions to appraise some aspects of the agency-communion distinction more adequately may be helpful.

The Independence of Masculinity and Femininity

The factor analytic studies indicate the nature of the content domains tapped by the androgyny measures. An important assumption further describing the interaction of the masculinity and femininity dimensions is that they are essentially independent from one another. This characteristic permits each dimension to have a unique impact upon behavior apart from the influence of the complementary dimension. Varying combinations of the dimensions may have different conjoint effects upon behavior.[1]

As noted in the chapter on measurement, correlations between the Masculinity and Femininity scales contained on a single measure range from $-.42$ to $+.47$, depending upon the measure and sex sampled. Another potentially useful criterion of scale independence is whether the measures contain primarily simple factors that draw only one type of item (masculine or feminine). Wilson and Cook (1984) determined that roughly 75% of the ANDRO, PAQ, and BSRI scale factors are simple factors, with a similar percentage of their items loading on these simple factors. The ACL measure had roughly half of its factors labeled as simple ones, and half of its items loading on these simple factors. Analyzing the PAQ, Helmreich, Spence, and Wilhelm (1981) reported negligible mean loadings of Masculinity scale items on the femininity factor and Femininity scale items on the masculinity factor, lending support to their conceptualization underlying the PAQ. In reviewing the androgyny measures as a group, however, Wilson (1980) suggested that "there is considerable cross-over of association" on these measures with "specific combinations of items which contribute to a lack of orthogonality" (p. 15).

These studies suggest that masculinity and femininity as currently measured are modestly related to one another, the degree depending upon the androgyny measure. Heilbrun (1981b) emphasized that the assumption of statistical independence may not accurately represent the actual relatedness of the dimensions. Failure to demonstrate statistical independence would not automatically indicate that the measure is a faulty representation of the dimensions. He argued instead that masculinity and femininity may not be totally unrelated. This argument is consistent with present data. He also suggested the intriguing possibility that the nature of the relationship between femininity and masculinity may vary as a function of level of the sex-role dimension. For example, preliminary data analyses indicated that as ACL masculinity scores increase, the femininity score decreases slightly, except for extremely masculine men, whose femininity scores suddenly drop. His data suggest that such variations deserve closer attention rather than simple dismissal on the grounds of sampling differences.

Summary

The primary assumption concerning androgyny is that masculinity and femininity are discriminable, meaningful dimensions. The major issue surrounding this assumption is whether androgyny measures represent femininity

---

[1]Myers and Gonda (1982) asserted that it is assumed that masculinity and femininity are orthogonal and cite the documentation of correlations between M and F as disconfirming evidence. In my view, a more accurate rendering of the basic assumption is what they define as separateness, or "existing as an entity or conceptual independence" (p. 515). Demonstration of adequate divergent validity for the use described here would not demand demonstration of no correlation between the dimensions which Myers and Gonda seem to require.

and masculinity as they are currently conceptualized. A related assumption concerning the nature of these dimensions is their independence from one another. This assumption is fundamental to research exploring each dimensions' unique effects upon behavior, as well as the dimensions' interactions.

Statistical analyses of the androgyny measures indicate that masculinity and femininity appear to be discriminable, meaningful dimensions as hypothesized. Factor analyses of the androgyny measures singly and as group portray the dimensions as currently measured to be typically more heterogeneous than homogeneous. Their content compares favorably to the theoretically defined instrumental/agentic and expressive/communal domains. The measures are modestly correlated with one another. These conclusions provide a basic foundation for other research which explores the effects of masculinity and femininity separately and in combination with one another.

CORRESPONDENCE BETWEEN MASCULINITY AND FEMININITY AND RELATED VARIABLES

If masculinity and femininity as currently conceptualized are indeed meaningful constructs, they should be successful in explaining to some extent a host of characteristics presumably associated with sex-role identity and behaviors. This is an important question for research. In Worell's (1978) words, a major thread in androgyny theory and research concerns "the extent to which the characteristics measured by any of these current sex-role scales reflect unitary traits or dispositions that are predictive of a wide range of behaviors, attitudes, and life-style choices" (p. 789). Ideally, a number of objective data sources should be explored to establish these associations (Mischel, 1970).

Validation research has taken two tracks. The first approach is to explore the convergence of masculinity and femininity with concepts viewed as explicitly related to them. Studies that attempt to relate sex-typed criterion variable measures to the corresponding scale (e.g., a "masculine" aggression measure with a Masculinity scale) help to establish the scale's construct validity.

An extensive cataloging of androgyny studies provided some evidence for the validity of the scales as a group. Taylor and Hall (1982) reported that about 93% of the analyses they surveyed showed a positive relationship between Masculinity scales and various measures they judged to be masculine sex-typed, and 80% showed a similar relationship between Femininity scales and feminine typed measures. The pattern of standardized coefficients (where available in the original articles) further supported the convergent and differential validity of the scales, with very similar results for both men and women.

The second approach to validational research is based upon an assumption of correspondence among various sex-role phenomena. That is, the pervasive impact of masculinity and femininity as portrayed by the androgyny (trait) measures should be reflected in close relationships with other types of sex-role related variables: for example, behaviors traditionally considered to be the province of one sex, and sex-role attitudes.

Looking at the unique conceptualizations concerning androgyny, only Bem's, and Spence and Helmreich's conceptualizations provided explicit hypotheses for how masculinity and femininity should be related to other types of variables in theory and in practice. Bem's research reflects the two-stage development of her androgyny model, with an early focus on behavioral flexibility giving way to an interest in cognitive processing variables. Spence and Helmreich's research is seemingly paradoxical but theoretically consistent in nature. They have employed a wide range of biographical, achievement, personality, and attitudinal variables believed to be associated with their trait conceptions of masculinity and femininity, but expected a modest relationship at best with these complex classes of variables. Pertinent evidence for each conceptualization will be discussed in turn, followed by a brief discussion of the role of situational factors in sex-role behavior.

Androgyny and Flexibility

Bem's earliest formulations of psychological androgyny emphasized the superior behavioral flexibility of androgynous persons. Freed from the need to conform to rigid behavioral standards for his or her sex, an androgynous person is able to engage in masculine, feminine, or a blend of these characteristics depending upon what is appropriate for the specific situation (cf. Bem, 1975). This flexibility should lead to more adaptive behavior (cf. Heilbrun & Pitman, 1979). Research on androgyny and flexibility used several criteria as signs of flexibility: performance of instrumental/expressive behaviors; comfort in performing sex-typed activities; performance on paper and pencil measures.

Instrumental/expressive behaviors. The first research strategy used in flexibility studies assessed whether androgynous persons could perform both instrumental and expressive behaviors in a laboratory situation. Bem assumed that only an androgynous person would be able to exhibit both types of behaviors, thus suggesting flexibility across situations. Different samples of persons were used in different tasks, so flexibility attributed to androgynous persons over situations was inferred through between-group comparisons (Heilbrun & Pitman, 1979). Bem later reanalyzed the results using multiple regression analyses and/or median split scoring (Bem, 1977) and modified her conclusions in some respects.

Bem (1975) elicited "masculine" independence by placing subjects under social pressure to conform their funniness ratings of cartoons to obviously false ratings presumably supplied by others. For both sexes, high masculine subjects did conform less frequently than low masculine groups, although the androgynous-undifferentiated comparison was not statistically significant. Differences in expressive behaviors were first assessed by observing self-initi-ated playing with a kitten (Bem, 1975). For men, differences among the sex-role categories were related largely to degree of femininity, whereas for women nurturant behaviors were related to both masculinity and femininity. The first and second most responsive were the androgynous and masculine women. Examinations of display of expressiveness with human targets also revealed differentiations between high and low feminine groups. Androgynous versus undifferentiated comparisons were not statistically significant (Bem, 1977; Bem, Martyna, & Watson, 1976).

These early flexibility studies demonstrated that some androgynous persons could perform masculine behaviors, whereas others performed feminine be-haviors. As Taylor and Hall (1982) pointed out, these studies support that androgynous persons are indeed high on masculine or feminine traits, but do not directly test the hypothesis of flexibility.

Performance of sex-typed activities. In another research strategy, Bem and Lenney (1976) hypothesized that androgynous persons' flexibility would help them to feel comfortable about performing either feminine or masculine ac-tivities. Bem and Lenney asked students to indicate which of a series of paired activities stereotypically masculine or feminine they preferred to demonstrate, and their degree of comfort in performing them. Only one subject was classifi-able as undifferentiated, so median split scoring was not used. Traditional sex-typed persons tended to show more avoidance of other-sex typed tasks than did androgynous or cross-sex typed persons, who did not significantly differ from one another.

Helmreich, Spence, and Holahan (1979) argued that subjects' ratings of anticipated comfort in performing *any* category of tasks would be related to their masculinity and femininity scores, because of associated differences in self-esteem and self-confidence. In general, Helmreich et al. (1979) predicted minimal relationships between preferences for and comfort in performing sex-typed tasks and PAQ masculinity/femininity, in contrast to Bem and Lenney's expectations for large, consistent differences with the BSRI. As predicted, masculinity and secondarily femininity scores were weakly related to prefer-ence and comfort ratings, to an even lesser degree for women. Androgynous or masculine persons showed the highest comfort ratings over all tasks and undifferentiated or feminine the lowest. Sex was a more powerful factor in determination of preferences and comfort levels than masculinity and femi-ninity per se. Harackiewicz and DePaulo (1982) recently replicated these results. Helmreich et al. (1979) concluded that the weak relationships with the PAQ scores suggests that "the androgynous are more flexible than others in the limited sense of manifesting a higher degree of both instrumentality and expressiveness in their behavior but that the extension of the flexibility notion to include sex-related behavior in general is unwarranted" (pp. 1642–1643).

To summarize briefly, performance of behaviors classified as instrumental or expressive appears to be affected by degrees of masculinity or femininity. However, androgynous persons' performance in these studies is not necessarily superior compared to the other sex-role categories. And, the hypothesis of flexibility pertains to the behavioral flexibility of *one* person *across* situations. These studies do not indicate whether any given androgynous person may be more flexible across situations. Generally, this within-subject flexibility in behavior has been inferred from how androgynous persons respond differently from other persons on paper and pencil measures.

Paper and pencil measures. Heilbrun (1981b) has interpreted the manner in which androgynous subjects endorse ACL adjectives as providing evidence about their flexibility. Heilbrun labeled androgynous individuals' endorsement of a more equal number of masculine and feminine characteristics as exhibiting "more flexibility in the domain of sex-role behavior than others who show all masculine and or all feminine attributes" (p. 23). Androgynous persons also endorse a greater number of adjectives on the ACL, which he interpreted as another type of evidence for a more extensive repertoire of behaviors. A third criterion for flexibility in his research has been consistency of self-description across imagined social situations. Heilbrun (1981b) concluded that "men actually demonstrate a more balanced utilization of masculine and feminine behaviors than do women" (p. 29) because of their less consistent self-descriptions. He did recognize that men are not necessarily less flexible in sex-role functions (e.g., assuming more duties at home), but viewed this as a separate issue from his definition of sex roles.

Another approach to infer within-subject flexibility has employed paper and pencil measures of experimenter-defined masculine and feminine characteristics with a single sample. Babladelis (1978) used a variety of personal orientation, interpersonal behavior and feelings, and creativity measures. Sex-role differences outweighed sex differences in responses. Most significant differences occurred between masculine and feminine groups. Orlofsky and Windle (1978) investigated differences among the BSRI sex-role categories on measures of interpersonal assertiveness (labeled as masculine), emotional expressivity or affect cognition (feminine), and the personal integration scale of the Omnibus Personality Inventory (Adjustment). Results again differed by sex, and did not clearly differentiate among the sex-role categories. High feminine male groups scored higher on affect cognition and high masculine men and women on assertiveness. Sex typing was seen to be associated with less effectiveness in cross-sex tasks but with a general sense of well being, an undifferentiated classification with low flexibility and self-esteem, and androgyny with high flexibility and self-esteem.

Summary. The research evidence suggests that androgynous persons may be able to engage in either masculine or feminine behaviors depending upon the situation. However, the flexibility studies as a group are not convincing. Differences between androgynous and other persons are not remarkable. The presence of differences by sex and lack of differences between androgynous and undifferentiated persons were not expected.

The most serious criticism of the studies is that they have not directly addressed the hypothesis of flexibility: the presumed ability of one androgynous person to engage in both feminine and masculine behaviors across situations. Use of different subjects for different studies provides a much weaker test of this hypothesis. The studies that infer flexibility from subjects' patterns of responses on personality measures also provide weak evidence in favor of this hypothesis. As Helmreich et al. (1979) argued, the flexibility assumed to accompany androgyny may not include flexibility in sex-role behaviors as well as traits. Kaplan and Sedney (1980) have also questioned the relevance of these laboratory studies for the behavioral choices which individuals must make in everyday life. The validity of this hypothesis about androgyny has not yet been demonstrated adequately.

Gender Schema Theory

Bem's (1981a) recent line of research focuses on cognitive processing differences between sex-typed and nonsex-typed persons. Her basic hypothesis is that sex-typed persons tend to divide the world into the classes of "male" and "female" according to culturally based definitions of masculinity and femininity, and to evaluate the world around them and themselves in these terms. Nonsex-typed persons are presumably not as sensitive to the gender (sex) connotations of personality characteristics and behaviors and do not use such connotations to shape their self-concepts and behavior. Bem (1981a) has emphasized the "process of partitioning the world into two equivalence classes on the basis of the gender schema, not the contents of the equivalence classes" (p. 356). In other words, her attention is focused on whether and how individuals respond to the world in masculine versus feminine terms, rather than what the two categories themselves encompass.

Validational studies have been designed to permit the inference that gender schema processing was responsible for differences between sex-typed and nonsex-typed persons on experimental tasks. Three categories of research have emerged: (a) differences in how sex-typed and nonsex-typed persons cluster experimental items along masculine versus feminine lines; (b) effects of hypothesized gender schema on speed of cognitive processing of certain items; and (c) the type of schematic processing of nonsex-typed persons.

Clustering of tasks. A number of diverse studies have addressed whether sex-typed persons are more likely than nonsexed-typed persons to categorize an experimental task in sex-linked terms. Bem (1981a) proposed that if sex-typed persons encoded pieces of information along sex-linked lines, thinking of one item in the masculinity/femininity cluster (as part of the gender schema) should facilitate remembering other items in the cluster. Bem reported that traditionally sex-typed persons were more likely to remember stimulus words clustered by sex (e.g., "bikini/nylons" as contrasted to "butterfly/dress") than were the other three BSRI sex-role categories, which differed negligibly from each other. Other memory studies were cited as confirming. In a modification of Bem's study, Mills (1983) reported that all subjects remembered sex-related words better than neutral words, but sex-typed subjects recalled sex-congruent items (e.g., feminine words by feminine women) better than incongruent words. Markus, Crane, Bernstein, and Siladi (1982) found similar results.

Andersen and Bem (1981) explored whether sex-typed persons would be more likely to respond to the physical attractiveness of the other sex in social interactions. This would be consistent with a greater readiness to monitor perceptions and responses in a sex-linked manner. They persuaded subjects that their unseen partners were attractive/unattractive on a number of dimensions. Although sex was a stronger determinant of social responsiveness than sex role, sex-typed persons were generally rated as more responsive to "attractive" than "unattractive" partners; there were no analogous differences for androgynous subjects. Bem (1981a) considered this study to provide further evidence for sex-typed individuals' special sensitivity to male versus female distinctions.

Hollinger (1984) proposed that the career choices of highly talented young women could reflect gender-schematic processing, because their assimilation of career-related information should have been consistent with their sex typing. For example, sex-typed women should show the greatest interest of all sex-role categories in traditional feminine occupations, where androgynous women should score higher than sex-typed women on "masculine" vocational interests and higher than masculine women on "feminine" interests. Hollinger's results were mixed and minimally supported her view of gender schematic processing. However, her study was an especially indirect test of the existence of schematic processing. Mills and Tyrrell (1983) also found no sex-role related differences in sex-typed encoding of occupational titles, although there were some sex differences in performance on their memory task.

Other studies have provided support to hypotheses that individuals differ in their sensitivity to the sex-linked connotations of information, and that sex-typed persons are more prone to use sex-linked connotations in information processing than nonsex-typed persons (LaFrance & Carmen, 1980; Lippa, 1977; Neimeyer, Banikiotes, & Merluzzi, 1981; Tunnell, 1981).

Speed of cognitive processing. Bem (1981a) proposed that it is easier for individuals to decide whether a particular attribute is self-descriptive if they employ gender-schematic processing, rather than the more laborious process of reviewing supportive evidence in memory necessary for individuals lacking the schema. Conversely, it should take gender-schematic individuals longer than others to make a judgment inconsistent with the schema (e.g., that a sex-typical attribute is not personally descriptive). Several studies have indicated shorter reaction times required for sex-typed individuals to endorse attributes traditional for their own sex than other attributes, and longer times to make schema-inconsistent decisions. Nonsex-typed individuals (androgynous and undifferentiated) do not show differences in reaction time according to type of item. Data for cross-sex-typed individuals are mixed or absent (Bem, 1981a; Markus et al., 1982; Mills, 1983). These data support the hypothesized differences between sex-typed and nonsex-typed persons in cognitive processing of sex-linked information.

Type of schematic processing. In a detailed discussion of schema, Markus et al. (1982) suggested that although most individuals understand the meanings attributed to "masculinity" and "femininity," only some individuals use these distinctions to describe and evaluate themselves (self-schema). Markus and her associates proposed two alternatives pertaining to the nature of the gender self-schemas of nonsex-typed persons: (a) Androgynous persons may have both masculine and feminine schema in their self-concept, whereas undifferentiated persons are aschematic (without masculine or feminine self-schemas); or (b) both groups are aschematic with respect to gender. Correspondingly, sex-typed persons could be experts in processing information relevant to their own schema only (e.g., masculine information relevant to masculine persons) or could be sensitive to gender-related information in general.

On the basis of their information-processing studies, Markus et al. (1982) argued that sex-typed persons may show more efficient processing of information relevant *only* to their sex typing (e.g., feminine items for feminine persons) compared to items that are neutral or identified with the other domain (e.g., masculine items for feminine persons) (see also Crane & Markus, 1982). Sex-typed persons' patterns of responses suggested that they did not have a particular sensitivity to and knowledge of the other sex-traditional dimension that could be expected if they had schemas relative to gender as a whole. Results were less definitive with respect to distinctions between androgynous and undifferentiated groups. Androgynous individuals' responsivity to both sets of attributes suggested incorporation of both masculine and feminine schemas. Undifferentiated persons appeared more aschematic in that they did not appear to be sensitive to either feminine or masculine attributes. Bem (1982) responded that gender schema theory requires neither certain patterns of speed, efficiency, and confidence in processing information nor a certain amount of knowledge pertaining to each dimension, as Markus and associates argue. The theory simply requires demonstration of the salience of gender connotations to sex-typed individuals, and a lack of salience for nonsex-typed individuals, which Markus et al.'s data do illustrate. Crane and Markus (1982) countered that Bem's theory fails to account for important differences between masculine and feminine sex-typed individuals. More research appears to be needed to determine the precise effects of gender schema on processing of information, now that the presence of an effect is recognized. The significance of cognitive processing differences between masculine and feminine, and between androgynous and undifferentiated persons also needs further study to clarify which of the interpretations of the data at the present time is more accurate.

Summary. Research on gender schema theory has provided some convincing support for Bem's hypothesis that sex-typed persons are sensitive to and utilize gender connotations of information in their cognitive processing in a manner that nonsex-typed persons do not. Sex-typed persons' responses in tasks eliciting self-descriptions and memory using a range of items suggest that they are especially sensitive to the sex-linked connotations of information. Nonsex-typed persons do not appear to differentiate among items according to their sex-linked connotations in a similar way. It is not yet clear whether sex-typed persons have schema relative to gender as a whole, or if their sensitivity is focused on information pertinent to their own sex. Possible differences in the schematic processing of androgynous and undifferentiated persons and the cognitive processing of cross-sex-typed persons also need to be clarified.

Most recent studies on gender-schematic processing address the impact of gender as a cognitive schema on processing information relevant to self-descriptions. Modest interrelationships between domains of sex-role related variables, as discussed in a later section (for example, between traits and attitudes), suggest that the impact of gender schema in sex-role domains other than self-descriptions needs to be independently explored. Andersen and Bem's (1981) study suggested its role in interpersonal perceptions. Mills (1983) argued that the use of gender schema as a cognitive schema by sex-typed and nonsex-typed persons alike may help to explain the pervasiveness of sex-role stereotypes. The promise of these cognitive processing theories in explaining sex-role related differences in behavior is evident in Crane and Markus' (1982) remark that "we have no difficulty in assuming that the manner in which gender has been incorporated into the self-concept influences not only cognitive behavior but most other forms of individual behavior as well" (p. 1197).

Validation of Spence and Helmreich's Conceptualizations

Two lines of research have explored essential aspects of Spence and Helmreich's conceptualization of masculinity and femininity: (a) the relationship between sex-role stereotypes and self-ratings, and (b) the trait-behavior connection.

Relationships between stereotypes and self-ratings. An important concern in the PAQ's development was to establish its independence from subjects' more general sex-role stereotypes. For the PAQ to be used as a measure of personality traits, individuals' self-descriptions should be minimally distorted by their perceptions of how the sexes do or should differ on these attributes. Correlations between PAQ self-ratings and ratings of the typical man or woman were found to be small and only occasionally significant. Spence, Helmreich, and Stapp (1975) concluded that self-ratings on these sex-related characteristics can be granted the same degree of confidence accorded other self-report measures.

However, Storms (1979) noted several methodological problems with their study, which make their conclusions worthy of further consideration: (a) Different item formats were used for each set of ratings; (b) use of bipolar, unidimensional scales encouraged ambiguous ratings at the scale midpoint; (c) correlations between scales designed to be uncorrelated should not be expected when essentially just the target of the rating is changed. That is, self-ratings and stereotype ratings done on uncorrelated scales should not be expected to be correlated themselves. Using a modification of Spence et al.'s procedure to correct these problems, Storms found positive, significant correlations (range: .17–.39) between matched PAQ Self-rating and Stereotype scales. Storms argued that these results do not necessarily challenge the validity of Spence et al.'s trait measure, however. Correlations were still rather small, and some stereotype-trait correlation should be expected, since sex-role trait development appears to be affected by stereotypes. Both studies indicate that the PAQ is not simply measuring subjects' general sex-role stereotypes, and that PAQ self-ratings can be studied as a distinctive type of sex-role variable.

The trait/behavior connection. More central to their conceptualization and the rest of the discussion in this section is the strength of the presumed trait/ behavior connection. Sex-role researchers have been prone to assume that there is a strong relationship between the sex-role traits of masculinity and femininity, and sex-role related behaviors. Research on androgyny and behavioral flexibility is a good example. In contrast, Spence and Helmreich (cf. 1978, 1979b, 1980) have repeatedly argued that relationships among sex-role traits and behaviors are likely to be moderate at best. In their view, sex-role phenomena are heterogeneous, complex, and multiply determined. Sex-role traits may *predispose* a person to behave in a given manner, but observable behavior is the result of a complex interaction of many factors. Even behaviors that directly reflect instrumental/expressive domains may not necessarily be expressed in any given situation by an individual high in the corresponding trait. Close associations between self-ratings on instrumental and expressive characteristics, and other sex-role related variables (e.g., attitudes or behaviors), should not be expected unless these other variables explicitly key into the instrumental/expressive trait domains. The trait-behavior connection is likely to be even more strained when the behavior is peripherally related to these domains.

Research using the PAQ tends to support this view. Spence and Helmreich (1978) interpreted their voluminous data on correlates of masculinity and femininity as illustrating the complexity of sex-role related phenomena. The weak relationship between PAQ scores and preference for and comfort in performing sex-typed tasks was as predicted (Helmreich, Spence, & Holahan, 1979) (see also Atkinson & Huston, 1984). Using the BSRI, Lippa and Beauvais (1983) found weak effects for masculinity and femininity on behavioral choices in the laboratory, which they labeled as supporting Helmreich et al.'s contentions. And, correlations between the PAQ and a measure of sex-role behavior (Orlofsky, 1981b), and actual performance of sex-role related behaviors in a laboratory setting (Klein & Willerman, 1979), were not high.

These conclusions, and what they imply, deserve a closer look. Research with androgyny measures other than the PAQ has yielded irregular, borderline, and frequently confusing results. Many of the empirical associations derived among the androgyny measures and other criteria could be interpreted either as meaningful because of their statistical significance, or negligible because of their small absolute size. Which of these interpretations of the data is true? Perhaps the assumption of close correspondence among various sex-role phenomena (traits/attitudes/behaviors) should be reevaluated in light of Spence and Helmreich's assertions.

Evidence for Correspondence Among Sex-Role Variables

Actually, most of the androgyny literature implicitly pertains to the presumed correspondence among sex-role variables, as researchers typically choose variables presumed to be related but not identical to measures of masculinity and femininity. Some examples of studies that address this correspondence more explicitly are in the areas of homosexual versus heterosexual comparisons, attitudes about sex roles, and specified sex-role behaviors.

Homosexual/heterosexual comparisons. It is commonly believed that homosexual individuals are higher in the other-sex typical traits than in sex-typical traits (e.g., gay men are more feminine than masculine). Traditional masculinity-femininity measurement often incorporated the belief that "deviation from the norm of one's own sex in M or F may imply deviation in sexual orientation or homosexuality as well" (Constantinople, 1973, p. 390). In accordance with this belief, Heilbrun (1976) considered homosexual/heterosexual differences to be evidence of validity for his ACL scales. A sample of gay men scored significantly lower on masculinity than heterosexual men, where for lesbian and heterosexual women the pattern was reversed. Heterosexual women also scored significantly higher on femininity than did lesbians, with no significant differences for men. Heilbrun noted, however, that significantly more gay men scored at least one standard deviation above the mean on femininity. Heilbrun and Thompson (1977) found no significant differences for men in ACL sex-role classification distributions. Among women, differences were significant, because of a very high incidence (60%) of masculine classification for homosexual women. These results were interpreted as indicating "the apparently greater importance of sex-role deviation (sic) in female homosexuality" (p. 77).

Other researchers have not adopted this criterion for androgyny measure validation, but have expressed a curiosity about whether sexual preferences might meaningfully covary with masculinity and femininity. In general, mixed results have been obtained for homosexual/heterosexual group comparisons, with some tendency for the former to respond in less traditionally sex-typed directions (cf. Bernard, 1982; Bernard & Epstein, 1978a, 1978b; Berzins et al., 1978; Cardell, Finn, & Marecek, 1981; Kweskin & Cook, 1982; Ward, 1974 in Spence & Helmreich, 1978). The relationship between sexual preference and femininity/masculinity is clearly not a definitive one.

Attitudes about sex roles. One type of sex-role variable often explored vis-à-vis masculinity and femininity is attitudes toward sex roles, or more specifically, attitudes about what constitutes desirable personality characteristics, attitudes, and behaviors for women. The correspondence between sex-role self-description and attitudes is an intuitive one. Persons whose self-descriptions characterize them as traditional for their sex (masculine men and feminine women) could logically be expected also to espouse traditional ideas about the sexes in general. In contrast, those whose self-descriptions are innovative in their embracing of both masculine and feminine dimensions might favor a more egalitarian, less prescriptive and dichotomous position concerning the sexes' behavior. Heilbrun (1981b) considered evidence for such a relationship as relevant to his ACL validation.

The data are relatively clear concerning this hypothesized association: the relationship is a loose one at best. Correlations overall are low. The most consistent relationship is between less traditional attitudes and higher levels of masculinity in women (Bridges, 1978; Heilbrun, 1976; Hogan, 1977; Jones, Chernovetz, & Hansson, 1978; Minnigerode, 1976; Orlofsky, Aslin, & Ginsburg, 1977. For other studies see Bibliography).

Specified sex-role related characteristics. Other studies have explored relationships between androgyny measure scores and other characteristics generally accepted as either masculine or feminine in nature. Two characteristics strongly identified with traditional masculinity are aggressiveness and athletic interests. Several studies suggest a relationship between these characteristics and masculinity as measured on androgyny measures. Hoppe (1979) found that BSRI-classified masculine males were more aggressive to an unseen (and imaginary) opponent than other men, before and during provocation. Persons classified as Type A personalities (aggressive, competitive, achievement oriented) are more likely to be classified as high masculine than those who exhibited few of these characteristics (DeGregorio & Carver, 1980).

High masculinity may be more frequent in samples of athletes (Myers & Lips, 1978; Spence & Helmreich, 1978) although they have also been characterized as less feminine rather than more masculine (Colker & Widom, 1980). High masculinity is apparently also characteristic of male and female athletic directors as well (Williams & Miller, 1983). Mills and Bohannon (1983) found their sample of college male football players and police cadets to score high on masculinity. Interestingly, more of their sample were classified as androgynous than masculine, and roughly 10% were classified as feminine. This was consistent with their prediction that although masculine characteristics are necessary for masculine stereotyped activities, feminine characteristics should be free to vary widely.

Orlofsky's (1981b) Sex Role Behavior Scale was explicitly designed to cover a variety of masculine and feminine role behaviors and interests. A series of studies analyzing the correspondence among sex-role behaviors, masculinity and femininity trait measures, and masculinity and femininity trait measures and sex-role attitudes led to the following instructive conclusions:

> In general, when the effects of sex were controlled, only minimal relationships were obtained between sex role traits and behaviors, traits and attitudes, and attitudes and behaviors . . . thus, contrary to traditional beliefs that sex roles are unitary phenomena comprising tightly intercorrelated traits, attitudes, and role behaviors, the present findings suggest considerable independence among these three levels. (Orlofsky, 1981b, pp. 938–939).

Commentary. The evidence presented here suggests that the relationship between trait femininity and masculinity, and other categories of sex-role variables (e.g., sexual preference, sex-role attitudes, and behaviors not directly tapped by the androgyny trait measures) are not strong. Androgyny theorists do not agree about what degree of association should rightfully be expected. Bem's original focus upon behavioral flexibility predicted a strong relationship between trait self-descriptions and behavior. The gender schema theory permits prediction of relationships between diverse variables because of their association in the gender schema (e.g., descriptions of self as shy and preference for the color pink may be linked as feminine within a gender schema). Spence and Helmreich's expectations for trait-behavior links are far more stringent: they would, in fact, regard a lack of association between the variables above as evidence for their view.

Three possible explanations may account for the observed lack of strong association. First, the androgyny concept may be a limited one, with minimal power to predict actual behavior. However, the studies do indicate *some* relationship among categories of sex-role variables. The modest size of the relationships documented thus far suggests that it is probably time to stop expecting simple confirmation of complex variables and processes. Second, past studies may have had serious psychometric and design errors that prevented documenting whatever relationships may be present. Although individual studies might be improved, at present there do not appear to be glaring errors in research methodology that consistently produce inconclusive results across studies. Finally, sex-role phenomena may be far more complex than previously thought, being multi-dimensional and multi-determined. This appears to be the most likely alternative.

The most conservative strategy to adopt in future work would be to assume that sex-role phenomena are multi-dimensional and multi-determined, and then proceed to clarify androgyny's conceptualization and assessment. Spence and Helmreich's repeated pleas for conservative hypothesizing and more systematic theorizing in sex-role research are echoed by other researchers. Lenney (1979a) suggested that sex-role behaviors are likely to be affected by cognitive (e.g., sex-role beliefs), affective (e.g., sex-role threat), and motivational (e.g., personal goals) factors as well as global self-descriptions. What she described as a jumble of findings minimally guided by theory can only be corrected by attending to the complex determinants underlying behavior. Worell (1978) called for attention to be given to such variables as value attributed to the activity, expectations for success, and desire to please self or others. Other researchers have recommended enriching current theoretical perspectives through recognition of the role of situational factors in sex-role related behaviors, including the behavior of self-description.

The Power of the Situation

The role of situational factors, well respected in other areas of psychological research, has been largely overlooked in androgyny research. Situational factors have begun to be recognized as potentially influential in sex by sex-role interactions. Locksley and Colten (1979) emphasized the importance of different situationally based contingencies and behavioral norms for the sexes. Situational demands can facilitate or inhibit expression of a trait, although they should not always supersede the power of the predispositions in determining behaviors (see also Kaplan & Sedney, 1980). Orlofsky (1981b) pointed out that the sexes are likely to differ more in sex-role behaviors than in traits, because deviations from behavioral norms are more likely to be noted by others. In fact, persons are likely to behave consistently with sex-traditional roles even when the behavior in question is not consistent with underlying personality traits. And, unconventionality in laboratory tasks may not transfer directly to unconventionality in "real-life" behaviors. Gilbert (1981) agreed that each sex is likely to be most comfortable with performance of same-sex activities, regardless of personality characteristics (cf. Helmreich et al., 1979; Lippa & Beauvais, 1983). In addition to general sex-based norms, individuals' perceptions of appropriate behavior on a situational basis must not be overlooked (Rowland, 1980).

Klein and Willerman (1979) skillfully demonstrated how situational demands may interact with traits and behaviors. They distinguished between typical (usual and average) behavior and maximal behavior performance, where maximum expression of a trait through associated behavior is explicitly encouraged. College women classified on the PAQ were placed in two small group situations for decision-making tasks. In the second situation, subjects were asked to be as dominant as possible. Significantly more rated dominance behavior was elicited in the second, maximal condition. The women as a group were significantly less dominant with male than with female confederates in the typical condition, but equally dominant in the maximal condition. CPI Dominance scores proved to be much more powerful predictors of laboratory behavior than were masculinity/femininity scores, although the latter scores were instructive in accounting for consistent differences in the groups' rank-orderings by dominance. Klein and Willerman concluded that women differentially exhibit or inhibit certain trait inclinations in various situations as a function of sex-role demands, and levels of masculinity and femininity can affect how these behaviors are enacted. According to Alagna (1982), sex-role identity and situational demands may each have important but separate effects on women's behavior, and the power of extrinsic factors in such situations may be more powerful for women than for men.

Androgynous persons may behave less predictably across various situations than do sex-typed persons. LaFrance and Carmen (1980) observed frequencies of sex-typical nonverbal behaviors during discussions with an instrumental or expressive flavor. Detailed analyses by BSRI sex-role category suggested that responses of androgynous persons revealed less cohesiveness of behaviors within type (masculine or feminine), less cross-sex avoidance, less differences between display of each type of behavior across situations, and fewer extremes of behavior, especially in a sex-consonant situation (e.g., an instrumental situation for men). LaFrance and Carmen characterized androgyny as the addition of some cross-sex behavior and deletion of some more extreme sex-consonant behavior. The flexibility of androgynous persons may denote a varied blending of masculine and feminine characteristics, with different combinations in each situation. Description of androgynous persons' behavioral tendencies may thus require careful analysis of a complex of situational factors.

One interesting theoretical twist concerns the question of causality. It is usually assumed that traits as expressed through self-descriptions somehow cause a person to behave in a particular manner, in a given situation. Two studies on masculinity and femininity suggest that the influence can also occur in the opposite direction: coping with crises arising at various points in the family life cycle may result in changes in self-perceived masculinity and/or femininity (cf. Abrahams, Feldman, & Nash, 1978; Feldman et al., 1981). These researchers interpreted complex trends for masculinity and femininity levels in both sexes in light of the sex-role demands each sex typically faced at various points in the family life cycle. In a theoretical paper on the adult male sex role, Moreland (1980) similarly proposed that men change their sex-role conceptions successively over the years to correspond to age-related demands placed upon them. These perspectives on how sex-role related self-descriptions may fluctuate over time in response to situational demands suggest that much could be gained from focusing on an interaction of person/situation factors rather than simply person characteristics.

Summary

A central assumption underlying androgyny is that masculinity and femininity have the power to explain a range of personality characteristics, attitudes and behaviors. As a group, androgyny studies have been performed to document the nature and extent of this power. The conceptualizations of Bem, and Spence and Helmreich provide some hypotheses about these interrelationships.

Bem's early emphasis upon the behavioral flexibility inherent in androgyny has received support through a variety of paper and pencil and laboratory studies. Androgynous persons appear to be capable of performing both feminine and masculine behaviors well. Cognitive processing differences between sex-typed and nonsex-typed persons offer an extremely promising area for future research. It appears that sex-typed persons utilize sex-linked connotations of information in their cognitive processing about themselves and others. This reliance upon gender distinctions has not been similarly observed in the cognitive processing of nonsex-typed persons. Gender schema theory may offer some explanations for sex-role related differences in behavior.

Two of Spence and Helmreich's assumptions about masculinity and femininity have also received some support. The correspondence between general stereotypes about the sexes' behavior and self-descriptions is not strong, as they have asserted. Of most importance to androgyny, relationships among various types of sex-role variables—for example, trait self-descriptions, sexual preference, attitudes about sex roles, and specific behaviors—are also not strong, as Spence and Helmreich also predicted. Recognizing the possible multidimensionality of sex-role variables may promote more detailed theorizing about the determinants of sex-role related behaviors and more finely honed measures of these sex-role variables. One of the factors that needs to be considered is situational factors, which may affect whether behavior in a given situation will be consistent with the individual's personality traits.

THE CONTRIBUTIONS OF
MASCULINITY AND FEMININITY

A basic assumption within the androgyny literature is that departure from traditional sex-role standards carries with it decisive psychological advantages for both sexes. Individuals stand to gain as much from incorporating femininity into their personality makeup and behavior repertoire as do others who embrace some much-needed masculinity. The personality ideal of androgyny is gained through a balance. The logic of this conclusion depends upon demonstrating that masculinity and femininity each have a powerful, positive impact upon behavior. Some evidence for this assumption is provided through the contrasting characteristics of the sex-role categories (see Tables 3.1–3.4, pp. 99–102). Obviously, masculinity and femininity each must have some impact in order for meaningful distinctions among persons classified by levels of both dimensions to emerge. What deserves closer attention, however, is whether each carries enough decisive advantages to merit labeling possession of high degrees of both dimensions as *maximally* desirable. Or, does one dimension play a perhaps complementary but subsidiary role?

Research Evidence

To demonstrate each dimension's power, the favorite research methodology is to analyze masculinity and femininity scores separately with dependent variable scores representing a variety of characteristics. As expected, femininity is positively correlated with nurturant behaviors, in the laboratory (Bem, Martyna, & Watson, 1976) and perhaps also with actual child rearing activities (Russell, 1978); empathy (Orlofsky & Windle, 1978; Spence & Helmreich, 1978; Thomas & Reznikoff, 1984); ability to send nonverbal cues (Zuckerman, DeFrank, Spiegel, & Larrance, 1982); frequency of self-assessed fears (Krasnoff, 1981); importance placed on marriage and the family (Doherty, 1979; Spence & Helmreich, 1978) and desired family size (Berzins et al., 1978; DeFronzo & Boudreau, 1977); and intimacy in relationships for women (Fischer & Narus, 1981b). Both self-rated femininity and ratings of a spouse's femininity are positively related to marital happiness, where masculinity is not (Antill, 1983). Femininity may predict category of major and occupational choice more powerfully than does masculinity (Harren & Biscardi, 1980; Harren, Kass, Tinsley, & Moreland, 1979).

However, masculinity wields greater predictive power in a number of areas: Adjustment (Adams & Sherer, 1982) and scores on emotional stability (Thomas & Reznikoff, 1984); extraversion (Thomas & Reznikoff, 1984); assertiveness (Lohr & Nix, 1982; Nix, Lohr, & Stauffacher, 1980; Orlofsky &

Windle, 1978); profeminist attitudes about sex roles in women (Baucom & Sanders, 1978); dominance trait measures and actual behavior (Klein & Willerman, 1979); fear of success, especially in women (Cano, Solomon, & Holmes, 1984; Gayton, Havu, Barnes, Ozmon, & Bassett, 1978; Orlofsky, 1981a; Spence & Helmreich, 1978); differences in achievement motivation and competitiveness (Olds & Shaver, 1980; Spence & Helmreich, 1978, 1979c); and reactions to competitive situations (Alagna, 1982; Welch & Huston, 1982); inner directedness (Evanoski & Maher, 1979); self-monitoring (Lee & Scheurer, 1983); ability to interpret nonverbal cues (Hall & Halberstadt, 1981); distinctions among women professionals, working "nonprofessionals," and women not employed outside the home (Welch, 1979); creativity (Harrington & Andersen, 1981); leadership behavior, styles, and concerns within groups (Astley & Downey, 1980; Inderlied & Powell, 1979; Spillman, Spillman, & Reinking, 1981); positive body image and sexual satisfaction in women (Kimlicka, Cross, & Tarnai, 1983); and even self-described expressivity in men's relationships with others, especially with other men (Narus & Fischer, 1982). Tabulation of a number of studies pertinent to psychological health indicated that masculinity is more consistently and strongly related to these variables than is femininity. This was true for both sexes (Taylor & Hall, 1982). Bassoff and Glass (1982) drew the same conclusion from their meta-analysis using femininity, masculinity, and a range of variables measuring adjustment, maladjustment, and pathology. They concluded that "androgyny is not distinguishable from masculinity, at least as a correlate of mental health" (p. 109). Masculinity has also been *negatively* related to depression to a degree that femininity is not (Berzins et al., 1978; Holahan & Spence, 1980), perhaps to incidence of psychosomatic symptomatology (Olds & Shaver, 1980) and to alcoholism and psychiatric symptoms in women (Beckman, 1978). In general, it is associated with superior self-rated adjustment, although femininity is not necessarily negatively correlated with adjustment (Silvern & Ryan, 1979).

The best documented and robust association in the androgyny literature is between masculinity and paper and pencil measures of self-esteem. Femininity is more weakly related, if at all. The stronger positive relationship of masculinity to self-esteem holds regardless of the androgyny or self-esteem measures used, and across samples (Antill & Cunningham, 1979; Bem, 1977; Berzins et al., 1978; Colker & Widom, 1980; Evanoski & Maher, 1979; Gauthier & Kjervik, 1982; Hoffman & Fidell, 1979; Kimlicka et al., 1983; Orlofsky, 1977; Sappenfield & Harris, 1975; Spence, Helmreich, & Stapp, 1975). This was true for a measure of social self-esteem as well as self-esteem associated with one's goal-achieving abilities (DeGregorio & Carver, 1980). In a convincing meta-analysis of the sex-role/self-esteem literature, Whitley (1983) concluded that although both masculinity and femininity accounted for a portion of the variance in self-esteem scores, the far weaker relation of femininity suggested that psychological well being is more likely to be a function of the extent to which one possesses masculine characteristics.

Explanations for Masculinity's Stronger Effect

Explanations for masculinity's better-documented power have focused upon the content of the androgyny measures and other measures used in androgyny research, the nature of femininity, and the masculine supremacy effect.

Some explanations indict the composition of the Masculinity and Femininity scales themselves. Researchers may have simply been less successful in analyzing the effects of femininity. Important, although at present largely unspecified, aspects of femininity may be omitted from extant androgyny measures; for example, an active "care-taking" nurturance (Richardson, Merrifield, Jacobsen, Evanoski, Hobish, & Goldstein, 1981).

Other researchers have suggested that femininity as assessed by the BSRI may be less socially desirable than masculinity (cf. Pedhazur & Tetenbaum, 1979). Taylor and Hall (1982) explicitly address several such arguments concerning the noncomparabilities of the scales. They noted that there is no systematic difference in social desirability for the scales, except for some sample fluctuations. Hall and Halberstadt (1980) had attributed the more robust relationship for masculinity to the more behavior-referenced nature of masculinity, contributing to the greater behavioral correlations in studies. Taylor and Hall viewed their own data on the comparable construct validity of masculinity and femininity to contradict this possibility. However, masculinity does appear to have greater variability than femininity in within-sex analyses, which could contribute to the statistically stronger effects. The variability suggests that "in this society, feminine traits are more uniformly claimed by women and avoided by men than is the case for masculine traits" (p. 361).

The empirical use of global measures of other constructs, especially self-esteem, may also obscure associations with femininity. Such global measures may be more fruitfully broken down into aspects differentially related to masculinity and femininity (cf. Flaherty & Dusek, 1980; Stake & Orlofsky, 1981). The type of self-esteem often included in self-esteem measures may slant the direction of the correlations in the direction of masculinity (Whitley, 1983). Thus, the use of more precise measures in research may indicate more subtle associations with femininity, which are currently obscured within the broader measures.

It has also been suggested that feminine characteristics require a certain corresponding level of masculine characteristics for their potency to be released. Femininity may be essential in some ways that would not be detected by examining its effect apart from levels of masculinity. For example, the interaction of masculinity and femininity rather than femininity alone may predict self-disclosure to intimate target persons (Stokes, Childs, & Fuehrer, 1981). Yager and Baker (1979) labeled masculine assertive behaviors as possible "precursors" required for implementing expressive skills. Analyses of the interaction of masculinity and femininity may clarify this moderating effect.

The favored explanation for the masculinity/femininity discrepancy has been named the *masculine supremacy effect*, pointing to the superior social utility value attributed to masculinity in American society today (Yager & Baker, 1979). Masculinity may simply confer more advantages at present. Unger (1976) noted how femininity is often equated with weakness, while Kenworthy (1979) tersely stated that "femininity often has an ideal but not functional value for those who possess it" (p. 235).

The advantages of masculinity over femininity have been frequently noted. Locksley and Colten (1979) declared that there is no proof that masculine and feminine sex-typed persons are similarly disadvantaged. Masculinity may inhibit some emotional gratification but does permit survival skills, access to important resources, and control over situations and interactions. Femininity, at least as defined on the BSRI, does not carry analogous skills. Masculine characteristics are obviously relevant to independent goal-directedness, achievement, and recognition by others, all highly valued attributes. Rowland (1980) labeled masculine characteristics as those that "represent to people characteristics which enable them to *control* (italics in original) their own environment and its effect on them" (p. 451). Masculinity's social rewards tend to be obvious and immediate (e.g., interpersonal control) (Yager & Baker, 1979). Individuals high in masculinity may be responded to by others in a way that heightens their self-esteem (Kaplan & Sedney, 1980). In contrast, femininity's rewards may be apparent only over the long run (e.g., better family relationships), with benefits that become salient to the person only through actual interaction with the environment (Bernard, 1980). Finally, the power of femininity may be underestimated simply because it is more socially acceptable to admit to or display masculine characteristics in a variety of settings (Hoffman & Fidell, 1979; Yager & Baker, 1979). (For an alternative view, see Korabik, 1982; Major, Carnevale, & Deaux, 1981.)

In brief, the possibilities for explaining femininity's less powerful impact are: (a) It has not been adequately assessed; (b) its effect is more subtle than that of masculinity; and (c) it really does have fewer unique positive benefits. All of these explanations can be valid. The manner in which femininity interacts with masculinity and other variables may prove to be instrumental in explaining its consequences.

Summary

A basic assumption in the androgyny literature is that both masculinity and femininity have a powerful, positive impact upon individuals. The endorsement of androgyny as an ideal assumes that its benefits occur because of this feminine/masculine balance. Research has consistently documented more numerous and stronger effects with masculinity than with femininity. Although some experts have pointed to measurement problems as the possible cause of this pattern, most explanations focus upon the greater social value attributed to masculine characteristics in our society.

The unequal power of the masculinity and femininity dimensions as currently measured may help to explain the irregular differentiations among the sex-role categories. Straightforward, theoretically reasonable distinctions would require both defining dimensions to contribute as expected. The contributions of femininity may be less potent and predictable than is desirable for some typological purposes.

THE USEFULNESS OF THE TYPOLOGY

The fourth major assumption in the androgyny literature is that specific combinations of masculinity and femininity have systematic, theoretically consistent effects on behavior. As discussed in the chapter on measurement, there are a number of methods used to represent these specific combinations. Several sex-role classifications have gained prominence in the androgyny literature. The first classification, based on a *t*-ratio scoring, has largely been replaced by a four-way classification based on median splits of the Masculinity and Femininity scales. The median split classification was originally proposed primarily as a shorthand for portraying the conjoint influence of masculinity and femininity (cf. Spence & Helmreich, 1979b, 1979c). Since then, the median split method has become so popular as a way to conceptualize masculinity and femininity that, as Spence and Helmreich (1979b) wryly described, it has been "accepted by some with uncritical enthusiasm as a kind of genuine typology, suitable for use on all occasions" (p. 1035). The categories are assumed to label valid types of persons who can be reliably expected to behave differently from one another in predictable ways.

The four-way sex-role classification has been employed in research with two implicit attitudes about the extent of its meaningfulness. In the more conservative approach favored by Spence, Helmreich, and associates, the categories are regarded simply as handy labels for partitioning segments of masculinity and femininity score distributions. All research hypotheses and variables are explicitly related to the conceptual definitions of the masculinity and femininity dimensions. These definitions are generally some variation of the classic instrumental/expressive distinction. Thus, characteristics of persons labeled "androgynous" are those characteristics predictable from considering the Masculinity and Femininity scale items used to derive the classification.

In an alternative, more theoretically speculative use of the classification, categorical differences indicate more pervasive person characteristics above and beyond those directly denoted by the masculinity and femininity scores.

This approach is ideally exemplified in Bem's (1981a, 1981b) discussion of unique modes of information processing hypothetically corresponding to sex-role classification from the BSRI. Other researchers using this approach may simply attempt to see what collection of diverse variables discriminate among the categories and explain why (or why not) these results occurred later. Whether the approach is theoretically based or strictly empirical, these more speculative uses assume that the classification method successfully distinguishes among persons who differ in ways other than their masculine/feminine self-descriptions.

The major research task in validating such use of the typology is to demonstrate that the categories are useful in explaining and predicting a range of behavior. In the case of the androgyny literature, there should be a theoretically meaningful constellation of characteristics that discriminate among the members of the categories. Most androgyny research has addressed just this question: Do individuals classified into the sex-role categories respond differentially with respect to designated variables in a sensible and reliable manner?

Characteristics of the Sex-Role Categories

Results of studies pertaining to how the sex-role categories differ as a consequence of their contrasting levels of masculinity and femininity are presented in Table 3.1–3.4. Statistically significant results are organized by category and sex.[2] The characteristics in these tables are drawn from the studies noted in parentheses. Characteristics listed under "sexes combined" are applicable to both men and women. Those referring to one sex were determined by within-sex analyses.

The summary descriptions should not be given too much weight, however. Meaningful information about the effects of masculinity and femininity is omitted, and some information included on the table may not be important. For example, only analyses showing a sex-role category to be significantly different from other categories were included. Some interesting trends have been omitted. For example, androgynous persons generally score the highest on self-esteem, although the statistical significance of this top ranking may not be reported (cf. Bem, 1977; Spence, Helmreich, & Stapp, 1975). Nonsignificant analyses by category are not shown, which can be as illuminating as the significant differences. Differences included on the table may also have been statistically significant, but small in absolute magnitude. Comparisons between high versus low levels of one dimension (e.g., high versus low masculinity)

[2]Olds (1981) provides a detailed comparison of a small sample of sex-typed and androgynous persons based on in-depth interviews with them. Although she stated that her discussion is based on statistically significant results, no data are reported. Her discussion appears to be more anecdotal in favor as a result, so is not included in this section. Nonetheless readers may find her comparisons to be stimulating.

Table 3.1. Characteristics of Androgynous Persons

Sexes Combined

High on dimensions of friendly-dominance (Berzins, Welling, & Wetter, 1976) and social poise (Berzins, Welling, & Wetter, 1978)

Characterized as outgoing, social, high in leadership, responsible, mature, socialized, high achieving, concerned about others (Baucom, 1980)

Attribute generally positive characteristics to themselves (Wiggins & Holzmuller, 1978)

Highest on self-esteem measure (Spence, Helmreich, & Stapp, 1975)

Rated by others as most likeable and well adjusted (Major, Carnevale, & Deaux, 1981)

Seen as highly attractive (especially by women) (Bridges, 1981; Kulik & Harackiewicz, 1979)

Highest ratings in assertion skills (Campbell, Steffen, & Langmeyer, 1981)

More self-disclosing to a variety of persons (Lombardo & Lavine, 1981; Stokes, Childs, & Fuehrer, 1981)

Not as likely to be differentially responsive to presumably attractive versus unattractive targets as sex-typed persons (Andersen & Bem, 1981)

Generally more favorable to egalitarian marriages and having an androgynous spouse (Pursell, Banikiotes, & Sebastian, 1981)

Scored highest in role consistency across situations (Heilbrun, 1976)

Evidence both masculine and feminine self-schemas in their information processing (Markus, Crane, Bernstein, & Siladi, 1982)

Men

As a group reviewed a "flat" profile of interpersonal variables (Wiggins & Holzmuller, 1978; Wiggins & Holzmuller, 1981)

Endorsed fewest undesirable adjectives as self-descriptive (Kelly, Caudill, Hathorn, & O'Brien, 1977)

Typically reported identification with a nonstereotypic mother (Heilbrun, 1978)

Highest on a measure of social cognition (Heilbrun, 1981a)

More football players and police cadets classified here (Mills & Bohannon, 1983)

Women

Highest on adjustment measure (Silvern & Ryan, 1979)

Rate their stressful life events as less undesirable than do others (Shaw, 1982)

Success facilitated problem-solving behavior; tended to internalize success, externalize failure (Welch & Huston, 1982)

Likely to prefer nontraditional careers (Clarey & Sanford, 1982)

Least likely to sex-stereotype occupations (Yanico, 1982)

More athletes classified here (Myers & Lips, 1978)

Reported feeling the least pressure to conform to others' expectations (Kleinke & Hinrichs, 1983)

Table 3.2. Characteristics of Masculine Persons

Sexes Combined
High on hostile–dominance dimension (Berzins, Welling, & Wetter, 1976)
Low on dimensions of dependency (Berzins, Welling, & Wetter, 1978) and friendly-submissiveness (Berzins, Welling, & Wetter, 1976)
Characterized as leadership-oriented, domineering, egotistical, demanding, temperamental (Baucom, 1980)
Lowest on measure of self reported anxiety (Erdwins, Small, & Gross, 1980)
Low in display of nurturant behaviors (Bem, Martyna, & Watson, 1976)
Likely to evidence masculine self-schemas in information processing (Markus, Crane, Bernstein, & Siladi, 1982)
Sensitive to expressive cues in rating others' masculinity/femininity (Lippa, 1977)

Men
More internal locus of control (Jones, Chernovetz, & Hansson, 1978)
Most conservative in attitudes about sex roles (Bem, 1977)
Athletes likely to be classified here (Myers & Lips, 1978)
Displayed the most aggressive behaviors (Hoppe, 1979)
Prone to exaggerate masculinity under threat conditions (Babl, 1979)
Likely to process information along sex-linked lines (Bem, 1981a; Mills, 1983)
Reported less problem drinking than others (Jones, Chernovetz, & Hansson, 1978)
Gay men less likely to be classified here (Spence & Helmreich, 1978)

Women
Highest on extraversion (Jones, Chernovetz, & Hansson, 1978)
Overrepresented in a sample of feminist women (Baucom & Sanders, 1978)
Endorsed fewest ideal sex differences (Orlofsky, 1981b)
Most liberal in sex-role attitudes (Jones, Chernovetz, & Hansson, 1978; Orlofsky, Aslin, & Ginsburg, 1977)
Likely to try to take control of a team problem-solving task (Baucom, 1983)
Reported selves as least religious (Hoffman & Fidell, 1979)
Lesbian women more likely to be classified here (Heilbrun & Thompson, 1977)

100

Table 3.3. Characteristics of Feminine Persons

Sexes Combined

High on dimensions of friendly—submissiveness (Baucom, 1980; Berzins, Welling, & Wetter, 1976) and dependence (Baucom, 1980; Berzins, Welling, & Wetter, 1978)

Low on dimension of hostile-dominance (Berzins, Welling, & Wetter, 1976)

Characterized as conforming, nonassertive, questioning ability to handle self (Baucom, 1980)

Reported selves as being more fearful (Carsrud & Carsrud, 1979)

Endorsed more psychosomatic symptoms than others (Olds & Shaver, 1980)

Reported the lowest grade-point averages (Olds & Shaver, 1980)

Displayed less independence in laboratory conformity study (Bem, 1975)

Likely to evidence feminine self-schemas in information processing (Markus, Crane, Bernstein, & Siladi, 1982)

Sensitive to expressive cues in rating others' masculinity/femininity (Lippa, 1977)

Preference for indirect interpersonal influence modes, and least liked by discussion group members (Falbo, 1977)

Men

Lowest in self-esteem (Jones, Chernovetz, & Hansson, 1978)

Schizophrenics more likely to be classified here (Berzins, Welling, & Wetter, 1978)

Most liberal in attitudes about sex roles (Bem, 1977)

Women

Lowest in activity, extraversion, and emotional stability (Thomas & Reznikoff, 1984)

Most conforming in a laboratory study (Brehony & Geller, 1981)

Least likely to use undesirable masculine objectives as self-descriptive (Kelly, Caudill, Hathorn, & O'Brien, 1977)

Rated sex-typed stimulus persons as more physically attractive than androgynous (Bridges, 1981)

Underrepresented in a sample of feminist women (Baucom & Sanders, 1978)

Greatest preference for occupations dominated by women (Clarey & Sanford, 1982)

Least approving of competitive conflict-management modes (Baxter & Shepherd, 1978)

Likely to process information along sex-linked lines (Bem, 1981a; Mills, 1983)

Somewhat biased in using feminine constructs to evaluate others (Tunnell, 1981)

Lowest on creativity measure (Jones, Chernovetz, & Hansson, 1978)

Reported fewest negative reactions to college social pressures, but most difficulty in adapting to a wide range of people (Kleinke & Hinrichs, 1983)

More likely to hesitate offering help as a bystander in emergency situations (Senneker & Hendrick, 1983)

Lesbian women less likely to be classified here (Spence & Helmreich, 1978)

Table 3.4. Characteristics of Undifferentiated Persons

Sexes Combined

Low on dimensions of friendly-dominance (Berzins, Welling, & Wetter, 1976) and social poise and intellectuality (Berzins, Welling & Wetter, 1978)

Characterized as alienated, withdrawn, poorly socialized, low in academic performance (Baucom, 1980)

Attributed generally negative characteristics to selves (Wiggins & Holzmuller, 1978)

Highest in depression (Burchardt & Serbin, 1982)

Lowest in self-esteem (Spence, Helmreich, & Stapp, 1975) and self-concept measures (Erdwins, Small, & Gross, 1980; Hinrichsen, Follansbee, & Ganellen, 1981)

Adolescents lowest in adjustment (Wells, 1980)

Rate their stressful life events as least meaningful compared to others (Shaw, 1982)

Rated by others as least likable and well-adjusted (Major, Carnevale, & Deaux, 1981)

Seen by others as least attractive (Kulik & Harackiewicz, 1979)

Lowest in self-reported intimacy with others (Fischer & Narus, 1981b)

Scored lowest in cross-situational role consistency (Heilbrun, 1976)

Men

Lowest on adjustment measures (Silvern & Ryan, 1979)

Endorsed the most undesirable adjectives as self descriptive (Kelly, Caudill, Hathorn, & O'Brien, 1977)

Typically identified with feminine mothers (Heilbrun, 1978)

Women

Lowest in self-esteem (Hoffman & Fidell, 1979)

Women with alcohol and psychiatric problems more likely to be classified here (Beckman, 1978)

Scored highest on measure of psychasthenia (Burchardt & Serbin, 1982)

Tended to be most pessimistic concerning reactions to women's success (Gackenbach, Heretick, & Alexander, 1979)

Lowest in nurturant behaviors (Bem, 1977)

have also proved to be valuable but are omitted from the tables. Not every study made every possible comparison among the category and sex combinations. For example, meaningful differences may have been reported for women alone simply because men were not included in the sample, or the subjects may have been preselected for study from a subset of the sex-role categories. Finally, an array of androgyny measures, scoring procedures, dependent variable measures, and research procedures are represented in the table (see measurement chapter for discussion). It would be prudent to interpret the results in "more-or-less" terms rather than as revealing striking contrasts among the categories.

Personality characteristics related to the traditional instrumental/expressive distinctions corresponded to levels of masculinity and femininity as expected. For example, masculine persons were achievement-oriented, assertive, and dominant; feminine persons were nurturant, sensitive, and tolerant. Masculine men and feminine women tended to behave the most predictably. Androgynous persons exhibited a blend of both dimensions and were routinely the favored ones, although they shared their adjustment advantages with masculine persons to some extent. Undifferentiated persons were clearly the worst off: more likely to report psychological problems, poorest social interactions, lowest in self-attributed positive characteristics. Some studies suggest there may be a meaningful differentiation between sex-typed (masculine and feminine) versus nonsex-typed (androgynous and undifferentiated) groupings; for example, on indices related to women's home versus career priorities or salience (Doherty, 1979; Yanico, 1981), cognitive processing (Bem, 1981a; Markus, Crane, Bernstein, & Siladi, 1982), and subjects' performance in a learned helplessness study (Baucom & Danker-Brown, 1979). However, this pattern may not be a strong one (Taylor & Hall, 1982).

What is obscured by such a straightforward summary of an extensive body of research is the complex patterning of results not included in the tables. Rarely did it occur that every category included in a study was significantly discriminated from each of the other categories. Most differences among the categories were simply of degree, usually with only modest differences in size. Commonly, a particular rank ordering emerged with differences reaching statistical significance on certain contrasts only. It is usually impossible to interpret from an isolated study whether this singling out of a specific comparison denoted a meaningful distinction among the designated categories or a chance effect.

In general, the results of androgyny research indicate that breakdowns by levels of femininity and masculinity can be quite informative, but do not yield the robust patterns of differences among the categories expected by some proponents of androgyny. Spence and Helmreich's predictions for relationships with expressive/instrumental characteristics are generally supported.

Critiques of the Typology

There is adequate evidence to conclude that the dimensions of masculinity and femininity are probably valuable in explaining certain aspects of sex-role related phenomena. What is less clear, however, is the usefulness of the popular four-way typology. Discrimination among the types is less than optimal. If the categorization is viewed as a "genuine typology" pointing to enduring distinctions among persons so classified, a number of possibilities can be entertained for these irregular distinctions. The particular variables chosen for discrimination purposes do not differentiate the groups adequately, whereas other variables may prove to be more successful. Second, the groups that are successfully delineated from one another may indeed stand out from the other groups in some unique and undetermined manner. Future research may shed light on the currently puzzling results. Or, the typology (and probably the theory underlying it) may be faulty.

However, if the classification is viewed merely as a useful shorthand for portraying the conjoint influence of masculinity and femininity, failure to find a meaningful ordering of the categories on specific variables may suggest other possibilities. For example, the variables were not sufficiently conceptually related to masculinity and femininity as defined by the androgyny measure of choice. Other variables less tangential to femininity and masculinity or a different androgyny measure may be more successful. Second, any experimental effects may be entirely attributable to one of the two dimensions, for example, masculinity. This overriding power would make levels of the other variable, and the classification by extension, largely superfluous. Finally, the statistical model for representing the conjoint influence of masculinity and femininity was inadequate. For example, a difference score or an interaction term may have been a better fit (cf. Spence & Helmreich, 1979b, 1979c). At the present time, all of these explanations for the irregular distinctions among the categories are feasible.

The unquestioned popularity of the median split based typology has recently attracted more criticism. The researcher who first suggested the median split scoring procedure that provides the typology has been most insistent in her opposition to how it is commonly perceived. Spence (1983) emphasized that the four-way typology was intended in a nominal sense to refer only to masculinity and femininity score combinations. Many investigators instead use these score combinations to represent quasi or actual types. This usage requires at least a theoretical model specifying how these different score combinations denote properties above and beyond masculinity and femininity scores alone. This theoretical model is largely absent. In a related article, Lubinski, Tellegen, and Butcher (1983) argued that data analyses do not support the existence of these emergent properties as is often implied.

Efforts to describe the characteristics of each category by present empirical procedures may promote some misleading conclusions. As Spence and

Helmreich (1978) pointed out, it may be fallacious to assume that combining a heterogeneous collection of independent statistical findings about any group of persons forms a valid description of them. Essential information on the relative importance of any one characteristic and the relationship between the characteristics is missing in this simple assembly of discrete observations. For example, the information that androgynous men tend to self-disclose freely (cf. Lombardo & Lavine, 1981) may indicate an important mode for manifesting their feminine expressiveness or may be a serendipitous observation. Data analyses based on the typology may not accurately represent the nature of masculinity and femininity's effects separately or in interaction. This does not necessarily preclude use of a median split method to refer to femininity and masculinity levels if preliminary analyses are performed to determine whether more complex interactions are indeed present (Spence, 1983).

Another problem with current use of the typology is the tendency to describe sex-role categories in terms of what they are *not*, as in the "undifferentiated folks are not like the others" hypotheses. Definition of a category by negation poses particular problems with measures largely reflecting socially desirable characteristics, since the unfortunate target is inevitably described in negative terms. Few efforts have been made to describe in a theoretically meaningful manner how and why undifferentiated persons might be expected to behave (other than being worse off than everyone else). As a result, why undifferentiated persons can also behave similarly to androgynous persons remains obscure.

To summarize, recent critiques of the typology have primarily focused upon the lack of a theoretical foundation for many studies utilizing the sex-role categories. Bem's (1981a) gender schema theory is unique in this respect. Better theory is needed to propose what properties accompany the categories beyond differences in expressive/communal and instrumental/agentic characteristics; to tie together diverse results meaningfully; and to hypothesize more clearly about the behavior of members of each sex-role category. Each of these purposes should be addressed by proponents of the typology.

Summary and Commentary

It is widely assumed in the androgyny literature that specific combinations of masculinity and femininity have a systematic, theoretically consistent effect on behavior. The four-way typology generated from some variation of median split scoring of Masculinity and Femininity scales has been the favored method for representing the levels of masculinity and femininity simultaneously in a person. The majority of androgyny research has explored the unique characteristics of persons falling into each of the sex-role categories. A brief overview of the research suggests the most robust relationships could be predicted from the expressive/communal and instrumental/agentic qualities built into the currently popular Femininity and Masculinity scales. This conclusion is consistent with Spence and associates' predictions. Androgynous and masculine persons apparently enjoy a healthy set of benefits. Beyond this, however, even a cursory look at the literature indicates its perplexing constitution. In general, the existence of the sex-role categories as unique entities with properties beyond those built into the Femininity and Masculinity scales has been assumed but not clearly documented.

A major problem in interpreting the androgyny literature as a body is that researchers have uncritically accepted the validity of the typology without attempting to think through its theoretical ramifications. Researchers need to provide a rationale for *why* persons variously classified into the categories should differ from one another on some criterion variable, a rationale that ideally should be rooted in a broader framework for sex-role phenomena. Instead, researchers have often been content to let the data speak for themselves. This empirical strategy is similar to earlier m-f studies that searched for any characteristics that differentiated between the sexes. Certainly, there is a core of meaning linking the diverse distinctions that emerge, but the reasons for their emergence and their significance remain hidden.

Spence and her associates have repeatedly argued that part of the confusion stems from the habit of attaching surplus meaning to categories that should be viewed only as convenient labels. In this view, these labels are appropriate where, and only where, they accurately portray the effects of masculinity and femininity in a given body of data. The burden falls upon researchers to inspect their data and determine if the use of the median-split method is indeed appropriate. Other representations of masculinity/femininity's effects, as Spence has also pointed out, are also valuable and can be more informative. How and why the typology is suitable in a particular study should be evident.

The classification system is a serviceable tool, but should not be regarded as an indispensable component of the androgyny concept, or for all purposes. In some cases, levels of masculinity and femininity alone may be insufficient to represent the complexity of sex-role related phenomena. For example, the presence of sex differences within sex-role categories that are obvious in the tables point to the importance of analyzing sex by sex-role interactions in addition to effects attributable to femininity/masculinity levels alone.

DIFFERENCES BETWEEN MEN AND WOMEN

One major consequence of the androgyny concept is reconceptualization of the sexes as similar in important respects rather than diametrically opposed to one another. The rationale for androgyny rests on the basic assumption that masculinity and femininity are not simply *the* typical and desirable province of one sex alone but are dimensions present in both sexes in varying degrees.

Although there are significant group sex differences in scores on measures of masculinity and femininity, the considerable overlap between the sexes marks the differences as ones of degree rather than kind. The sex-role typology derived from the Masculinity and Femininity scales on the androgyny measures uses the same criteria, labels, and in most cases, combined-sex score distributions to classify men and women. The fifth basic assumption in the androgyny literature is that sex (gender) and the dimensions of masculinity and femininity interact to produce variations in behavior.

At the present time, the status accorded sex differences within the androgyny literature is an uncertain one. One outcome of the switch in emphasis from between- to within-sex differences has been a tendency on the part of some researchers to downplay sex differences in sex-role related behaviors. For example, the hypothetical characteristics of androgynous persons will be discussed without reference to the individual's sex, and data gleaned from research using a single-sex sample will be generalized as suggestive of people in general. Yet, other researchers have asserted that important sex differences in androgyny literature must not be overlooked.

Many professionals would be uncomfortable with Pedhazur and Tetenbaum's (1979) insistence upon using biological sex as the appropriate and necessary criterion for discriminant validation of the BSRI scales. These professionals might agree, however, that the potency of sex-specific norms in governing behavior should not be underestimated. Locksley and Colten (1979) argued cogently that "situations are structured with respect to sex at both institutionalized and informal social levels, and . . . differential contingencies influence the behavior of males and females, their dispositions to behave in varying ways, and consequently their perceptions of self as an actor in general . . . we should expect to find sex differences in the frequencies of certain types of behavior" (p. 1027).

This argument appears obvious in the case of traditionally sex-typed and cross-sex-typed persons. By definition, masculine men and feminine women describe themselves in a manner traditional for their sex and thus in accordance with sex-specific norms. These sex-congruent persons would not be expected to behave identically to their sex-incongruent peers (feminine men and masculine women). Whereas the system of social rewards and costs enforcing traditional sex-role behavior supports sex-congruent typing, the same system works against sex-incongruent typing. Colwill and Lips (1978) noted that "out-of-role" behavior has a different impact upon others' judgments than does expected behavior, so judgments concerning masculine or feminine behaviors will be influenced by the person's sex. Conformity and nonconformity to sex-role norms may be expected to be rooted in different sets of perceptions, background factors, motivations, and so on. In this way, sex differences among feminine and among masculine persons are easily predictable.

The more difficult conceptual question arises for those sex-role categories in which both males and females are displaying nonsex-typed characteristics: androgynous and undifferentiated. How and why do men and women who have presumably transcended sex-typical standards of behavior behave differently? How can these sex differences be consistent with the conceptualization of androgyny? The simplest answer to the latter question is the previously stated assumption that sex and sex-role differences interact to produce unique and complex patterns of behavior. A brief look at the existence of sex differences in the androgyny literature can suggest the scope of this interaction.

Sex Differences in Androgyny Research

Some of the topic areas in which sex as well as sex-role differences have consistently emerged include: (a) psychological health; (b) attitudes about sex roles; (c) biographical correlates of androgyny; (d) career-related variables; and (e) interpersonal sensitivity.

Psychological health. The often-stated assumption that masculinity and femininity contribute additively to androgyny's benefits was supported by early research indicating positive relationships between masculinity/femininity and self-esteem in both sexes, with the same rank-ordering of the sex-role categories (androgynous, masculine, feminine, undifferentiated) (Spence, Helmreich, & Stapp, 1975). More recent research has indicated that femininity is more weakly related to self-esteem than masculinity, and a significant relationship for femininity when present is limited to women alone (Antill & Cunningham, 1979; DeFronzo & Boudreau, 1979; Flaherty & Dusek, 1980; O'Connor, Mann, & Bardwick, 1978). Lamke (1982) and Wells (1980) reported different patterns of relationships among masculinity, femininity, and self-esteem for adolescents. Two other studies have found a stronger relationship between sex-role variables and measures of psychological health for women than for men: undergraduate and psychiatric outpatients' scores on a version of the Minnesota Multiphasic Personality Inventory (Burchardt & Serbin, 1982), and the effects of combinations of Type A personality and masculinity on social anxiety and depression (DeGregorio & Carver, 1980).

Attitudes about sex roles. Attitudes about what constitute desirable personality characteristics, attitudes, and behaviors for women have been the focus of interest here. The results of studies relating these attitudes to masculinity and femininity have not been conclusive, but generally have held better for women than for men. Less traditional attitudes appear to be associated with higher levels of masculinity in women (Bridges, 1978; Heilbrun, 1976; Hogan, 1977; Jones, Chernovetz, & Hansson, 1978; Minnigerode, 1976; Orlofsky, Aslin, & Ginsburg, 1977). Bem (1977) reported that for men alone liberal attitudes were *negatively* related to BSRI masculinity. Looking at correlates of sex-role attitudes, Orlofsky (1982) concluded that sex-role attitudes affect the type of sex-role characteristics desired by men for their ideal dating partner, but not for women. Atkinson and Huston (1984) reported complex relationships among sex-role attitudes, masculinity and femininity, and performance of feminine and masculine-typed household tasks that differed by sex.

Biographical correlates of androgyny. The intriguing issue of what causes sex-role related differences has been explored in the androgyny literature primarily through efforts to delineate patterns of family background variables. Somewhat divergent patterns by sex have been implicated in eventual sex-role classification. Relative degrees of masculinity and femininity are postulated to be differentially affected in men and women by their sibling family structure (Lamke, Bell, & Murphy, 1980; Shaw & Rodriguez, 1981) and fathers's participation in household tasks (DeFronzo & Boudreau, 1979). Men and women classified into the same sex-role categories have reported different parental child-rearing practices as being most salient (Kelly & Worell, 1976).

Spence and Helmreich (1978) have reported the most extensive data on associations between masculinity/femininity and respondents' perceptions of and relations with their parents. Few young men reported identifying with their mothers, where for young women the influences of fathers and mothers were rated about equal more often, or they were about equally divided between both parents. Young women were generally more responsive to their parents' masculine characteristics than the sons were to their feminine characteristics. Sons were likely to score high in feminine characteristics only if both parents or the father was perceived as androgynous. For young women, androgynous typing was most likely to result if both, or secondarily either parent, was androgynous. Spence and Helmreich concluded that patterns for young women's development are probably more complex than those for men.

Career-related variables. A heterogeneous assortment of studies on topics pertinent to career choice and motivational variables also indicates sex and sex-role interactions. There may be a relationship between sex typing in women and expectations for success in mathematics and physical science classes, which is not present for men (Brewer & Blum, 1979). The relationship of femininity and masculinity to career decision-making variables appears to vary by sex (Moreland, Harren, Krimsky-Montague, & Tinsley, 1979). Spence and Helmreich (1978) suggested that the nature of achievement motivation may be the same for both sexes, but the sexes may differ in the mode of expression of the motivation. Complex patterns of sex and sex-role category differences and similarities were found on a measure of components of achievement motivation (Work and Family Orientation Questionnaire). For example, androgynous and masculine women scored higher than their male peers on the Work subscale. On the Personal Unconcern scale, labeled as similar to fear of success measures, feminine men and androgynous women reported the least concern. In another study utilizing the same androgyny and achievement motivation measures, femininity was positively associated with Mastery, and Competitiveness with masculinity in men only (Olds & Shaver, 1980). Observing the behavior of male and female subjects in a competitive situation, Alagna (1982) suggested that women's competitive behavior and self-evaluations may be more affected by peer approval than those of men.

Interpersonal sensitivity. Personal characteristics facilitating sensitivity to others may reasonably be expected to be related to femininity in both sexes. Sex may play a role as well. Relationships between PAQ scores and empathy have appeared to be stronger for women than for men (Spence & Helmreich, 1978). The relationship was more pronounced for men on a presumably similar measure of Affect Cognition (Orlofsky & Windle, 1978). Although display of nurturant behaviors has been associated with femininity in both sexes, for women masculinity may also be important (Bem, 1975).

Other studies. The studies reported above are representative of sex differences found in the androgyny literature. Many others have been reported: the nature of self-descriptions (Wiggins & Holzmuller, 1978, 1981); self-disclosure and intimacy in relationships (Fischer & Narus, 1981b; Lombardo & Lavine, 1981); perceptions of and responses to individuals varying in physical attractiveness (Andersen & Bem, 1981); descriptions of ideal other-sex persons/partners (Kimlicka, Wakefield, & Goad, 1982; Orlofsky, 1982; Silvern & Ryan, 1983); responses to simulus persons varying in sex role (Korabik, 1982); relationships among daydreaming style, depressive moods, and masculinity and femininity (Golding & Singer, 1983); locus of control (Brehony & Geller, 1981); predictors of tolerance for ambiguity and cognitive complexity (Rotter & O'Connell, 1982); perceptions of own and others' guilt about sex and hostility (Evans, 1984); adjectives the members of the sex-role categories use to describe themselves (Baucom, 1980); flexibility in terms of indices of laboratory competitive/cooperative task behaviors (Heilbrun & Pitman, 1979); factors distinguishing the sex-role categories in discriminant analyses (Bernard, 1980); even preferences for cartoons (Brodzinsky, Barnet, & Aiello, 1981) and willingness to participate in a study on erotica (Kenrick, Stringfield, Wagenhals, Dahl, & Ransdell, 1980).

Commentary

What do all of these reports about the presence of sex by sex-role interactions indicate? As a group, they suffer from shortcomings characteristic of research on sex differences in general. Numerous studies indicating no significant sex differences are not reported here. A correlation that was significantly different from zero in one sex but not for the other sex does not necessarily mean that the difference between the correlations themselves is significant. Finding significant main effects for certain variables within one sex, but not the other, is not identical to demonstrating a significant interaction with sex (Maccoby & Jacklin, 1974). Differences among the androgyny measures as a group make analysis of sex differences across measures challenging to accomplish. Current thinking about androgyny does not comprehensively discuss the impact of sex on masculine and feminine characteristics and behaviors. All in all, a lucid analysis of how and why these diverse sex differences exist is not possible at this point.

The androgyny literature suggests that the process, likelihood, and implications of becoming androgynous may be different for men and women. Block and associates (Block, 1973; Block, Von der Lippe, & Block, 1973) suggested that the self-evaluation in light of personal and social values that androgyny connotes may be especially difficult for women to handle because of their socialization. In contrast, a young man's tempering of his agentic qualities with mutuality and interdependence may be easier to accomplish, since challenging social norms involves agentic qualities that he already possesses. Whether or not it is easier for one sex to become androgynous, and that is still debatable, the sexes are confronted with quite different baselines for desirable sex-related characteristics and behavior. The piquant blending of masculinity and femininity for any given person is likely to be colored by his or her experiences with these sex-based standards.

Men may be less likely to opt to develop androgynous preferences, roles, and behaviors. From an early age, females show a greater preference for adopting aspects of the traditional other-sex role than do males (cf. Brown, 1957; Gilbert, Deutsch, & Strahan, 1978; Jones, Chernovetz, & Hansson, 1978; Strahan, 1975). In particular, feminine interests may appear taboo to men (Lippa & Beauvais, 1983). This tendency is predictable from the masculine supremacy effect hypothesis: women have more to gain now from becoming more masculine than men would from femininity, whose benefits are often unseen, underplayed, and devalued.

Implications of androgynous typing for men and women may be quite different. When compared to traditional sex typing, androgyny may connote superior adjustment for women only (Deutsch & Gilbert, 1976; Silvern & Ryan, 1979). Heilbrun (1981a) interpreted sex differences in the androgyny literature on self-esteem and adjustment to indicate that androgyny may connote clear advantages for women only, because femininity is generally correlated positively with adjustment indices for women but not for men. Androgynous men may have more conflict than androgynous women about possession of other-sex typical characteristics (Silvern & Ryan, 1983).

Androgynous men and women may not behave similarly. On the basis of preliminary data, Heilbrun and Pitman (1979) speculated that how androgynous women anticipate responses to their behaviors inhibits them from behaving in an identifiably masculine or feminine manner in social situations. In contrast, androgynous men would use flexibility in behavior in a more goal-directed fashion, to obtain maximum reinforcement. Alternatively, Heilbrun (1981a) suggested that a possible greater defensiveness among androgynous women may permit them to overcome potential sanctions against cross-sex behavior, whereas the less well-defended androgynous men may find it more difficult to utilize their broadened sex-role potential. Both explanations emphasize the importance of identifying mediating processes to account for sex by sex-role interactions.

There may also be sex-specific costs to becoming androgynous as well. Both sexes are subject to social disapproval for displaying certain other-sex characteristics. The evocative labels of "pushy broad" and "sissy" are not applied symmetrically to members of both sexes. Social support for women adopting aspects of the masculine role appears to be more widespread than it is for men becoming more feminine. However, expansion of roles for women may bring with it painful family-career conflicts not experienced by men in the same form at the present time.

The question of how and why men and women become androgynous is open for speculation, and may evoke different answers depending upon what aspect of androgyny is considered (e.g., personality traits, behaviors, cognitive schemata). Androgyny may have different, but as yet poorly understood, connotations for men and women. Theoretically based articles attempting to predict and to explain the nature of the sex by sex-role interaction across all levels of masculinity and femininity are lacking. A good start for researchers and practitioners might be to assume that the characteristics associated with masculinity and femininity are present in both sexes, but their origins, influences, and consequences for both sexes may not be identical. In a society still organized along sex-distinctive lines, failure to respect its power reflected in the characteristics and behavior of those who have somehow managed to transcend its prescriptions as well as in those still loyal may be misleading, inaccurate, and unfair.

Summary

A notable feature of the androgyny literature is the emphasis upon similarities between and differences within the sexes. The status given to sex differences in the literature is an uncertain one. Androgyny researchers have frequently underplayed or overlooked sex differences in their emphasis upon differences in femininity/masculinity levels existing in women and men alike. However, other researchers have argued that sex differences must not be underestimated. Sex differences in traditionally sex-typed (masculine or feminine) persons are intuitively reasonable. Sex differences in nonsex-typed persons are more difficult to predict and explain because these men and women have presumably avoided conformity to sex-traditional standards of behavior. The fifth basic assumption about androgyny is that sex (gender) and masculinity/femininity interact to produce variations in behavior.

The androgyny literature contains numerous reports of sex differences including studies of psychological health, attitudes about sex roles, biographical correlates of androgyny, career variables, and interpersonal sensitivity. The nature of the sex by sex-role interaction is not well understood. It appears likely that the origins, influences, and consequences of varying levels of femininity and masculinity are not identical for the sexes.

ANDROGYNY AS AN IDEAL

An important assumption concerning the androgyny concept is that androgyny represents an ideal of human functioning, blending the best of masculinity and femininity. This ideal runs counter to traditional values, which upheld masculinity for men and femininity for women as the ideals. Some frequently cited early research suggested that a combination of masculinity and femininity provides the maximum benefits rather than simple adherence to sex-typical standards (cf. Block, Von der Lippe, & Block, 1973; Heilbrun, 1968; Mussen, 1962). This novel perspective with an inherent sex-role value appealing to many researchers led to a series of studies to validate that androgyny does indeed denote the most favorable combination of masculine and feminine characteristics.

Researchers testing this assumption have typically defined psychological health by paper-and-pencil measures (e.g., measures of adjustment), or diagnostic criteria (e.g., persons specifically identified to have psychological problems versus a general population sample). Studies to be reviewed in this section are classified as those using: (a) paper-and-pencil measures of adjustment with the general population; (b) meta-analyses of numerous studies on mental health; (c) identified client populations; and (d) studies on psychological development. Studies on self-esteem reported elsewhere are also relevant.

Some of the studies are correlational in nature, relating masculinity/femininity raw scores to other variables of interest. Generalization of these data to the popular four-way typology may or may not be defensible. It is probably safer to view such studies as relevant to the general assumption about masculinity and femininity rather than casting light upon the characteristics of the androgynous type per se.

Studies with the General Population

Analyses have been performed with global measures of adjustment and with more specific measures of characteristics believed to have an impact on adjustment, most notably locus of control and anxiety.

Global measures. The most obvious and simplest analysis of adjustment is performed using self-ratings on global measures. Orlofsky and Windle's (1978) analyses with the Personal Integration scale on the Omnibus Personality Inventory yielded positive relationships between adjustment and possession of BSRI characteristics labeled as sex-typed. Most researchers have reported less sex-traditional results. In several studies, masculinity has been shown to bear a somewhat stronger relationship to indices of adjustment than femininity (Adams & Sherer, 1982; DeGregorio & Carver, 1980; Hoffman & Fidell, 1979; Lubinski, Tellegen, & Butcher, 1981). Femininity may not be negatively related to adjustment, however (Silvern & Ryan, 1979). In fact, high femininity may be important for male adolescents' adjustment whereas masculinity is crucial for female adolescents (Lamke, 1982; Wells, 1980).

Hinrichsen, Follansbee, and Ganellen (1981) reported that androgynous persons consistently rated themselves higher on psychological health and self-concept scales than did those in other sex-role categories. Burchardt and Serbin (1982) suggested androgynous persons to be the most "symptom-free" of the groups. However, results of other studies do not uniformly favor androgynous persons. Logan and Kaschak (1980) found no differences among the BSRI sex-role categories on various mental health measures. A lack of significant differentiation between sex-typed and androgynous adolescents was reported by Wells (1980). In Hoffman and Fidell's (1979) extensive interviews of adult women, few reliable differences between sex-role categories paired by level of masculinity were found. Although high feminine and high masculine women tended to make different life choices, neither group appeared to be less adjusted. However, undifferentiated persons appeared to be the most poorly adjusted (cf. also Burchardt & Serbin, 1982; Wells, 1980). Hoffman and Fidell suggested that women with strong traits of any kind are better off than the undifferentiated (low/low) person, especially when women's life situations require behaviors consistent with their self-descriptions.

Locus of control. Locus of control is a trait referring to the degree to which persons believe that they can control events by their own behavior (internal locus of control) versus events that are out of their control (external) (cf. Rotter, 1966). Locus of control measures have not proven to be helpful in documenting androgyny's superiority. Borderline or nonsignificant associations between locus of control and androgyny measures appear to be the rule (Bem, 1977; Berzins et al., 1978; Johnson & Black, 1981) although the relationships may vary somewhat depending on the measure used (Brehony & Geller, 1981). Masculinity may bear a somewhat stronger relationship to internal locus of control (Evanoski & Maher, 1979), although androgynous along with feminine men may score as more external than masculine men (Jones et al., 1978).

Anxiety. Studies with anxiety scores of presumably normally functioning persons have indicated anxiety (or at least the willingness to admit anxiety) and femininity are positively related when traditional m-f measures are used (cf. Biaggio & Nielsen, 1976; Cosentino & Heilbrun, 1964). With androgyny measures, masculine respondents have tended to score lower on overt anxiety than feminine persons (Carsrud & Carsrud, 1979; Erdwins, Small, & Gross, 1980). In contrast, Jordan-Viola, Fassberg, and Viola (1976) found small but statistically significant correlations between masculinity and anxiety for women feminist group members and college students, and positive correlations between the BSRI *t*-ratio androgyny score and anxiety for college students and working women.

It would be consistent with other research for the two high masculine groups (androgynous and masculine) to respond similarly to anxiety measures. An interesting study on compensatory masculinity suggests that masculine and androgynous men may respond differently to a perceived sex-role threat which implicitly generates anxiety (Babl, 1979). Masculine men were speculated to follow a "hierarchical organization of compensatory avenues" following a sex-role threat, where expressed masculinity is exaggerated first, or antisocial responses are used if first available. Emotional responses may be denied or distorted. The androgynous males are also vulnerable to threat but may respond idiosyncratically by *de-emphasizing* masculinity. Thus, relationships between sex-role characteristics, anxiety, and subsequent responses may represent complex interactions involving situational characteristics.

To summarize, masculinity appears to have a somewhat stronger positive relationship to adjustment in the general population than femininity, as suggested by studies using global adjustment, locus of control, or anxiety measures. The data tend to be mixed, however. Femininity is also not negatively related to adjustment in either sex. There is some tendency for androgynous persons to score as the most adjusted, although again the tendency is not a strong one.

These studies were performed using relatively small samples of subjects. The second research strategy, meta-analysis, summarizes across a large number of less specifically defined groups of subjects and measures of adjustment.

Meta-analyses of Studies on Mental Health

Two studies attempted to draw broad conclusions about the relationships between masculinity and femininity, and a variety of mental health variables through meta-analysis. Bassoff and Glass (1982) provide a good description of meta-analysis: "In a meta-analysis, statistical results from many studies are converted to a common metric which reflects the strength of association between the variables studied. By analyzing these findings statistically, one can reach broad conclusions about the empirical evidence in a given area of research. A meta-analysis assumes that related but different variables can be combined" (p. 105).

Taylor and Hall (1982) reported on the direction and size of masculinity and femininity's main effects for a heterogeneous grouping of studies pertinent to psychological health. Masculinity was positively related to measures of psychological health more consistently than was femininity (91% of the associations tabulated across measures versus 79% for femininity). The effects were also considerably stronger for masculinity, as shown by the size of the statistics. Bassoff and Glass (1982) provided a more extensive analysis on mental health. They concluded that androgynous and masculine subjects scored higher on measures of mental health over a range of studies than did their more feminine peers. Again, masculinity proved to be much more powerful than femininity in its contribution to positive psychological health, to the point that Bassoff and Glass suggested that femininity may be an irrelevant component of androgyny's mental health advantages. The correlations between masculinity and mental health did not significantly differ by type of subject (e.g., university students versus others). Correlations were also similar regardless of what sex-role measure was used in the original study. The results favoring masculinity are consistent enough across diverse studies to suggest that the conclusions in favor of masculinity are stable.

In the studies reported so far in this section, the subjects are presumed to be normally functioning in general, or, in the case of the meta-analyses, results are not reported by specific types of psychological problems. A third research strategy employs groups of persons labeled as less adjusted than the general population because of help-seeking or psychopathological behaviors.

Studies with Identified Populations

Variations from sex-typical sex roles have traditionally been regarded as signs of serious psychological disturbances. A few recent studies have explored the independent relationships of masculinity and femininity to various categories of psychological disturbances. The criteria for classification into some specific category are often not specified, and the heterogeneous nature of some categories (e.g., "neurosis") diminishes the usefulness of the results.

Help-seekers. Consistent with the sample preferred in most psychological research, "help-seekers" typically studied have been college students requesting services at a university counseling service. Heilbrun (1976) found proportionately fewer ACL classified androgynous and more undifferentiated women in a client than in a nonclient undergraduate group. Holahan and Spence (1980) compared clients with nonclients on an extended version of the PAQ, which incorporated undesirable masculine (M−) characteristics (e.g., arrogant, cynical, hostile) and feminine (F−) characteristics pertaining to a lack of sense of self and to verbal-aggressive qualities. The groups did not differ significantly on the positive femininity (F+) items, but clients were significantly lower on positive masculinity (M+) and higher on the negative characteristics. Correlations of the scales with specific types of problems were generally small and of borderline significance. Finally, using community rather than college samples, Nettles and Loevinger (1983) reported no significant differences between couples in marriage counseling and couples not in counseling in PAQ classification or in frequency of mismatching in PAQ category for the couple.

Identified groups. Analyses using identified patient or client populations have yielded some predictable trends, but no powerful relationship with masculinity and femininity. Berzins et al. (1978) concluded that "within both sexes, psychopathology appears to be associated with normatively low masculinity scores and among men but not women, with somewhat elevated femininity scores" (pp. 135–136). This general association has found some support in the case of neurosis and schizophrenia in men (LaTorre, Endman, & Gossman, 1976). Thomas and Reznikoff (1984) reported more high feminine and fewer high masculine women in a psychiatric inpatient sample than in a normal sample. There are largely inconclusive results concerning alcohol abuse in women and men, although these persons may be more likely to be low in masculinity (especially undifferentiated) (Beckman, 1978; Berzins et al., 1978, Kondo, Powell, & Penick, 1978; Penick, Powell, & Read, 1984; Powell, Penick, & Read, 1980). In Jones, Chernovetz, and Hansson's (1978) sample of college men, feminine men tended to score higher on a measure of neuroticism and to report more drinking problems than their contemporaries (although these tendencies may not be severe enough to warrant classification as psychological problems). Virtually no data are available on drug abuse. Berzins et al. (1978) labeled some male and female opiate addicts as masculine and feminine (bordering on undifferentiated) respectively. Finally, a few studies have explored the relationship between masculinity and femininity, and psychosomatic problems with no conclusive results (Fisher & Greenberg, 1979; Hoffman & Fidell, 1979). Masculinity may be associated with coronary-prone behavior of college students (Nix & Lohr, 1981), and high femininity/ low masculinity with number of psychosomatic symptoms reported (Olds & Shaver, 1980).

Depression. Depression has been more extensively studied. It appears to have a negative relationship to masculinity, as indicated by Berzins et al.'s (1978) sample of clinically depressed women, Burchardt and Serbin's (1982) heterogeneous group of inpatients, and Holahan and Spence's (1980) students seeking counseling at a university counseling service (cf. DeGregorio & Carver,

1980). Several studies have focused upon understanding how levels of masculinity and femininity may affect reactions to depression-inducing experiences and different patterns of depression.

Baucom (Baucom & Danker-Brown, 1979; Baucom, 1983) explored how levels of femininity/masculinity may affect how individuals cope with situations that induce feelings akin to depression. An apparently unsolvable problem-solving task induced temporary feelings of depression, lack of motivation, and helplessness in subjects. These temporary mood and cognitive changes are considered to be similar to those occurring in clinical depression. Baucom and Danker-Brown (1979) concluded that differential susceptibility to helplessness is a function of sex roles rather than sex. Sex-typed persons may share a lack of flexibility and resilience following a loss of control, but masculine persons may have a history of greater success in avoiding the uncontrollable situations that may produce depression. In a later study, Baucom (1983) reported that high and low-masculine women responded to their environment in very different ways after learned-helplessness induction: high masculine women made choices to attempt to regain control of the task, whereas low masculine women rarely chose to regain control, and in fact often preferred to avoid subsequent tasks altogether. This preference to avoid control occurred even after a successful rather than helplessness-inducing experience. Baucom suggested that this lack of control may help to explain the high rate of depressive symptoms in women.

Golding and Singer (1983) concluded that masculinity and femininity predict styles of daydreaming and normal depressive experiences better than biological sex. Androgyny was associated with positive daydreaming, fewest self-reported feelings of inefficacy, and moderating of mind-wandering and dependency, all of which are often related to depression. In general, both femininity and masculinity were part of a general positive orientation to life which was negatively correlated with feelings of incompetence.

Golding and Singer proposed that there may be two qualitatively different patterns of depression that are related to masculinity and femininity. Low femininity accompanied a self-critical depressive style characterized by guilt-ridden daydreaming. The presence of femininity and lack of masculinity were associated with a dependent depressive style. Mind-wandering appeared in both depressive styles.

Baucom and Golding and Singer's studies were conducted with presumably well-functioning college students. It is not clear whether the results of the studies are applicable to individuals with serious depression. However, the studies suggest that both masculinity and femininity may be associated with general coping styles that may influence development of depression.

Studies on specific categories of psychological disturbance have generally shown some tendency for lowered levels of masculinity to occur in groups with identified psychological adjustment difficulties. Data pertaining to femininity have been mixed.

Androgyny and Psychological Development

A final category of studies shares a common hypothesis that androgyny represents a stage of psychological development superior to that of nonandrogynous persons. An early series of studies by J. H. Block (1973) suggested that higher levels of psychological development may be "associated with the development of self-concepts reflecting an integration of the agentic concerns, self-enhancement and self-extension, with the satisfactions deriving from communion and mutuality" (p. 522). Recent research indicates that androgynous persons tend to receive the most favorable scores or classifications on various indices of psychological development (Amstey & Whitbourne, 1981; Nettles & Loevinger, 1983; Orlofsky, 1977; Schiff & Koopman, 1978; Tzuriel, 1984).

Commentary

Is androgyny truly an ideal? At this point, data generally point to its benefits but are inconclusive. High masculinity rather than a high masculine/feminine blend is generally associated with positive adjustment criteria. Studies reported in Tables 3.1–3.4 lend some confirmation: androgynous persons have consistently displayed the most positive self-descriptions, situation-appropriate behaviors, interpersonal skills and sensitivity, and achievement motivation. To some extent, these benefits are shared with masculine or feminine persons. Why is the evidence favoring androgyny over all possibilities not more compelling, considering the weight given to this idea by proponents of androgyny?

In the androgyny literature, acceptance of androgyny as an ideal is predicated upon other basic assumptions concerning the nature of masculinity and femininity outlined earlier. These have received varying degrees of empirical support. Masculinity and femininity as currently measured do appear to be meaningful, discriminable dimensions corresponding to the instrumental/expressive distinction. They are not simple dimensions, however, and implications of unique aspects of masculinity/femininity for behavior are only beginning to be addressed. Relationships with target behaviors are not as self-evident as first expected. These relationships are likely to be tempered by a complex of situational variables and personality processes. Several fairly stable conclusions have emerged, however: (a) Masculinity is a stronger predictor of good adjustment criteria than is femininity, at least as they are currently measured; (b) persons low on both sets of characteristics are least favored, even if the benefits for those high on both dimensions are not always clear-cut; and (c) not surprisingly, sex (gender) shapes behavior to some extent. All of these complexities of theory and research argue against unconditional acceptance of the "androgyny is ideal" equation.

In recent years, the equation of "androgyny is ideal" has changed its status from a basic premise accepted without question into a hypothesis that invites amendment and qualification. With this perspective, new questions are born. For example, research reported earlier in this chapter has suggested that femininity's influence is not absent, but is more situationally or life-stage specific in ways that are poorly understood. Persons classified into different sex-role categories may respond distinctively to stressful situations (e.g., threat to masculinity, induced helplessness) with varying personal consequences. The importance of situational factors in eliciting and modifying behavior are overlooked. Sex differences in what constitutes adjustment in a sex-typed society might be expected to be present, but have not been well explored. Wells' (1980) study on adolescents and Hoffman and Fidell's (1979) survey of adult women suggest that sex typing and cross-sex typing may not be undesirable for some individuals. These examples indicate that judgments about what constitutes "optimum" psychological health cannot be made simply on the presence or absence of certain psychological characteristics without considering how these characteristics may interact with other facets of psychological functioning.

Two examples of new directions for research on the consequences of androgyny are the effects of undesirable aspects of masculinity and femininity, and possible negative consequences of androgyny.

Negative aspects of masculinity and femininity. Part of androgyny's apparent superiority thus far may be attributable to researchers' nearly exclusive interest in positive aspects of masculinity and femininity. Androgyny has been typically defined in terms of positive characteristics alone, which can be readily ascertained from the composition of the androgyny measures. It should be no surprise that individuals singled out for their consistently high endorsement of diverse favorable personality characteristics should also perform well on a number of measures and tasks related to overall adjustment, self-esteem, and interpersonal confidence. Spence, Helmreich, and Holahan (1979) extended the PAQ to include socially undesirable feminine and masculine characteristics and found it to be promising in analysis of personal adjustment problems. Extensions of masculinity and femininity definitions may permit finer distinctions among people who do well because of global self-esteem (and incidentally femininity and masculinity), and those who enjoy androgyny's presumed benefits (or suffer its consequences) because of their masculine and feminine characteristics.

Negative consequences of androgyny. Refinement of understanding about androgyny's consequences may well include recognition of some costs as well as benefits from possessing high degrees of masculinity and femininity. If androgyny represents a valid and frequently encountered group of persons, ranging from 20% to 30% of the population as indicated by the measures' normative frequency distributions, these persons are not likely to be freed from possessing any personality characteristics or typical response patterns that could cause them problems. For example, androgynous men (Wiggins & Holzmuller, 1978) and women (Kelly, Caudill, Hathorn, & O'Brien, 1977; Wiggins & Holzmuller, 1978) are likely to use undesirable trait adjectives to describe themselves. Some of these largely hypothetical negative characteristics or problems that androgynous persons might report are those that probably occur for reasons that are irrelevant to sex roles (e.g., enduring reactions to traumatic situations). Androgynous persons might simply have an equal chance of acquiring these characteristics or problems. Of greater concern to androgyny theorists and researchers is whether androgyny itself may carry some specific liabilities that have not been recognized.

Since androgyny connotes combinations of personality characteristics and/or behavioral tendencies anomalous to traditionally sanctioned standards of sex-role related behavior, the potential for problems in interpersonal and intrapersonal functioning may be present. Some of the negative consequences may be the result of negative reactions of others. Forisha (1978) suggested that androgynous persons may suffer anxiety and moodiness because of consequent social pressures. Androgynous typing may not be viewed by the other sex as ideal (Gilbert, Deutsch, & Strahan, 1978; Kimlicka, Wakefield, & Goad, 1982).

Other consequences may arise from intrapersonal conflict of various types. Silvern and Ryan's (1983) sample of androgynous men viewed femininity as valuable for an ideal person but less so for their own sex. They may be faced with recognizing characteristics within themselves about which they feel ambivalent. For some of Kaplan's (1979) clients, an androgynous balance proved to be dysfunctional. Unable to integrate their masculine and feminine characteristics well, these persons were vulnerable, inhibited, and unable to direct their behavior effectively. Mere possession of both sets of characteristics was not sufficient for their adjustment. The behavioral flexibility emphasized by Kelly and Worell (1977) could be a mixed blessing. Kelly and Worell proposed that behavioral conflict within androgynous persons could occur in some situations if conflicting response tendencies are elicited. Androgynous persons may be generally skilled in avoiding these potentially conflict-ridden situations, but could experience some discomfort when having to weather them. Androgynous persons may also suffer from ambiguity in social situations which structured sex roles typically eliminate for sex-typed persons (Kaplan & Sedney, 1980).

Another form of intrapersonal conflict faced by androgynous persons may center around decision making. In their study of college women's career decisions, Tinsley, Kass, Moreland, and Harren (1983) proposed that androgynous women with liberal sex-role attitudes may have a more difficult time making career decisions than their more sex-traditional peers. College men and women typically choose sex-traditional careers, which would fit with traditional individuals' attitudes and self concepts. Less traditional persons, however, may have more trouble selecting a career that provides the same degree of consistency for them.

The degree to which androgyny causes problems may differ among persons and settings. Some androgynous persons could experience conflict if their same-sex ideal is sex-typed, according to Garnets and Pleck's (1979) theoretical analysis. That is, they could perceive their own characteristics as discrepant from their ideals. Rotheram and Weiner (1983) emphasized the importance of person-environment match. For example, androgynous persons in traditional relationships may feel dissatisfied. Additionally, while androgynous persons may be at an advantage in dual-career relationships, a masculine sex role may be more adaptive in certain work settings. Some of their small sample of androgynous professors did report more work stress than others. Androgynous persons may be most adjusted in situations which reward both feminine and masculine attributes (Kaplan & Sedney, 1980).

In summary, research indicates that androgynous persons are in many respects apparently better off than other types, but this is only a partial answer. The data are most convincing when gathered with paper-and-pencil measures of intuitively (and in some cases empirically) related measures. More complete answers await analyses of "real-life" demands and behaviors. Nor is it known what about femininity and especially masculinity produces the advantages: their subfactors, their individual impact, the nature of their conjoint influence, and related but distinct personality and environmental characteristics and processes.

SUMMARY

Theory and research on psychological androgyny are based upon a number of common assumptions about the nature of masculinity and femininity, and their impact upon behavior. In this chapter, research pertinent to each assumption was briefly reviewed and summarized.

The first assumption is that masculinity and femininity are discriminable, theoretically meaningful dimensions. Any hypotheses about the effects of the dimensions rest upon this basic assumption. A related assumption is that these dimensions are basically independent from one another. The assumption of independence supports hypotheses about the unique and conjoint impact of these dimensions upon a range of behaviors. Statistical analyses of current androgyny measures indicate that the content of their Femininity and Masculinity scales generally represents the expressive/communal and instrumental/agentic distinctions respectively. Their content thus corresponds well to theoretically based definitions of masculinity and femininity. The Femininity and Masculinity scales are not highly correlated with one another, as was desired. However, the multidimensionality of some androgyny scales, and some differences in factor structure across the measures as a group suggest that the measures tap different aspects of masculinity and femininity to some extent.

The second assumption is that the masculinity and femininity dimensions have important implications for various types of behavior. Bem, and Spence and Helmreich have provided explicit statements about how masculinity and femininity should be related to other types of variables. Bem has posited the existence of relationships between feminine and masculine self-descriptions and a range of sex-role related variables. Her early work predicted that androgynous persons should display superior behavioral flexibility across situations. Research clearly indicates that androgynous persons can perform either feminine or masculine behaviors well. However, the behavioral flexibility of single androgynous persons across situations, the actual intent of Bem's hypothesis, has not been adequately demonstrated. Her more recent focus on gender schema predicts that diverse sex-role related variables may be related to one another by virtue of gender schema. She proposes that sex-typed individuals are likely to use masculine/feminine distinctions to evaluate information pertinent to self and others, whereas these distinctions are not salient for nonsex-typed persons. Research suggests that sex-typed persons are indeed more prone to process a variety of information along sex-linked lines.

In contrast to Bem's hypotheses of relationships among diverse sex-role variables, Spence and Helmreich emphasize that the connection between femininity and masculinity self-descriptions and other sex-role variables is not likely to be strong unless these variables are explicitly related to the instrumental/expressive trait domains. Research on sexual preference, sex-role attitudes, and sex-role behaviors supports their assertion. Sex-role phenomena are likely to be multidimensional and multidetermined, rather than exhibiting a straightforward connection to masculine and feminine traits. In particular, the role of situational factors needs to be recognized.

In general, the research pertaining to the assumption about the implications of the femininity and masculinity dimensions indicates that the dimensions are in fact probably related to many aspects of behavior, but that the dimensions do not account for differences in sex-role related behaviors by themselves. Spence and Helmreich and Bem would probably agree that regardless of whether masculine/feminine self-descriptions are cast into a trait or a cognitive processing model (or other models for that matter), cause-effect statements attempting to link these self-descriptions to other behaviors are overly simplified and misleading.

The third basic assumption is that femininity and masculinity each have a powerful impact on behavior. The view of androgyny as an ideal rests upon its hypothesized incorporation of the benefits derived from possession of each dimension. This assumption has received partial support. Femininity does have good predictive value for some characteristics. However, research has documented much stronger and more frequent effects for masculinity. Although some researchers have pointed to possible measurement problems in assessing femininity's effects, this discrepancy in results probably accurately reflects the greater value accorded masculine characteristics in our society.

The fourth major assumption in the androgyny literature is that specific combinations of masculinity and femininity have systematic, theoretically consistent effects on behavior. The presumed impact of various masculinity/ femininity combinations has been most typically explored by comparing individuals classified into one of four sex-role categories by means of a median-split method. The members of each sex-role category are generally expected to behave differently from one another in predictable, theoretically meaningful ways.

Although breakdowns by level of masculinity and femininity can be quite informative, a review of the unique characteristics of the sex-role categories did not provide the robust patterns of differences among the categories expected by some proponents of androgyny. Spence has cogently argued for viewing the four-way classification simply as one way to portray the effects of masculinity and femininity, rather than as a representation of enduring distinctions extending above and beyond masculine/feminine self-descriptions. Proponents of the typology need to provide a careful rationale for expecting differences among the categories that are not directly connected to the feminine/masculine definitions built into the androgyny scales.

The fifth basic assumption is that sex (gender) interacts with levels of masculinity and femininity to produce variations in behavior. The status given this assumption in the literature is unclear. The prevailing focus in the androgyny literature is upon within-sex rather than between-sex differences, although some theorists and researchers have cautioned against underestimating the power of sex-differentiated norms in society. Sex differences in addition to sex-role related differences have been reported in the androgyny literature. Although the nature of the sex by sex-role interaction is not well understood, the correlates and consequences of masculinity and femininity may differ to some extent for the sexes. Androgynous men and women, who share an absence of traditional sex typing, may still differ from one another in important respects.

The final assumption is that androgyny is an ideal, blending the benefits of both feminine and masculine dimensions. Numerous studies have been performed to demonstrate that androgyny does denote the most favorable combination of masculine and feminine characteristics. Androgynous persons tend to score as the best adjusted on a variety of measures, although supporting data are not extensive. More data are available to support masculinity's stronger relationship to adjustment than femininity. Femininity is not necessarily *negatively* related to positive adjustment in either sex. Recent perspectives have moved away from accepting androgyny as an ideal toward considering the interaction of situational factors with masculinity/femininity and adjustment, negative aspects of the dimensions, and possible negative consequences of androgyny. Androgyny may carry some specific liabilities for individuals that have not been recognized.

Chapter 4
FUTURE DIRECTIONS FOR RESEARCH

This chapter will suggest some directions for androgyny research in the future. On the basis of the research discussed in the previous chapter, conceptual issues that deserve further attention will first be discussed. These issues as a group focus upon the complexity of sex roles, and the need to refine theory and assessment of masculinity, femininity, and androgyny. Future research should not only expand upon current research, but should attempt to correct some of its shortcomings. Some of these shortcomings, which have reappeared throughout the androgyny literature over the years, will then be reviewed. The chapter will close with some specific recommendations for the design, implementation, and analysis of androgyny studies.

ANDROGYNY AS CONCEPT AND MODEL

Androgyny was reintroduced into the psychological literature a decade ago, and quickly gained popularity as a new sex-role option and topic for research. Has androgyny fulfilled its original promise as a central concept in modern sex-role theory and research? Or should it be retired as a concept with considerable appeal but limited usefulness?

The answer to these questions depends upon one's perspective. Certainly, the research in Chapter 3 indicates that early assumptions about androgyny's nature and impact have to be modified considering the complexity of research results. In retrospect, early assumptions about androgyny's characteristics seem naive, if well intentioned.

On the other hand, androgyny theory and research have been stimulated by, and in return clarified certain key assumptions about sex roles in general and femininity and masculinity in particular. Over time the focus has expanded from studying the concept of androgyny per se to examining the nature and consequences of the broader masculinity and femininity dimensions themselves. In some respects, androgyny has changed its status from simply describing a new sex role option, to representing a new framework for the study of masculinity and femininity. This new and broader perspective on masculinity and femininity is the basis for the androgyny model.

Androgyny as Model

Androgyny as model incorporates but goes beyond the assumptions underlying the concept of androgyny. It is assumed that femininity and masculinity
are unique, independent dimensions present in women and men alike. These
dimensions have an impact upon diverse aspects of an individual's functioning, whether singly or in interaction with one another. A range of sex-role
personality characteristics, attitudes, and behaviors is assumed to exist between and within the sexes. The focus of the model is upon describing and
explaining this range of sex-role related similarities and differences. It is also
assumed that these similarities and differences between men and women can
be described as the product of complex sex-role socialization and maintenance
processes applicable to both sexes. The androgyny model of masculinity and
femininity places the concept of androgyny within a broader context for the
study of sex roles.

The primary purpose of theory and research within the androgyny model is
to propose explanatory mechanisms to account for sex-traditional and nontraditional characteristics. Whereas research on androgyny as a concept typically
attempts to define the correlates of this sex-role type (perhaps as compared to
others), research positioned within the more general androgyny model points
to factors or processes involving masculinity and femininity that can explain
multiple variants of sex-role phenomena (often including androgyny).

The contrast between a focus upon androgyny as concept and androgyny as
model can be most clearly seen in comparing the perspectives of Spence and
Helmreich with those of their lesser known colleagues as a group. Spence and
Helmreich have shared with their colleagues the assumption of the independence, variability, and potential value of the femininity and masculinity dimensions in women and men alike. Their colleagues have puzzled over the
poor discriminations of androgynous types from others, the "best" way to
denote androgynous types, and the intermittent presence of between-sex differences among people who had presumably transcended such identification.
At the same time, Spence and Helmreich have argued for a focus upon the
significance of the femininity and masculinity dimensions, and for the need to
select among a variety of data analysis techniques to fit the data and the
researchers' purposes. For Spence and Helmreich, androgyny is a helpful label
within a broader perspective rather than the focus of interest itself. They also
emphasized the importance of recognizing the multiple determinants of sex-
role related behaviors beyond personality characteristics. These determinants
include sex-based norms and other situational variables.

What difference does it make whether androgyny is viewed as a concept by
itself or as part of a more general model for the study of sex roles? The
difference lies in how past and present androgyny research is viewed, and the
promise of androgyny for future research on sex roles.

The Implications of the Androgyny Model

The androgyny model differs from more traditional views of sex roles as outlined in Chapter 1 in several important emphases. First, the androgyny model assumes that between-sex differences in behavior are often present, but not predestined by biological sex. Members of one sex may be more likely than the other sex to exhibit certain characteristics, for example, dominance and men, but by no means do all men and only a few "deviant" women necessarily have these characteristics. Second, these between-sex differences are likely to be modified by complex individual and environmental variables. (See Klein & Willerman, 1979, for an example of how dominance behavior in women can be elicited and modified.) Third, individual (or within-sex) differences are given far greater attention than provided in earlier views of sex roles. Researchers expect variations from the sex-typical norm and analyze for them. Finally, in the androgyny model traditional sex-role identities and behaviors are not by definition most desirable for men and women. The implications of a much broader range of sex-role related characteristics for both sexes are explored.

Early research exploring alternatives to traditional sex-role conceptions generally focused upon androgyny as a new sex-role option. Differences in behavior were generally attributed to characteristics of the person alone. Research on androgyny as sex-role option has had some limited success. Androgynous persons do not always behave in a manner different from others, particularly masculine persons. The blending of masculinity and femininity may not contribute to androgyny's benefits as originally assumed. Masculinity may be considerably more powerful than femininity across a number of dimensions, most notably in self-esteem and personal adjustment. This conclusion contradicts early hypotheses about androgyny's benefits. Androgynous persons have apparently not entirely transcended sex-based norms for behavior, because there are significant differences in the characteristics of androgynous women and men. Finally, androgyny may not be a sex-role "ideal." Androgynous persons may suffer from some unique problems because of their sex-typing. In brief, early hypotheses about androgyny's characteristics have not received the clear-cut empirical support that was first expected.

To some extent, all researchers expect that their initial conceptions will have to be tempered in light of subsequent research. In androgyny research, part of the necessary reexamination may be due to an initial oversimplification of masculinity and femininity, also characteristic of preandrogyny research. Previous work on m-f (traditional masculinity-femininity) and the folk wisdom about female/male differences that provided its focus have made masculinity and femininity appear to be less complicated than they are. These dimensions seem simple in nature: intuitively meaningful, easily defined, with a pervasive impact on individual's functioning.

The idea of androgyny is also straightforward in conception. In some professionals' eyes, androgyny represented a predictable blend of two sets of familiar sex-typical characteristics. For some, androgyny is a type, or a single unitary construct representing an enduring predisposition and/or behavioral style possessed by a fair segment of the population. Androgyny research frequently meant simply dividing the bipolar m-f continuum into two separate ones, and labeling those persons not falling at either extreme as nonsex-typed (or androgynous) rather than the old pejorative term of "deviant."

What is missing from such straightforward conceptualizations is an appreciation of how androgyny fits within the broader study of sex roles. Valuing of traditional sex roles was only one problem that sex-role researchers saw with traditional perspectives. Another problem, more troublesome to researchers, was that these preandrogyny perspectives did not attend to the presence and causes of between-sex similarities and within-sex differences that researchers observed. The simple addition of another type to the sex-role pool does not address these issues adequately.

Instead, the androgyny model of masculinity and femininity provides a way to look at sex-role phenomena with an appreciation for its complexity. Rather than asking "What are the consequences of having an androgynous sex-role identity?", research in the broader androgyny model typically asks, "How can we better understand the diversity of sex roles, including androgyny, given these new assumptions about them?" Part of this appreciation for complexity involves an awareness of the role of environmental factors in sex-role behavior. That is, individuals do not behave in a certain manner simply because they have specified personality characteristics. Their behavior is also shaped by factors present in the environment around them.

When androgyny is defined as part of a model rather than simply as a sex-role type, the contributions of previous research and directions for future research become more apparent. Research has well documented the meaning of masculinity and femininity on the androgyny measures and some of their implications for behavior. The multidimensionality of sex roles has become more obvious as well as the interaction of personal predispositions with environmental factors. The need to examine between-sex differences in conjunction with within-sex differences has also been shown. Finally, it is clear that what constitutes sex-role adjustment cannot be easily prescribed in terms of one sex-role type, whether this type is traditional sex typing (as in preandrogyny research) or androgynous typing.

The trend in sex-role literature recognizes that androgyny as a concept can only be understood in terms of broader psychological principles. A personality type alone does not determine behavior; individuals do not behave in a social vacuum; individuals are affected by the same environmental conditions in different ways. The androgyny literature suggests some directions for future work in the study of sex roles, consistent with the view of androgyny as model. Directions for future work include: (a) expansion of current assessment of masculinity and femininity; (b) recognition of the multidimensionality of sex-role variables; (c) a more temperate view of the importance of the four-way typology; (d) a more sophisticated conception of the meaning of androgyny; and (e) explorations into the causes of sex roles and their change, particularly during adulthood.

FUTURE DIRECTIONS FOR RESEARCH

Assessment of Masculinity and Femininity

Professionals' view of masculinity and femininity as a result of research is inevitably shaped by the androgyny measures' success in assessing these dimensions. A significant amount of androgyny research has been validational in nature: to explore the meaningfulness of femininity and masculinity as currently operationalized, in relation to one another and to other variables presumably linked to these dimensions as currently defined. These studies have revealed the recurrence of instrumental/agentic and expressive/communal distinctions among androgyny measures. Validational studies have generally also been successful in substantiating the correspondence of these dimensions to intuitively related characteristics (e.g. masculinity and aspects of achievement motivation), especially for masculinity. Heilbrun (1981b) has argued that the influence of the dimensions presumably sampled by the measures is probably *underestimated* because of problems plaguing all personality assessment. Two critiques of the androgyny measures paradoxically support this possibility.

Critiques of androgyny measure content. In developing the androgyny measures, researchers utilized a variety of item selection procedures based on criteria including subjects' judgments of sex typicality, judgments of social desirability based on sex, and researchers' personal definitions of masculinity and femininity (see Chapter 2). Locksley and Colten (1979) and Myers and Gonda (1982) have questioned the validity of deriving self-description androgyny measures from presumably global sex stereotypes. The diversity of items incorporated into the measures and the responsiveness of stereotypic ratings to differences in rating methodology (cf. Myers & Gonda, 1982) introduces questions about what the instruments are actually measuring. However, as Spence and Helmreich (1979b) argue for the PAQ, the performance of the measure suggests that stereotypes can be successfully used as the basis for a personal trait measure. And, it is clear that each androgyny measure assesses something related to psychological differences between the sexes that discriminate among members of a single sex as well.

Locksley and Colten (1979) and Myers and Gonda (1982) have also questioned the importance of the characteristics sampled for individuals' self-perceptions and behavior. Myers and Gonda reported that when individuals are given an opportunity to describe themselves as they are in various situations, a small percentage of the descriptors overlap with femininity and masculinity content. Many other types of characteristics are apparently important to individuals, which are not included on androgyny measures (in this case, the BSRI). To my knowledge, no sex-role researcher has ever claimed that sex roles and masculinity/femininity in particular are the single primary determinants of self-perceptions and behavior, but simply that they are potentially powerful factors to consider. It is noteworthy that content related to masculinity and femininity may enter into as *much* as 10% of an individual's self-descriptions, as reported by Myers and Gonda.

Obviously, some important aspect of sex-role phenomena is being tapped by the measures. A central question for androgyny research is whether masculinity and femininity are adequately represented in current androgyny measures. To some extent, this question has been answered affirmatively through psychometric analyses as described in earlier chapters. However, research summarized in Chapter 3 suggested that future sex-role research might benefit from a careful look at ways to expand assessment of masculinity and especially femininity.

Expansion of femininity/masculinity definitions. Researchers might consider whether current androgyny measures capture the essence of the instrumental/ agentic and expressive/communal distinctions. For example, Richardson, Merrifield, Jacobsen, Evanoski, Hobish, and Goldstein (1981) asserted that androgyny measures do not tap the more active, caretaking components of femininity and achievement orientation of masculinity. Researchers have also paid little attention to the negative aspects of femininity and masculinity as first described by Spence, Helmreich, and Holahan (1979). These negative aspects may provide some evidence for the effects of possessing low degrees of positive dimensions. Preliminary analyses suggest a negative association between possession of the positive trait (e.g., PAQ masculinity) and the negative cross-sex characteristics (e.g., feminine-typed verbal passive/aggressiveness). Also, the presence of specific masculinity and femininity factors contained within the androgyny scales (see Chapter 2) suggests that much could be gained from analyzing what specific aspects of femininity and masculinity might be most influential in a given situation. Thus, expanding the content of Femininity and Masculinity scales and distinguishing among aspects of these dimensions could be informative.

Assessment methods other than self-description. One interesting possibility for future research is development of measures that describe individuals' levels of femininity and masculinity by methods other than self-descriptions. One example is asking others to rate a person on the androgyny measure. Androgyny measures have already been used to describe subjects' sex-role ideals (cf. Silvern & Ryan, 1983) and could easily be used to describe subjects themselves as seen through the eyes of others. Or, individuals' masculinity and femininity could be described by others observing their behavior within a situation or over time. These divergent measures could prove useful in corroborating the validity of current conceptions of masculinity and femininity. These unique measures could also provide some illuminating glimpses into the multidimensionality of sex-role related characteristics. For example, what is the correspondence between individuals' self-ratings and others' ratings of their masculinity and femininity? What is the relationship between these different types of ratings and a variety of behaviors?

Androgyny measures appear to be successful in assessing central components of the expressive/communal and instrumental/agentic distinctions underlying current definitions of femininity and masculinity. Researchers find self-descriptions to be an easy and meaningful behavior to elicit. However, the androgyny model suggests the importance of exploring the complexity of sex roles by considering alternate styles and content of measurement.

The dualistic conceptualization of masculinity and femininity is another aspect of current androgyny measurement that deserves closer consideration.

The Duality of Masculinity and Femininity

The dualistic conception of femininity and masculinity as separate dimensions coexisting in everyone has replaced the bipolar conception that posited them as mutually exclusive opposites of a single dimension. The dualistic framework frees these dimensions from identification with one sex alone and enriches the descriptions of sex-role options beyond the "either-or" dichotomization.

However, the dualistic conception is only one framework possible for analyzing sex-role variables, and may not adequately account for all variables that fall within the purview of sex-role theory and research. For example, Kaplan's (1979) hybrid characteristics (e.g., assertive dependency), which emerge from a synthesis of the two dimensions, cannot be readily classified within the dualistic definitions. Individuals classified as androgynous because they have eliminated masculinity and femininity as separate dimensions through sex-role transcendence (cf. Hefner et al., 1975) may also not be adequately defined using the two dimensions. Certainly, both hybrid characteristics and sex-role transcendence are meaningful topics for exploration by sex-role experts, but may not receive proper attention because they do not easily fit into the conceptual scheme. The same thing was true for androgyny until new conceptions of masculinity and femininity permitted it recognition.

Developmental theorists have outlined stages of development in sex-role terms that also do not fit easily into the dualistic framework. For example,

Knefelkamp, Widick, and Stroad's (1976) adaptation of Perry's cognitive stage model describes how women change their interpretations of women's role in society and consequently their views of themselves. Women at the highest stage must reconcile diverse personal themes within themselves into a personal identity and commit themselves to living out this personal balance within a relativistic world. This description is consistent with definitions of androgyny, but extends significantly past masculinity and femininity as currently described. Gilligan (1982) brilliantly outlines differences in men's and women's moral development, founded upon contrasting premises and evolving through separate progressions. The end result is a mature convergence for both sexes. In Gilligan's words, "to understand how the tension between responsibilities and rights sustains the dialectics of human development is to see the integrity of two disparate modes of experience that are in the end connected" (p. 174). To explain this synthesis of human experience in terms of masculinity and femininity dimensions as currently formulated would appear to be a case of shrinking the insights to fit within the conceptual boundaries rather than expanding the model to accommodate a wider range of possibilities.

The point is simply that the current conceptualization of masculinity and femininity should not blind researchers to aspects of sex roles that deserve careful study but do not fit nicely within the framework. A commitment to understanding the complexities of sex-role phenomena requires a recognition of possible limitations of present conceptual tools, and a willingness to integrate what *does* work with other insights. One such important insight is the recognition that different categories of sex-role variables do not necessarily covary as was previously thought.

Multidimensionality of Sex-role Variables

Early androgyny research assumed a close correspondence between sex-role related personality traits, attitudes, and various types of behaviors, analogous to preandrogyny research. That is, traditionally sex-typed persons were predicted to express conservative sex-role attitudes and to behave in sex-traditional ways. Spence and Helmreich have long argued for independent conceptualization and study of different types of sex-role variables. Research on the lack of close correspondence among these presumably related aspects of sex roles corroborates their predictions.

A meaningful core may unite cultural stereotypes, self-descriptions, attitudes, behaviors, and so on. Beyond this core, it appears safest to assume that the factors that describe and influence individuals' conceptions of themselves as men/women may not be the same as those characterizing their attitudes about the rightful functions of the sexes, or those that elicit sex-typical behaviors in a given setting. With the exception of Orlofsky's (Orlofsky, 1981b; Orlofsky, Ramsden, & Cohen, 1982) work on sex-role behaviors, recent androgyny research has focused upon the correlates and consequences of self-descriptions in personality traits. This focus is consistent with Huston's (1983) commentary about sex-role research in general. As Huston argued, personality traits represent only part of the picture. Her matrix of sex-typing variables outlines 20 different categories of variables meriting study, and self-perception of femininity/masculinity represents one option.

The lack of correspondence among different types of sex-role variables needs to be explored rather than ignored. Why is there a poor correspondence between personality traits and sex-role behaviors? What factors might enhance a close correspondence between categories of sex-role variables?

Individual differences. It appears reasonable to assume that there are individual differences in the degree to which personality traits (or more precisely, self-descriptions) are closely associated with other sex-role variables. For example, some sex-typed individuals may report conservative role attitudes or behave in a sex-traditional manner in a given situation, whereas others may not do so. Varying degrees of correspondence among types of sex-role variables may also be seen among androgynous persons. Exploring patterns of and reasons for the correspondence among sex-role variables may shed some light upon what causes differences in sex roles in adulthood.

Interacting variables. One possibility beginning to be explored is the presence of variables that interact with personal dispositions to produce variations in behavior. Garnets and Pleck's (1979) analysis of sex-role strain provides an example of such an interaction. They hypothesized that "the relationship between sex typing and adjustment is moderated by two variables: the individual's ideal for his and her own sex, and the degree of the individual's sex role salience" (p. 274). For high *sex-role salient* persons, discrepancies between an individual's perceptions of personal masculine and feminine characteristics (real self-concept) and qualities rooted in sex-role norms that they believe their sex should possess same-sex ideal, produces *sex-role strain*, and leads to devaluation of self. When sex-role salience is low, sex-role strain stemming from real/same sex ideal discrepancies is low. Garnets and Pleck suggested that the concept of sex role salience can refine predictions made about the association between sex typing and adjustment.

Level of self-esteem may affect the likelihood that sex-typed individuals will perform sex-typed versus nonsex-typed behaviors. Nadler, Maler, and Friedman (1984) suggested that for individuals who tend to evaluate themselves poorly, behaving in a manner discrepant with sex typing may cause negative feelings. These individuals would be unlikely to behave in nontraditional ways. Other sex-typed individuals who evaluate themselves more highly may also typically engage in sex-typed behaviors. These persons may also choose to behave in a nontraditional manner if the cost of *not* doing so is high, without the cost of negative feelings suffered by low-esteem individuals. This interaction of self-esteem may also be pertinent to differences in the behavior patterns of androgynous and undifferentiated persons, who are both nonsex-typed but report highly discrepant levels of self-esteem.

Sex-role attitudes and behaviors may also interact with femininity/masculinity traits with varying results. For example, Yanico (1981) proposed that attitudes about sex roles influence the relationship between sex-role identity and career choices. A woman with a masculine sex-role identity and nontraditional sex-role attitudes might make different occupational choices than a masculine woman with traditional sex-role attitudes. Similar differences might be found for persons whose behavior repertoires contain varying proportions of masculine and feminine-typed behaviors. A person classified as androgynous by personality trait self-descriptions who has a primarily masculine-typed repertoire might be expected to behave quite differently in a situation than an androgynous person with an androgynous behavior repertoire.

The nearly exclusive focus upon personality trait sex typing (and androgyny) may have grouped together individuals who differ in important ways other than their self-descriptions. If these differences are significant, failure to account for them would result in confusing patterns of data. That is, in research it may be illuminating to distinguish between androgynous persons with high versus low sex-role salience, or sex-typed persons with traditional versus conservative sex-role attitudes. These combinations of variables may well prove to be more interesting and ultimately more explanatory than concentration upon personality trait self-descriptions alone.

The focus upon personal predispositions in the form of traits is a familiar one in psychology. However, the androgyny literature has shown that masculine/feminine self-descriptions do not always correlate with similarly typed behaviors or attitudes as expected. Part of this lack of correspondence is attributable to the role of situational factors, which will be discussed shortly. This lack of correspondence also indicates that sex role is a multidimensional construct that includes but goes beyond familiar personality characteristics. Explanations for sex roles need to extend beyond assuming that personality directly causes behavior in some manner. More complex interactions among variables are likely to occur, and these interactions have not been studied well.

This emphasis upon the multidimensionality of sex-role variables and a lessened emphasis upon personality traits by themselves suggests that description of persons by levels of traits may not be sufficient for some research purposes. The third direction for future work is implementing a more moderate view of the value of the sex-role typology.

Limitations of the Typology

The four-way typology was originally suggested as a convenient mode of representing the conjoint influence of masculinity and femininity. Some professionals came to regard it as an all-purpose, durable personality typing classification, although major androgyny theorists have largely adopted it more cautiously for descriptive rather than prescriptive purposes. As research in Chapter 3 indicated, use of the typology has yielded some puzzling and controversial results. If researchers view the typology as the only valid way to represent the feminine and masculine dimensions, they might generalize their doubts about the typology's validity to conclusions about the value of the androgyny model itself.

Researchers may hesitate to recommend unquestioned use of the typology for a variety of reasons. Some researchers are well aware of the shortcomings of the androgyny measures and scoring procedures upon which the typology is based. Others may recommend its use only for particular research purposes. Still others have viewed sex-role classification to imply an unnecessarily static view of sex roles and masculinity and femininity, and prefer to consider them as products of person-environment interaction, which are open to change. Other researchers see an individual's current sex-role classification as one step in a progression of life changes. These researchers would be interested in examining projected variations in masculinity and femininity over time as a function of age and/or developmental stage.

The typology has been a valuable tool, but it is not universally applicable for all analyses of masculinity/femininity, and is not foolproof. Its limitations can be recognized without necessarily dismissing the value of the androgyny model of masculinity and femininity. Alternative methods of describing individuals' relative degrees of masculinity and femininity are better suited for some purposes and types of data. It is reasonable to assume that if sex-role related phenomena are complex and multidimensional, descriptive methods may need to be likewise.

When researchers use the four-way typology, they should attempt to provide a rationale for why members of the sex-role categories should behave differently from one another. Spence and Helmreich would argue that the rationale should reflect differences attributable to the masculinity/femininity trait distinctions, although Bem's gender-schema theory suggests that explanations may not necessarily need to be trait-based. The failure to provide such a rationale makes it difficult to sort out differences among the categories that are random, from those that might be meaningful to consider further.

In addition, low/low scorers or undifferentiated persons deserve a closer look. Research has documented their general negative pattern of characteristics, most notably lower self-esteem and higher scores on various measures of maladjustment. Is their poorer performance in research in general because of their low self-esteem, or is the low self-esteem an indication of a more pervasive syndrome or response style? Their degree of similarity to androgynous persons also needs to be clarified. Clearly, there are some important differences between undifferentiated and androgynous persons (see Tables 3.1–3.4). Yet, Bem (1981a) has stated that these groups share an absence of sex typing, which presumably causes them to behave in some similar ways as well.

To summarize briefly, the typology provides one straightforward way to analyze the effects of femininity and masculinity. Recurring questions about the meaningfulness of the typology suggest that researchers should routinely consider other methods as well. When the four-way typlogy *is* used, researchers should specify why they expect differences among the categories to emerge. Such hypotheses could be invaluable in addressing the complexities of sex roles posited in the androgyny model.

The failure to provide a theoretical rationale for research expectations is also pertinent to the fourth recommended direction for androgyny research: reevaluation of the meaning of androgyny.

The Meaning of Androgyny

On the most basic level, androgyny simply indicates a particular blending of masculine and feminine characteristics. As suggested in this chapter, it can also label a model of masculinity and femininity, embodying some recently formulated assumptions about how these dimensions can and do interact. Major theorists and researchers have rapidly abandoned or avoided altogther a focus on androgyny per se in favor of a broader perspective on the properties and import of masculinity and femininity. For many professionals, however, what is most appealing about the androgyny model is its explicit recognition of the existence of nonsex-typed persons. This type of person was not openly acknowledged in preandrogyny formulations and signifies new alternatives for both sexes in a time of sex-role change.

Interest in clarifying the implications of androgynous typing has produced a body of studies addressing what Taylor and Hall (1982) denote as substantive issues in androgyny research. In this research, hypotheses about the consequences of various levels of masculinity and femininity feature characteristics not immediately obvious from the dimensions' content on androgyny measures. Thus, individuals describing themselves as possessing high levels of instrumental/agentic and expressive/communal characteristics are hypothesized to be flexible in their sex-role related behaviors across situations. Or, they are hypothesized to represent an ideal type with distinct mental health advantages over others.

Research on the implications of androgyny has suffered from four main problems: (a) a lack of theoretical rationale provided for studies; (b) the potential for researchers' sex-role values to color their hypotheses and conclusions; (c) oversimplification of definitions of androgynous persons; and (d) failure to account for between-sex differences.

Lack of theoretical rationale. Research on substantive issues is more troublesome than research that simply validates the content of the masculinity and femininity dimensions. Researchers have a greater burden to document the reasoning behind their studies than in validational studies, because substantive issues extend beyond obvious implications of the dimensions' content. Bem has recognized this responsibility through her speculations about how and why sex-typed persons process information differently than nonsex-typed persons, and how the BSRI may be able to distinguish these two groups. Unfortunately, many other researchers, especially those generating studies to demonstrate that androgynous persons are better at everything, have not done likewise.

This failure to develop comprehensive, potentially testable rationales supporting research hypotheses has yielded a bewildering mass of articles lacking conceptual bridges to unite them. For the consumer of the literature, it becomes more difficult to know who or what to believe about the nature and implications of androgyny.

The influence of sex-role values. The omission of a theoretical rationale is related to the second problem in research on androgyny's substantive issues. The notion of androgyny by its very nature embodies a new set of values about sex roles, and is probably most attractive as a concept to those who personally value less stereotyped roles for the sexes. As was true for preandrogyny sex-role research, these values can subtly shape empirical designs and the conclusions drawn from researchers' observations. A conclusion that the positive relationships between high masculinity/femininity and paper-and-pencil measures of self-esteem demonstrates decisively that androgyny is ideal, reflects more the values of the researchers than the data itself. Similarly, interpreting limitations within recent literature as proof that androgyny is not a viable concept also appears extreme.

The widespread endorsement of hypotheses such as androgyny's flexibility and ideal nature may mean that these hypotheses correspond closely to professionals' own experience about sex-role consequences, and in this manner receive real-life validation. However, androgyny research can extend and modify professionals' own observations. Because of the possibility that personal sex-role values may affect how professionals view androgyny and its consequences, professionals need to be especially careful to examine their own assumptions and conclusions.

Oversimplification of androgyny. Androgyny has typically been defined as possession of certain levels of masculine and feminine personality characteristics. Individuals classified as androgynous may actually be more diverse in nature than this simple definition suggests. Grouping together individuals with diverse characteristics under one category may obscure some meaningful differences among them which could clarify androgyny.

For example, Bem (1981a, 1982) and Markus and associates (Crane & Markus, 1982; Markus, Crane, Bernstein, & Siladi, 1982) have discussed whether androgynous persons possess both masculine and feminine schema, or whether they are aschematic with respect to gender. It is conceivable that *both* types of persons may be represented in androgyny research, and that each type may behave distinctively as a result of their cognitive processing.

Persons classified as androgynous because of personality traits may show differences in their sex-typed behavior patterns. LaFrance and Carmen (1980) characterized androgynous behaviors as the addition of some cross-sex behaviors and deletion of some of the more extreme same-sex behaviors. The specific patterns of additions and deletions may well differ across androgynous persons, which may result in differences in their behavior.

Finally, an early hypothesis in the androgyny literature was that androgynous persons are able to determine the most situational appropriate behavior to perform, and can perform a range of masculine and feminine-typed behaviors comfortably. With the emphasis upon individual differences in the androgyny model, it would not be surprising to find differences among androgynous persons in their sensitivity to environmental cues, the breadth of their behavioral repertoire, and their willingness to engage in certain behaviors. In gender schema theory, androgynous persons' freedom from attending to sex-linked cues in a situation presumably leaves them open to behave for a variety of reasons, so that differences among androgynous persons' behavior might be expected. Research has not begun to explore the possibility of complex differences among androgynous persons.

Sex differences in androgyny. The different implications of androgyny for the sexes need closer examination. Some professionals have suggested that the origins, correlates, and consequences of androgyny might not be the same for both sexes, and that in fact androgyny's hypothesized benefits may be enjoyed primarily by women. Few studies have explicitly attempted to examine these sex differences (see Heilbrun, 1984 for a recent exception). Instead, androgynous men and women have typically been compared as part of a broader study conducted for some other purpose. This problem is part of a more general tendency of failing to consider explicitly the interaction of between-sex and within-sex differences.

To clarify what androgyny means for individuals, researchers need to be careful to: (a) separate their values from their hypotheses and conclusions;

(b) provide a theoretical rationale for their hypotheses; (c) consider ways to refine their definitions of androgyny; and (d) look for between-sex interactions, as well as the possibility of other interactions described elsewhere in this chapter.

Issues of Causality

Throughout the issues raised in the chapter runs a common concern for explanation and prediction in addition to simple description. It is now clear that complex patterns of sex-role related differences are neither determined by, nor independent from a person's sex. Individual women and men often share similarities as well as differences. Levels of femininity and masculinity appear to be meaningfully related to some of these differences. Apparently, there is no simple cause-effect relationship between feminine/masculine personality traits and sex-role behaviors of various types. What is not at all clear in the androgyny literature is how and why these complex between and within-sex differences occur. Three promising areas for future work to address these questions are the interaction between an individual and the environment, theories linking sex roles in childhood and adulthood, and sex-role change in adulthood.

Person-environment interaction. Part of the explanation of sex-role related differences probably lies in analysis of person-environment interactions. Locksley and Colten (1979) asserted that situation-specific factors may interact with or supersede the effects of masculine and feminine personality traits. The environment may provide individuals with powerful cues about how they ought to behave. Sex-typed individuals may be particularly sensitive to sex (gender)-linked cues (cf. Bem, 1981a). Androgynous persons may be particularly skilled in picking up more general cues about what are the most adaptive or rewarding ways to respond (cf. Kelly & Worell, 1977). These environmental cues may vary across situations.

Social learning theory (Mischel, 1970) has also emphasized how performance of a particular sex-role behavior is influenced by the rewards or punishments that a person expects to receive. This possibility has received some attention in sex-role research based upon children and adolescents (Huston, 1983). Although it is reasonable to assume that adults behave in sex-typical or atypical ways at least partly to obtain acceptance and avoid disapproval, embarrassment, and so on, androgyny researchers have not explored this possibility.

The interaction of personal and environmental factors may be particularly helpful in explaining sex/sex-role interactions. Locksley and Colten (1979) stressed the impact of sex-based norms upon behavior. These norms may be common across situations, but are not necessarily applied or enforced consistently.

Individual characteristics may interact with these sex-based norms to produce differences in behavior. Klein and Willerman's (1979) study suggested that sex-based norms may elicit behaviors, but personal masculinity/femininity may affect how these behaviors are performed by a person. According to Bem's gender schema theory, individuals are not equally susceptible to identifying themselves and environmental cues by sex. Thus, sex-based norms and anticipated rewards and punishments may interact with personal characteristics to produce differences in behavior that are poorly understood.

Sex roles in childhood and adulthood. Explanation and prediction of behavior within the androgyny model have been hampered by the lack of perspectives linking the literature's nearly exclusive focus upon adults to sex roles in earlier years. Over the years, most sex-role theory and research has considered acquisition during the childhood years. Some of the understanding gleaned from this work may also be pertinent to understanding sex roles in the adult years, if careful theoretical transitions are made. Bem's and Spence and Helmreich's theoretical statements may provide starting points for such theoretical bridges.

Sex-role change in adulthood. Androgyny literature has also not considered the issue of sex-role change in adulthood. This is paradoxical, in light of how professionals have been concerned with the stresses accompanying sex-role change today, and have extensively discussed how to encourage individuals to become less sex-typed.

Certain individuals may find it easier to change than others. For example, the sex-role related behavior of gender-aschematic individuals might be relatively easy to change, because they are presumably not internally motivated to match their perceptions and behavior to pervasive sex-typical standards. Individuals engaged in lifestyles inconsistent with their personal sex-role identity might also be more likely to change, as in the case of masculine women who are full-time homemakers.

Sex-role changes may also reflect a maturational trend in adult development, as suggested by some development perspectives in androgyny (cf. Hefner, Rebecca, & Oleshansky, 1975). These perspectives imply that all individuals do not necessarily progress through all of the sex-role stages. Sex-role change may thus represent some developmental progress not present in another adult.

The question of change in sex roles is complicated by issues of directionality. It is generally assumed that personality traits cause certain behaviors, which describes a unidirectional change process. Change may actually be bidirectional: changes in environmental demands, attitudes, and so on may cause individuals to change their self-evaluations in terms of femininity/masculinity just as the reverse may be true. Feldman, Biringen, & Nash's (1981) research suggested that an individual's self-description in terms of masculinity and femininity may change in response to family demands. Sex-role self-descriptions may be involved in a reciprocal relationship with other person variables, so that each variable has an effect upon the other. Tinsley, Kass, Moreland, and Harren (1983) proposed such a reciprocal relationship between sex-role identity, cognitive complexity, and sex-role attitudes.

In summary, the androgyny model highlights the need for explanation and prediction in addition to description of sex roles. Research has documented the existence of complex sex-role related differences without simple cause-effect relationships between feminine/masculine personality traits (or sex-role identity) and sex-role behaviors of various types. Analysis of person-environment interactions, the relationship between sex roles in childhood and adulthood, and the occurrence of sex-role change in adulthood may be instrumental in generating these missing explanations within the androgyny model.

Summary

The focus of the androgyny model is upon describing, explaining, and predicting the range of sex-role related similarities and differences between men and women, including androgyny. This model incorporates some of the essential assumptions supporting androgyny as a concept, but extends significantly beyond them. In the androgyny model, androgyny as a concept fits within a broader framework for the study of sex roles which recognizes the complexity of the factors and processes involved in the multiple variations of sex roles. Androgyny research summarized in the last chapter suggests some future directions for theory and research within this model.

First, researchers can broaden and refine their assessment of femininity and masculinity. Current androgyny measures successfully incorporate instrumental/agentic and expressive/communal distinctions in their masculinity and femininity scales respectively. These masculinity/femininity descriptions could be expanded by focusing upon different aspects of the trait distinctions, including negative aspects of masculinity and femininity, or by attending more closely to the unique factors included on each scale. Researchers could also use methods other than self-description to assess an individual's masculinity/femininity, such as ratings of others. Alternate styles and content of measurement may help to represent the complexity of sex-role variables more adequately. Researchers should also consider what types of sex-role variables and processes may not fit into the dualistic framework now characterizing the masculinity and femininity dimensions.

Second, sex-role variables appear to be multidimensional in nature rather than unidimensional as was previously thought. The lack of a close correspondence among presumably related types of sex-role variables (e.g., between personality traits and behaviors) deserves closer attention. There may be some important individual differences in the degree to which these aspects of sex roles covary within an individual. Some variables, such as sex-role salience or attitudes, may interact with personality predispositions to produce certain specific patterns of behaviors. It appears obvious that personality traits alone do not cause behaviors. The multidimensionality of sex roles suggests that complex interactions among variables are likely to occur, and these interactions have not been extensively studied.

Third, the popular sex-role typology is not the only way to represent the influence of the masculinity and femininity dimensions. A range of descriptive methods is needed to address the complexity and multidimensionality of sex-role variables and processes. Researchers who use the typology should attempt to predict how and why they expect the members of the categories to behave differently. These theoretical statements may help to sort out the frequently puzzling presence or lack of differences among persons labeled according to their self-reported levels of femininity and masculinity.

Fourth, understanding about what androgyny actually means has probably been hampered by four problems in the androgyny literature. Researchers have frequently not provided a clear rationale for their hypotheses about androgynous individuals' unique characteristics. It has also been easy for researchers' own values to affect how they view androgyny and its consequences. These views can color how they plan and interpret androgyny research. Third, individuals uniformly classified as androgynous may be quite diverse in various characteristics (e.g., in cognitive processing, behavioral repertoire, and actual performance of behaviors). Failure to distinguish among these individuals may obscure some important differences among them. Fourth, researchers should examine more closely the possibility that androgyny's origins, correlates, and consequences may not be the same for men and women.

Finally, issues concerning how and why complex between and within-sex differences occur are relevant to many areas of sex-role research in the future. Analyses of person-environment interaction including environmental cues, rewards for behavior, and powerful sex-based norms should replace an emphasis upon the impact of person variables (e.g., traits) alone. Theoretical statements linking sex-role acquisition and behavior in childhood with sex roles in adulthood are needed. How and why sex-role change might occur in adulthood has also not been given adequate attention. Certain individuals may find it easier to change than others, for largely unspecified reasons. Change itself is likely to be a bidirectional process, where the personality self-descriptions stressed in androgyny research promote and are conversely affected by changes in other types of characteristics.

The androgyny model recognizes that the concept of androgyny rests within a broader set of assumptions and observations about the nature of sex roles. Sex roles must be understood in relation to a complex interrelationship among diverse variables encompassing the person and the environment. Androgyny itself gains its meaning from an appreciation of the broader psychological processes maintaining sex-role related differences. Future androgyny research should follow in the footsteps of Bem and Spence and Helmreich in deemphasizing the androgynous type itself, in favor of examining what may produce and maintain the range of sex-role variations, including androgyny.

This section has mainly emphasized ways in which the conceptualization of sex roles can be expanded in future research. These ideas provide the content of studies. However, researchers can also improve future research by refining *how* these ideas are studied. Recurrent problems in androgyny research methodology will next be discussed, followed by a list of suggestions for carrying out studies in the future.

RESEARCH METHODOLOGY CRITIQUE

To the delight of graduate students and the dismay of those synthesizing the androgyny research, empirical studies on psychological androgyny are plagued with a number of methodological problems. Although trivial ideas can be and are successfully tested with sound research methodologies, the most exciting conceptualizations can easily be buried under sloppy procedures. Part of the problem in integrating all of the results presented in Chapter 3 is attributable to the mixed quality of research methodologies employed by the researchers. Some problems are perhaps unavoidable; others evoke only frustration in the serious reader. The brief critique presented in this chapter is one such response and is meant to prompt a more critical attitude rather than to provide a comprehensive listing of methodological failings. Worell's (1978) excellent review incorporates unreferenced prototypes of problems from published and unpublished work, and should serve as a primary source for the interested reader. Lenney (1979a, 1979b) also outlines important issues to consider.

The Theoretical Basis/Statement of Hypotheses

Any good study should begin with a review of pertinent literature and a cogent statement of research hypotheses. This section is, all too frequently, much weaker than is necessary in androgyny research. The ready availability of androgyny measures has encouraged a wealth of studies in search of a purpose, with researchers hoping to find *some* relationship among several measures. Literature reviews may be done in a cursory fashion, listing only the favorite studies in the field at the time and omitting other easily retrievable, more relevant sources. The value of Bem's work is undeniable, yet does not represent all androgyny research. Apparently other perspectives are not often considered for some unspecified reason. This narrow view can inhibit the integration of the various perspectives into a more meaningful whole.

While androgyny studies are often unconnected to one another, as noted earlier in this chapter the general study of androgyny is isolated from other areas of psychological research. Complex determinants of behavior, including cognitive orientations, motivations, and person-environment interactions are often overlooked. Exclusive reliance on global self-descriptions as determinants of behavior prevents exploration of more sophisticated interactions from the start. Conversely, when extensions to other realms of behavior are made, they need to be accompanied by a thoughtful rationale so as not to appear to be "fishing expeditions."

When hypotheses are stated, they may not be appropriate for the androgyny measure used, which makes negative findings difficult to interpret. If the hypothesis addresses either too broad a band of behaviors or characteristics tangential to the androgyny concept, it is challenging to sort out from garbled results whether the theory, construct, scale, or design is at fault (cf. Worell, 1978). Even more troublesome are the hypotheses of the "androgynous types will score higher because they're better" variety. Expectations should be based on more than stereotypes alone. Where possible, hypotheses should order dependent variables by their expected degree of association with androgyny, a step very helpful when a mass of variables is tapped (Lenney, 1979b).

One common but easily remedied shortcoming of research is failure to state alternative hypotheses (Lenney, 1979a). Especially in the type of exploratory work characteristic of much of the androgyny research, it is quite conceivable that divergent results may be theoretically meaningful. Development and subsequent discussion of competing hypotheses may help to clarify broader theoretical issues than is possible with exploration of only one possibility. Alternative hypotheses are not always necessary or even appropriate in a given study, but should be routinely considered in the planning of any study.

A major problem which especially distressed Worell (1978) is the failure to examine sex by sex-role interactions meaningfully. This failure has taken several forms: (a) collapsing men and women into a single group for analysis by sex-role category alone; (b) ignoring possible effects due to sex role in favor of analyzing only male versus female distinctions; or (c) using sex differences as a criterion for validity of the Masculinity and Femininity scales, effectively misunderstanding the purpose of the scales. As Worell stated, "although gender (sex) and sociocultural sex roles are not completely independent of each other, they are by no means isomorphic" (pp. 781–782). Such confusions can be easily remedied.

Sampling Procedures

As in many psychological studies, the favorite subject group is undergraduate college students. This poses a special problem in androgyny research in that there is some evidence that relative degrees of masculinity and femininity may vary somewhat over the life span. Students also represent a specialized subgroup in terms of socioeconomic status, career goals, racial or ethnic background, and intelligence. These factors may all have some impact on sex-role related characteristics and behavior.

Sampling procedures and the sample itself may be insufficiently described. How and why a particular group was chosen may be unrevealed, as well as the percentages of these initially contacted who did agree to participate. Characteristics of the sample beyond sex are often left unspecified.

Extremes of sample size may be problematic. Very small samples make the meaningfulness of statistical analyses questionable, especially with the still smaller frequencies in the cross-sex typed categories. On the other hand, very large samples may encourage injudicious interpretation of statistically significant results when the actual effect size is quite small.

As Worell (1978) pointed out, sampling issues extend to the use of contrast or control groups as well. There should be grounds for assuming that the groups differ and are similar to the experimental groups along desired dimensions. Especially when comparisons are made between "maladjusted" and "adjusted" groups, it should not be assumed that members of the contrast group are free of problems because they did not seek help.

Use of Androgyny Measures

As should have been clear from Chapter 2, the measures are not interchangeable. Frequently, articles do not provide the reasons for selection of a given measure. Important differences between the measures should be considered and may be illuminating in discussion of results as well.

The androgyny measures are occasionally modified by the researcher: shortened, lengthened, factored, or varied in method of administrations. Reasons for such modifications should be explicitly stated, and the impact upon data analysis and interpretation of results should be taken into account rather than ignored.

Most androgyny research has utilized paper-and-pencil tasks to measure both masculinity/femininity and other variables believed to be associated with them. Frequently these other measures are not accompanied by information regarding their characteristics, reliability, and validity, making explanation of the data a real challenge. The ease of using paper-and-pencil measures in research has obscured the potential value of other types of variables and research strategies, for example, activities engaged in or behavioral observations. As Worell (1978) indicated, use of paper-and-pencil measures alone can introduce the problem of "method variance" where significant relationships are confounded by commonalities in *how* the variables are measured.

Scoring Procedures

As Spence and Helmreich (1979c) amply demonstrated, different scoring procedures for the same androgyny measure are based on divergent views of the relationship between masculinity/femininity and other variables, and may not represent equally well the nature of the relationship. Reasons for choice of scoring procedures should be based on more than convention alone whenever possible. Occasionally researchers develop their own scoring procedures, some with no clear rationale for doing so. New procedures can be invaluable in understanding the relationship between sex-role related variables, but can add to the chaotic mass of research when not explicitly discussed vis-à-vis other, more commonly utilized methods. The lack of follow-up on new scoring procedures by other researchers in subsequent studies makes evaluation of the merit of the new procedure tricky to accomplish.

Most current scoring procedures rely upon mean scores or medians to calculate an individual's relative standing on masculinity and femininity. The numerical values of these statistics, especially when computed on that sample only, are necessary to enable cross-sample comparisons of results.

Use of Experimental Procedures

Worell (1978) discussed some methodological issues pertinent to designs other than the standard paper-and-pencil correlational study. In clinical analogue studies, subjects are expected to give diagnoses, labels, and treatment or adjustment evaluations to stimulus persons who vary on sex role or sex. It is assumed that generalization to actual clinical situations can be fairly made, which may not be an accurate assumption to make. In use of task performance and behavior sample designs, how people actually do behave in "real-life" situations is examined. Major issues here include: (a) criterion or construct validity—whether the task/situation reflects correctly the variable of interest; and (b) sex-role validity—whether the task represents a type of behavior meaningfully related to the specific sex-role dimensions tapped by a given measure. Information about how the experimental tasks were chosen is frequently lacking or insufficient, or when present can suggest that the task is inappropriate for the domain of sex-role behavior in question.

A problem most notable in interpersonal rating tasks is improper replications of previous tasks (Worell, 1978). Procedures and instructions to subjects may not be followed exactly as they were in the original study, which limits the replication study's usefulness for that purpose.

Use of Statistical Analyses

The problem of choosing and using appropriate statistical analyses can be avoided through expert consultation. Unfortunately, the analyses may seriously detract from the value of the empirical data. Researchers are sometimes uncertain about the choice of their procedures, which is apparent occasionally in the use of an inappropriate statistical test. T tests are certainly not appropriate for every study, but more complex analyses (e.g., factor analyses) are not automatically superior for a given type of question. Analyses need to fit the hypotheses and type of data collected.

Two of the most frequently encountered statistical problems are sample size and use of multiple test statistics. Inadequate sample sizes for the specific analyses used may result in artificially deflated or inflated results. Researchers are also fond of performing every possible statistical comparison between the variables without adjusting the alpha level for nonindependence of the statistical tests. Such statistical results are misleading. At best, performance of many statistical analyses, some devoid of rationale, can confuse the reader and resemble more a card game with frequent deck shuffling than a planned series of comparisons chosen to test certain explicit and thoughtful research hypotheses. Follow-up tests should also be clearly motivated less by hopes to find *something* salvageable from the data and more by a systematic step-by-step examination of the data.

Researchers also need to be consistently disciplined in their interpretation of the data. Statistical significance is not necessarily the same as practical significance: correlations of less than .20, for example, are not very impressive except in their smallness. Alpha levels should also follow conventional usage, with departures duly justified.

Discussion of Results

As Worell (1978) stated, "negative findings do not necessarily imply a useless theory, a questionable construct, or an invalid sex-role scale" (p. 781). Alternative hypotheses or inadequate designs may produce these results as well. These possibilities should be considered even when the data fall in the desired direction, especially when the possibilities concern subject-specific or situation-specific factors not obvious to other readers. Instead, the reader is often left with puzzling questions about the equally puzzling presence (or lack) of statistically significant results.

Possible limitations to the generalizability of results are not supplied nearly as often as promises of ultimate answers. Some researchers have a tendency for grandiosity in expounding on the meaningfulness of their data. Conclusions may bear little relationship to the "near-significant" or statistically significant but modest statistics yielded in the analyses. Ideas for the future research directions are rarely described, thus inhibiting continuity in the field in general (as well as the reader's positive anticipation of the researcher's future work).

RECOMMENDATIONS

Few of these research problems are unavoidable. Most can be corrected or eliminated with some advance planning and prudence. Worell's (1978) suggestions were invaluable in composing this prescriptive list.

Theoretical Basis/Statement of Hypotheses

1. Provide a clear, theoretically sound rationale for expecting relationships between sets of variables. Avoid what Worell (1978) calls a "contest between white hats and black hats" because "androgynous persons ought to be better at everything" (p. 779).
2. Define phenomena of interest clearly and consistently, with some respect for conventional usage of terminology.
3. Do library homework conscientiously. The reference list of this book alone should suggest other researchers may have something to offer.
4. Consider alternative perspectives on androgyny seriously, to determine where the proposed research may best fit and contribute.
5. Question its relevance to psychological (personality, social, behavioral, etc.) research in general. How will it fit into the larger picture?
6. Make sure that the hypotheses can be addressed meaningfully by the particular androgyny measure chosen.
7. Specify direction and/or ordering of results expected via the research hypotheses whenever possible.
8. If the sex-role typology is used, specify how and why differences among the categories should occur.
9. Consider the appropriateness of competing hypotheses, and if possible plan to analyze for them in the course of the research.
10. Be sure to distinguish between sex and sex-role main effects, and analyze for interactions between them.
11. When feasible, try to state ahead of time the potential meaningfulness and/or limitations of the findings.
12. Be aware of the conceptual issues discussed in chapters here and in other resources. There is no need to reinvent an already crooked wheel.

Sampling Procedures

1. Try to use samples other than undergraduate college students, where appropriate, of course. Where students are an appropriate sample, state *why* if not obvious from the research hypotheses.
2. Describe sampling procedures and characteristics of the sample and its parent population clearly.
3. Choose sample size to fit the study rather than forcing analyses to fit sample size whenever possible. Recognize how to interpret results sensibly in light of the sample.
4. Select contrast or control groups wisely with explicit criteria in mind as well. Control for what is essential to control.

Use of Androgyny Measures

1. Be aware of theoretical and psychometric distinctions among the various androgyny measures, and choose with foresight.
2. Where pertinent, present the rationale for modifying standard androgyny measures, and the new version's convergence/divergence with the original. Consider these aspects in interpreting results.
3. Be as faithful in documenting other measures chosen for use as with the androgyny measures. Recognize their strengths and liabilities too.
4. Consider the usefulness of research strategies other than paper-and-pencil measurement for particular research questions.

Scoring Procedures

1. Choose scoring procedures with an eye toward the expected relationship between the variables.
2. When new scoring procedures are utilized, describe the rationale for doing so and their comparability to other more commonly-used methods. Explicit statistical comparisons between methods are usually easy to effect in data analysis.
3. Consider following up on unique scoring methods proposed earlier if they appear to have merit.
4. Provide descriptive statistics for the sample's masculinity and femininity score distributions. Note unusual discrepancies from other studies if present.
5. Avoid sex/sex-role confounding. Use cut-off points for classification based on combined-sex samples, and use raw scores to eliminate this criterion-group problem. If this procedure is judged to be clearly inappropriate or impossible to implement, be sure to discuss why alternative procedures are preferable and/or meaningful in light of this issue.

Use of Experimental Procedures

1. Make sure that generalization from analogue to real-life settings is defensible. It is better to err on the conservative than on the generous side.
2. Attend to criterion or construct and sex-role validity issues in studies using task performance and behavioral samples. Pretest tasks to determine their sex-role relevance and value. Choice of tasks should reflect sociocultural standards (sex role) rather than simply sex differences of endorsement, unless between-sex differences in response are of sole interest.
3. Specify task selection and performance procedures clearly enough so that adequate replication or extension is possible.

4. In replication studies, be faithful enough to the original research plan so that the label of replication can be preserved. Altered replications are fine, when intentional.

Use of Statistical Analyses

1. Consult a statistical expert if helpful. It may save the study later.
2. Choose and apply statistical procedures carefully. Be aware of a particular procedure's essential assumptions and limitations.
3. Make sure that the sample size is adequate for desired procedures. If questionable, point out how it is questionable.
4. If multiple tests are performed, determine if the capitalization upon chance variations which accompany dependent observations will cause problems for data interpretation.
5. Be parsimonious in numbers of analyses performed. Be considerate of the reader's potential confusion in assimilating complicated analyses by presenting data clearly and concisely with appropriate summaries.
6. Make sure it is obvious which analyses correspond to which hypotheses.
7. Whenever possible, use preplanned follow-up tests to preserve the congruence with the theoretical rationales.
8. Be ruthless in recognizing nonsignificant results. (Remember that these may be theoretically meaningful as well.)
9. Remember that some intended and serendipitous overlapping of personality measures can frequently be expected. Explore ways to control for these statistically where needed, or be prepared to account for this overlapping in discussion of results.
10. Consider the feasibility of using masculine and feminine raw scores in data analyses to circumvent classification and scoring issues.

Discussion of Results

1. Reflect the theoretical rationale in interpreting the results.
2. Explore fallibility of the design and analyses as well as that of androgyny theory, terms, and measurement in accounting for nonsignificant results.
3. Formulate alternative hypotheses in discussing results whenever possible. Use them as guides for subsequent studies.
4. Make discussion of results parsimonious and credible.
5. Provide clear guidelines whenever possible pertaining to the generalizability of the results.
6. Attempt to discriminate between statistical and practical significance of results

Chapter 5
ANDROGYNY IN PRACTICE

As reviewed earlier in this book, proponents of androgyny generally hold certain basic assumptions about the nature of femininity and masculinity. Positive aspects of masculinity and femininity are assumed to have important consequences for human behavior. A combination of both dimensions should have the most desirable implications for individuals of both sexes, rather than exclusive possession of one set of characteristics as traditionally assumed. Androgyny is thus a highly desirable sex-role alternative, replacing traditional sex-based distinctions as the ideal.

The earliest research on psychological androgyny focused upon demonstrating the mental health benefits of androgynous typing. Bem and her colleagues' work on behavioral flexibility (Bem, 1975; Bem & Lenney, 1976; Bem, Martyna, & Watson, 1976) was based on the hypothesis that "whereas a narrowly masculine self-concept may inhibit so-called feminine behaviors, and a narrowly feminine self-concept may inhibit so-called masculine behaviors, a mixed or androgynous self-concept may allow an individual to freely engage in both masculine and feminine behaviors" (Bem, 1975, p. 634). Other early research documenting high levels of self-esteem in androgynous persons (cf. Spence, Helmreich, & Stapp, 1975) was consistent with assumptions about androgyny's superiority.

Many psychological practitioners adopted these hypotheses about androgyny's flexibility and adaptability as the core of a new sex-role ideal. Traditional sex roles were seen as maladaptive because exclusive reliance upon them prevented development and expansion of the positive, sex-atypical domain. Reliance on one domain indicates a failure to develop one's psychological potential to its fullest. In contrast, androgynous persons are presumably able to develop this potential through transcending sex-based restrictions traditionally placed upon their sex (Forisha, 1978; Foxley, 1979).

This conception of androgyny as extending one's personality and behavioral alternatives is apparent in recent literature on psychological practice concerning sex-role issues. In this chapter, negative aspects of traditional sex roles will be briefly reviewed. Assumptions about androgyny (and traditional sex typing) have been incorporated into counseling interventions aimed at helping men and women overcome sex-role based restrictions. Examples of these interventions will also be discussed. In counseling clients toward androgyny, practitioners must be aware of certain basic conceptual and values issues. An outline of these issues will be followed by one model for sex-role counseling that can be used with both male and female clients.

COUNSELING FOR ANDROGYNY: A RATIONALE

Traditional Sex-role Characteristics and Problems

As summarized in Chapter 1, certain characteristics have been traditionally associated with each sex. These sex-based associations are generally well known by members of a particular society. These stereotypes represent what characteristics are widely considered to be typical and/or desirable for one sex to possess. Stereotypes are by their very nature overgeneralizations and the existence of a man or woman precisely fitting these dispositions is probably mythical, except as projected through popular media (compare the enduringly popular images of Marilyn Monroe and John Wayne). Any given real individual is probably best characterized by a combination of the stereotypes to some degree. There is a dark side to the stereotypes as well: Men are also considered to be emotionally inexpressive and unskilled in interactions with others while women are labeled as passive and dependent. The negative implications of these pervasive sex-role stereotypes have caught the attention of mental health practitioners in recent years.

It is widely believed today that strict adherence to sex-appropriate standards for characteristics and behavior can adversely affect the psychological well-being of both sexes. Gove (1979) persuasively analyzed sex differences in the epidemiology of mental disorders. His perspective emphasized differential sex-role stresses present from early childhood into adulthood, which are related to the incidence of certain emotional disorders. The patterns of mental health problems experienced by the sexes can be predicted to some extent by extrapolation from their sex-role stereotypes.

In the case of women, as Brodsky and Hare-Mustin (1980) succinctly stated, "certain variables associated with women's sex roles may have an impact on the development of mental illness: nonexpression of negative feelings, taking roles which satisfy a male partner, passivity, learned helplessness, exaggerated femininity, and other-directedness" (p. 391). Unger (1979) added role conflicts and role strains, less control over stressful life events, and lack of real power. Some specific disorders that women suffer more frequently than men are depression, the battered woman syndrome (as victim), psychotropic drug abuse, agoraphobia, psychological maladjustment following rape or incest, eating disorders, miscellaneous problems associated with low self-esteem, social withdrawal, guilt, self-depriving and self-destructive behaviors, and general nervousness (cf. Brodsky & Hare-Mustin, 1980; Fidell, 1981; Hall & Havassy, 1981; Herman, 1981; Levy, 1981; Meyerowitz, 1981; Unger, 1979; Walker, 1981; Weissman & Klerman, 1979).

For men, their traditional masculine sex role has been labeled as "hazardous to (their) health" and responsible for health problems and shorter life expectancy (Harrison, 1978). Meinecke (1981) proposed that men's higher mortality rate may be attributed to a combination of biological predispositions for certain health problems with stresses from trying to conform to the traditional masculine sex role. O'Neil (1981a) also discussed sex-role strains and conflicts as problematic for men, as well as the need to validate oneself continually in all areas. Issues concerning restrictive emotionality with its overdeveloped cognitive and rationalistic communication patterns, and problems related to control, power, and competition are believed to have widespread effects on men's interpersonal, career, home and family, and physical functioning.

Specific problems seen more frequently in men include destructive hostility and aggressiveness, pathological self-indulgence and impulsiveness, anxiety over failure and/or lack of success (actual or anticipated), initiator of sexual abuse and rape, battering wife syndrome (as abuser), emotional rigidity, compulsive self-proving behaviors and associated reflexive aggressive acts, and more frequently successful suicide attempts (cf. Goldberg, 1979; Herman, 1981; Lester, 1979; O'Neil, 1981a; Skovholt, 1978; Unger, 1979; Walker, 1981).

Some of these characteristics are portrayed well in the following case example. A woman requested short-term professional help with a pending career decision. She was considering acceptance of a full-time job offered her after years of volunteer work with a social service agency. She was not sure she could handle the perceived stresses and responsibilities of paid employment and was afraid of her husband's explosive temper if she modified her management of home responsibilities in any way. She described other long-standing personal problems, which she attributed to her "weak nerves": feelings of depression, anxiety, crying spells, and eating binges followed by periods of intense guilt. The picture of her husband emerged as equally bleak: an ambitious, successful, independent businessman who worked around the clock, drank heavily, worried constantly about finances, and had attacks of angina at age forty. He generally avoided emotional contact with his wife except for expressing infrequent sexual interest and all-too-frequent low frustration tolerance and anger. These partners' problems may be seen to some extent as extreme consequences of traditional sex-role socialization of men and women.

Traditional sex-role socialization may contribute to many psychological problems more characteristic of one or the other sex including those illustrated in the example above. As O'Neil (1981a) stated, "men and women have each learned only about one-half of the attitudes, skills, and behaviors necessary to cope effectively in life" (p. 64). Both sexes would benefit from the permission and the skills to engage in the complementary attitudes and behaviors that they do not possess, or are unwilling or not permitted to manifest. Becoming more androgynous should alleviate these problems for both sexes, whether androgynous functioning connotes a tempering of the extreme quality of sex-appropriate characteristics (in Bakan's terms, unmitigated agency and communion) or a willingness to consider viable behavior alternatives (cf. Bem, 1976). Counseling around sex-role issues to increase the options for both sexes and to alleviate the negative consequences of sex-role socialization can take the forms of moderating extreme sex-role characteristics, facilitating expression of less traditional characteristics, adding to existing sex-traditional response repertoires, and developing entirely new characteristics blending the masculine and feminine together. All of these goals can represent counseling for androgyny.[1]

GENERAL PERSPECTIVES
ON COUNSELING FOR ANDROGYNY

Counseling for androgyny represents a new focus for sex-role related interventions in counseling. Until recent years, a sex-typed identity was considered to be essential for mental health. Practitioners frequently intervened to help sex-role nonconformists, especially women, to develop a more "appropriate" sex-role identity, attitudes, and behaviors (see American Psychological Association, 1975 for some examples of these attitudes and practices among practitioners). Now practitioners espousing androgyny tend to view traditional sex roles as problematic, and are likely to encourage clients to become less sex-stereotyped.

"Counseling for androgyny" is a broad term encompassing a diverse range of interventions designed to move individuals away from traditional sex-role characteristics and behavior. Practitioners supporting androgyny are likely to share the assumptions that: (a) Sex roles are learned early in life. The impact of sex-role socialization continues throughout life. (b) Sex roles have a pervasive impact upon an individual's self-perceptions, relationships with others, and behavioral options. (c) Certain specific problems are typical of each sex because of sex-role socialization. That is, each sex has a predisposition to develop certain types of psychological problems as a result of sex-role socialization (for examples, see pp. 152–153). (d) Finally, at least some negative aspects of sex roles can be corrected through counseling interventions. Current counseling interventions for men and women aimed toward fostering less sex-typed functioning will be reviewed below.

Androgyny as focus for counseling. Some professionals have recently begun to incorporate the concept of androgyny explicitly in their writings and psychological practice. Worell (1980) noted that theory and research on androgyny

---

[1]To avoid awkward terminology, the generic term "counseling" will be used to refer to psychological interventions offered by a range of professional mental health practitioners including, but not limited to, counselors, psychologists, psychiatrists, and social workers.

have significant implications for counseling practice and training programs. Kenworthy (1979) describes androgyny as an important concept useful in integrating a new set of cultural values about the sexes into counseling practice. Both practitioners and clients are able to recognize and examine their sex-related expectations during the therapeutic process. Clients do not initiate counseling when their lives are in balance, but when their roles no longer work for them. These clients then need to develop a more flexible, androgynous adjustment. Androgyny offers options and choices to people who are blocked, who are facing new life situations, or who are trying to adjust to a changing world (Franks, 1979). Individuals are encouraged to implement a life style appropriate for them toward an ideal of mental health identical for the sexes (Foxley, 1979).

In order for this to occur, both sexes need to become aware of the impact of sex typing on their sense of identity and their lives in general (Doherty, 1979), and of the benefits of androgyny. How the situational appropriateness of instrumental and expressive behaviors may vary depending upon the situation needs to be stressed (Gilbert, 1981). Identity issues are especially central to young adults, who are exploring personal values and lifestyles during a time in which they are likely to conform to traditional modes of thinking and behavior (Baker, 1980). For these clients, Baker viewed androgyny as particularly relevant, but also very helpful in considering career, marital, and sexual problems.

Recommended interventions. The types of changes which should occur in counseling for androgyny depend upon the needs of the individual client (Kaplan & Sedney, 1980). Baker (1980) recommended a combination of remediation, supportive, and prevention approaches. Remediation may be particularly important for clients whose sex-traditional attitudes and behaviors are ineffective for them. People in transition periods who feel "stuck" in life may need new life options and behaviors. Those experiencing dissonance between sex-typed and androgynous attitudes and behaviors that they simultaneously possess can benefit from assistance in reconciling the discrepancies. Other clients may be committed to androgynous styles of behavior and may elicit negative reactions and pressure to change from others. The distress these responses cause may thus prompt androgynous persons to seek counseling. Supportive group activities may provide role models for persons moving away from sex-traditional standards and some external validation for their newly developing androgynous attitudes and behaviors. Growth-enhancing activities such as workshops and classes can prevent through self-exploration and education some problems that may be caused by traditional sex roles.

Foxley (1979) similarly regarded a variety of interventions as helpful, and especially favored groups to help persons learn from one another. Consciousness-raising, assertion, and decision-making groups may all foster less stereotyped attitudes and life styles. She provides an extensive listing of types of groups in her text. Foxley implicitly labeled any interventions designed to counteract sex-role stereotyping as promoting androgyny, and detailed interventions that practitioners can use in a number of different institutional settings. Sargent (1977) developed an extensive manual that could be used in a small group workshop or class format, with self-awareness and subsequent growth as the targets. Her assumption was that examination of personal attitudes and life experiences with the help of structured exercises, group discussion, and selected readings can overcome past sex-role prescriptions for behavior in favor of a more androgynous perspective. Emphasizing the centrality of restrictive self-concepts in sex-role problems, Kahn and Greenberg (1980) asserted that behavioral skill training methods may be insufficient to change clients' perceptions of themselves and their options. They recommended the use of stimulation methods to foster these changes, including journal writing, internal dialogues, and exploration of imagery and fantasy.

A variety of techniques may be appropriate for both sexes. Franks (1979) cautioned that counselors may not want to use identical techniques for them, however. Modified goals and interventions may be necessary to recognize each sex's unique background and needs.

Practitioners' values and goals. Regardless of activities chosen to encourage androgynous functioning, Gilbert (1981) warned mental health service providers to be aware of how their own values about sex roles may affect their practice. Bear, Berger, and Wright (1979) listed the tasks for practitioners dealing with changing sex roles of both sexes as: (a) coping with personal involvement in perpetuating traditional sex-role standards; (b) understanding the difficulties faced by persons who attempt to adopt nontraditional sex-role behaviors; and (c) examining institutional constraints that may work against these nontraditional sex-role behaviors. For both sexes, counseling for androgyny must entail values clarification and support of clients pursuing new sex-role options for themselves.

This process requires special skill and patience on the part of the practitioner. Kaplan (1979) emphasized that this process must be delicately handled by the practitioner. The first step may be to encourage clients to bring new opposing, potentially threatening capacities and traits to the surface. This must be carefully directed so that the client is not pushed to a premature organization of traits. Kaplan and Bean (1976) proposed that clients working for change may follow the "pendulum principle," where they swing from one extreme of characteristics and behavior to the other, until a gradual modulation is achieved. Practitioners need to be patient through this slowly developing change process, mindful of the importance of establishing interrelated modifications in traits and the clients' life situations.

The way that practitioners present themselves as individuals may affect clients' willingness to self-disclose and satisfaction with counseling. Clients may be most comfortable with a high feminine (especially androgynous) practitioner, although the supporting evidence is mixed and highly tentative (Banikiotes & Merluzzi, 1981; Feldstein, 1979, 1982; Highlen & Russell, 1980).

Counseling for androgyny is likely to have complex consequences for clients. The concept of androgyny may well appear to be foreign to many in the clients' environment, for whom traditional sex stereotypes still have power. Practitioners who use androgyny as a mental health ideal must be prepared to help clients deal with the consequences generated from opposing such powerful stereotypes. Androgynous behavior may in fact elicit expressions of sexism, especially when the behavior is performed by a woman. Men may also face negative reactions from others and personal dissonance in performing more feminine behaviors. With the help of practitioners, clients must make clear choices and prepare for their possible consequences (Franks, 1979; Kenworthy, 1979).

Summary. Counseling for androgyny requires clients and practitioners to become aware of the impact of traditional sex typing and of the benefits of some sex-role alternatives. The process of counseling may involve remediation of present sex-role related problems, support for those who are already less sex-traditional, and prevention of future problems stemming from traditional sex roles. A variety of counseling interventions may be appropriate depending upon the needs of the individual client. Practitioners must be aware of how their own sex-role values may influence their work with clients. Practitioners must also be patient through the change process, and must be ready to help clients deal with the consequences of sex-role changes.

ANDROGYNY AS AN IMPLICIT PERSPECTIVE

Although the literature on modifying traditional sex roles has proliferated in recent years, in most cases androgyny is mentioned briefly as a goal in counseling, if at all. Perspectives have focused on exploring the unique sex-role problems of one or the other sex, relatively independently of the other sex. Although the concept of androgyny has played a largely philosophical role in these discussions, a brief overview of some selected literature can provide a good idea of how professionals today are working to encourage less traditionally sex-typed behavior in their clients.

Counseling Men

The literature on counseling men has generally focused upon dealing with traditional men's problems with emotional expressiveness and power/competition. The goal of counseling with men is to awaken them "to the limitless ways in which they can reinvent themselves and their situations" (p. 104) by resocializing them into a more androgynous mode (Marino, 1979). This can be challenging to initiate in counseling. O'Neil (1981b) noted how interpersonal communication based upon emotions and intimacy is considered negative within the traditional masculine sex role. Bruch (1978) analyzed the interaction between the typical man and counseling situation to be a poor person-environment match: the man with his inhibited emotional processing, his rational thinking, and his emphasis on action, and the environment with its emphasis on self-expression, emotions, and interpersonal relationships. Men may be reluctant to enter into counseling at all, may discuss their problems logically and factually, and may feel threatened by their perceived loss of power (Downing, 1981). Central tasks of counseling men involve dealing with their desires for intimacy, power, and reduction of pain. Yet as clients they have been characterized as "hidden," and simultaneously appreciative and resentful of counselors' power to grant them permission to feel and be what they have denied (Scher, 1981).

Encouraging men to become fully engaged in the therapeutic process is a delicate task. Obtaining and maintaining participation is a critical problem (cf. Washington, 1979). Scher (1979) labeled initiation of counseling as a humiliation for some men. A combination of acknowledging the client's sense of pride and strength, while working slowly to gain the trust of the client by "exercising restraint, candor, and affection" (p. 254) is likely to be successful in establishing a good working relationship. For women practitioners, this process may be somewhat easier to accomplish as men may be more accustomed to being emotionally intimate with a woman. However, men may be uncomfortable about doing what they perceive as admitting lack of omnipotence to a woman. Defining the therapist/client power differential as temporary may help (Downing, 1981; see also Carlson, 1981).

Strategies. The first step in the formal counseling process per se is assessment of the man's own sex-role conflicts and strains (O'Neil, 1981a). As much as possible, the client should be actively involved in goal-setting, and is likely to favor rapid progress toward well-delineated goals once the commitment to counseling is made. Areas of content likely to be covered include: how occupational structures today encourage men to overvalue work and devalue family relationships and responsibilities (Bear et al., 1979); the masculine mystique and its devaluing of and fear of femininity; competition and power issues; homophobia and general lack of intimacy with men; sexual dissatisfaction (O'Neil, 1981a, 1981b).

To explore these issues, the practitioner needs to proceed carefully, teaching the client to express feelings and thoughts. This process may be tricky because typically both the practitioner and client have needs for power, control, and competition, although perhaps for different reasons (Scher, 1979). The client may be simultaneously striving for control and expecting the "expert" to perform (Toomer, 1980). The practitioner may be reasonably assured that the client is not manipulating emotions, however, and the client should respond well to explorations of immediate interactions and of behavior dynamics in a direct fashion (Scher, 1979).

Marino (1979) listed a number of suggestions helpful in counseling men, including: (a) avoid using "whys," since men may already be adept at explaining their behavior; (b) use gentle but persistent prodding to encourage the men to explore feelings; (c) observe nonverbal messages about how men may be resisting strong emotions (e.g., crossing their arms, breathing patterns); (d) encourage men to examine how they may be denying important aspects of themselves that are inconsistent with the traditional male stereotype (e.g., their need for others); and (e) use behavioral rehearsals to test out new behaviors in a step-by-step manner. Practitioners have been encouraged to use a number of techniques to assist men in exploring new sex-role options, including reading lists, consciousness-raising groups (a real favorite), guided practice for new behaviors, in-service education and on-the-job training, and public education about men's sex-role problems (cf. Bruch, 1978; Heppner, 1981; Marino, 1979; O'Neil, 1981a). Programs structured around a stimulus film, sketches, and songs can initiate sex-role exploration (Croteau & Burda, 1983; Gelwick & Heppner, 1981; Wade, Wade, & Croteau, 1983). Lewis (1980) described a workshop designed to develop openness and intimacy between men using dyadic and small group self-disclosure exercises and physical contact. Group leaders can modify standard group interaction and values clarification activities to stimulate self-exploration (cf. Heppner, 1983). The hoped-for outcome is what Crites and Fitzgerald (1980) termed the competent male: using internal criteria for achievement, success, and excellence, relating to women as equals, cooperating rather than competing.

It is extremely important for practitioners to be aware of the extent to which others (including themselves) may hold traditional values about men's behavior. Bear, Berger, and Wright (1979) asserted that it is often easier for counselors to support a woman who desires to be upwardly mobile than it is to support a man who may wish to concentrate on more humanistic ventures such as raising his children. The socialization of professionals (which practitioners themselves have survived) may make such implied threats to work-related values difficult. The male client pondering life options deviant from those traditionally upheld for men may anticipate powerful opposition from family, friends, and broader institutions. Bear and associates recommended that the counselor: (a) understand the nature of the client's own work and family pressures; (b) help the client develop ways of negotiating new life style arrangements; (c) focus on values clarification; (d) help the client enlist the cooperation of his spouse or partner; and (e) give permission for and support deviant but personally rewarding options (cf. also Berger & Wright, 1980).

In summary, current perspectives on counseling about men's sex-role issues focus on the need for men to overcome emotional restrictions and their emphasis upon power and control. Recognizing how these can complicate the therapeutic process, practitioners have recommended awareness of underlying dynamics coupled with values clarification on both sides. Understanding of male clients' reluctance to self-disclose, to yield personal control of the situation, to admit the need for help, and to be nurtured are essential for laying the foundations for therapeutic success.

Counseling Women

Much more literature is available on sex-role counseling for women than for men. Identification of sex-role issues with women exclusively has become almost automatic over recent years. For example, an issue of *Professional Psychology* devoted to "Sex Roles, Equality, and Mental Health" mentions men only in passing throughout the issue (Sobel & Russo, 1981). Concern with women's unique mental health problems has produced an extensive body of research in less than two decades (cf. Brodsky & Hare-Mustin, 1980).

Discussions of counseling women have been linked to consideration of women's disenfranchised position in society. Gove and Tudor's (1973) classic article carefully argued that women's higher rate of emotional problems stems from their single, restrictive, powerless, stressful role. Traditional modes of counseling/psychotherapy have been perceived as perpetuating women's oppression through a patriarchal system (cf. Chesler, 1972; Franks, 1979; Unger, 1979). The traditional mental health system has been viewed as helping women to adjust to a restrictive social reality for them (Marecek & Kravetz, 1977). Feminist practitioners espousing new sex-role values have sought models that can represent their sex-role ideals and serve as meaningful guides to the therapeutic process. Awareness of sociopolitical aspects of sex-role interactions has formed the essence of counseling with women in recent years.

Perspectives in counseling. Rawlings and Carter (1977) described three models of mental health that form the basis of women's counseling today. The *normative* model prescribes behavior conforming to traditional sex-role standards of society. The *androcentric* model supports male-oriented values (e.g., achievement, competition) at the cost of denigrating feminine values. The *androgyny* model recognizes the need for women to integrate and balance the masculine and the feminine. In Rawlings and Carter's view, the "strong woman" goal inherent in the androcentric model is scarcely superior to the traditional feminine ideal. A balance between the feminine and the masculine is needed.

Two somewhat overlapping but distinguishable approaches to counseling women have been proposed as ways to achieve this healthy balance in clients: nonsexist therapy and feminist therapy. Rawlings and Carter emphasized that both approaches encourage clients to determine their own lives freed of sex-role prescriptions, and attempt to equalize power between the sexes. The difference lies in the importance placed on sociopolitical analyses of sex roles.

Nonsexist therapy focuses on the process of individual change. The scope of sexism in society is recognized, as is the value of alternative lifestyles. Each client is seen as a unique individual rather than solely as a member of her sex. The personal effects of women's lack of power are understood, and individuals are encouraged to develop their own traits and lifestyles without regard for sex-role prescriptions for behavior.

A set of values and goals is shared by nonsexist practitioners. Rawlings and Carter listed three basic principles: (a) Practitioners do not use their professional power to strengthen sex-traditional behavior patterns in their clients. Practitioners equally value nonstereotypic attitudes and behaviors; (b) practitioners do not diagnose clients' problems in terms of conformance/nonconformance to traditional standards; and (c) sex-biased testing instruments are not used. These principles are natural outgrowths of the nonsexist values these practitioners hold (cf. also Marecek & Kravetz, 1977).

With its emphasis on individual change and more flexible sex-role standards, nonsexist therapy appears to be similar to what Kaplan (1976) terms psychotherapy as resocialization. Personal pathology is frequently attributed to overly sex-typed behavior patterns. The practitioner's task is to determine deficiencies in the client's upbringing related to sex-role socialization, and then serve as an "ideal parent" helping the client to correct these deficits. Doherty (1979) described how women with different sex-role classifications may present unique problems in counseling. Feminine women may present a limited, inhibited view of self. Masculine women may need to explore the ramifications of their competitive style and their self-doubts. Undifferentiated women may have withdrawn from dealing with identity issues. A nonsexist practitioner would help each individual to determine the best options for herself independent of sex-role prescriptions. Nonsexist practitioners would find these principles equally applicable to their work with men. The interventions described in the section on counseling men are consistent with these principles.

Feminist practitioners also espouse these standards, but believe that they do not go far enough. In feminist therapy, the emphasis is placed upon a critique of society and social institutions at large, advocating the need for sociopolitical as well as individual change. Women's problems are understood from a political/economic power analysis that is rooted in a radical-socialist perspective on sex-role change. Values of feminist therapy include: (a) no value placed on social class distinction; (b) the importance of economic and psychological autonomy for women; (c) emphasis on equal power in friendship, love, and marriage; and (d) a goal of social-political change rather than adjustment to the status quo (Rawlings & Carter, 1977). Rawlings and Carter also make explicit some of the strategies used in feminist therapy, such as: (a) communicate explicitly any personal values relevant to work with clients; (b) use sex-role analysis as a therapy technique to help make clients aware of sex-related expectations placed upon them; (c) help women explore economic and social barriers to their goals; (d) enter into a specific contract with the client specifying the client's own goals for treatment; (e) emphasize self-help, equal power, trust, sharing of knowledge between client and practitioner (including material in case records and psychological test results); and (f) avoid using diagnostic labels, diagnostic tests, counselor interpretation, and indirect communication styles. Groups are viewed as powerful means to help women take control of their own lives. The emphasis throughout is upon self-help, personal growth, and equal power (cf. also Marecek & Kravetz, 1977).

To review briefly, both nonsexist and feminist practitioners consider understanding the results of the sex-role socialization process to be essential, and view nontraditional sex roles as viable and in fact preferable for many women. The principles listed above serve as a concrete expression of the practitioners' values about women. Especially for feminist therapy practitioners, the content of what is discussed may be quite different from that in traditional therapy, as is the degree of importance placed upon practitioner direction and expertise.

Practitioners have also become aware of how women's career development has been shaped by sex-role socialization processes. Vocational psychology has not addressed women's unique patterns and needs (cf. Tittle, 1983). Many practitioners have misconceptions about women and work, do not challenge women's vocational choices that are not congruent with their interests and abilities, do not know how to use vocational counseling materials to women's benefit, and do not know how to help women integrate complex role demands and personal needs (cf. Farmer, 1976; Fitzgerald & Crites, 1979; Harmon, 1977; Vetter, 1973). These authors are representative of many in the field who would recommend vocational counseling to help each individual woman make decisions within the context of other values and commitments. These professionals indicate that vocational counseling for women must be based on knowledge of stereotypes and barriers to women's vocational development, careful individual assessment of strengths and life goals, and judicious use of vocational materials and life planning perspectives. These vocational counseling approaches would probably be best classified as nonsexist (rather than feminist) in focus. (For a recent view on men's career issues, see Skovholt & Morgan, 1981.)

Strategies. Despite the proliferation of articles discussing counseling women, relatively little mention is made of interviewing techniques or intervention strategies particularly suited for women. In an issue of *The Counseling Psychologist* (1979) devoted to counseling women, authors were asked to describe specific principles for counseling specific subgroups or problems with women. Most authors recommend knowledge of the problem areas, psychological assessment in nonstereotypic terms, and an ability to apply basic counseling skills flexibly. These are compatible with the principles adopted by Division 17 Ad Hoc Committee on Women of the American Psychological Association (1979).

Two unique interventions have emerged from recent work with women. Assertion training teaches women (and men) how to stand up "for one's basic interpersonal rights in such a way that the rights of another person are not violated in the process. It is a direct, honest, and appropriate expression of one's thoughts, feelings, and beliefs" (Jakubowski, 1977a, p. 147). A variety of techniques are used including didactic training, cognitive restructuring, behavioral rehearsal, and group interaction exercises (Jakubowski, 1977b). Change in sex-role belief systems, self-concepts, and behavioral repertoires are commonly cited positive outcomes.

The second major innovation has been the use of consciousness-raising (C-R) groups. The emphasis in C-R groups from the beginning has been on making women aware of their position in society as second-class citizens, and analyzing women's problems in terms of their common experiences rather than as individual failures (cf. Whiteley, 1973). The sharing of experiences, analysis of issues from a common perspective, use of other women as role models, and erasing many women's feelings of isolation have been viewed as therapeutic. Brodsky (1977) discussed how understanding C-R groups' dynamics can be helpful in individual counseling. Marecek and Kravetz (1977) have similarly stressed the value of women's groups as collective self-help efforts.

Gulanick, Howard, and Moreland (1979) blended components of C-R groups and assertion training into a six-week group program designed to help feminine women become more androgynous. Women were first provided a brief discussion of assertion, sex-role stereotyping, achievement/competition, self-esteem, or expression of negative emotions by the leader and then were encouraged to share their own feelings and experiences. A behavioral rehearsal or group exercise component facilitated assertion skill development. Members were also encouraged to apply the information to their own life situations during the intervening week. Clark-Stedman and Wolleat (1979) adapted issues commonly covered in C-R groups into structured activities for middle-school young women.

Regardless of preferred techniques, the process of change for women can be a painful one. Sherman (1976) noted how women face both an internal and external resistance to change. They need permission to change, the power to do so, and time to change gradually.

A Comparison of Approaches

Recent literature on counseling men and women is based upon recognition of the negative effects of traditional sex-role socialization. An interesting trend can be observed in comparing the literature available for each sex. Although an oversimplification, it appears that practitioners with women have been most interested in modifying the philosophy and goals of working with women, while essentials of interviewing techniques have not been given the same attention. In contrast, writers about men have been more likely to accept the general philosophy of counseling/psychotherapy while recommending specific revisions in style, types of questions asked, and so on. There is nothing in the men's literature to date comparable to the radical changes proposed in feminist therapy, while comparatively little space in the women's literature has been devoted to issues such as how to formulate goals or elicit a client's cooperation in the counseling process.

This difference may reflect the tenor of traditional counseling approaches rather than a systematic over or under-evaluation of either facet of the process. Because of their sex-role socialization, women may have typically felt more at home than men in the therapeutic process, which is characterized by self disclosure, exploration of emotional responses and belief systems, and focus on interpersonal relationships and intrapersonal dynamics (cf. Bruch, 1978). Instead, feminists have been incensed by traditional counseling's "patriarchal" nature: its use of authority and power, encouragement of dependency in clients, and reliance on traditional sex-role standards (cf. Chesler, 1972). Feminists saw the need to develop a unique practitioner and client relationship characterized by equality and an awareness of sociopolitical sex-role issues. This is the essence of feminist therapy. Writers on men noted how the traditional atmosphere and process of counseling were not suited to most men's defense against emotionality and their unwillingness to admit the need for help. Before changes could be accomplished with these men, practitioners must be skillful in persuading them of the negative aspects of their socially valued role and in engaging them in the therapeutic process.

The literature for both sexes emphasizes the need for clients to become aware of the impact of traditional sex-role socialization and of alternatives to traditional sex-role characteristics that they did not previously consider. Counseling involves a process of "resocialization" where clients are carefully encouraged to explore and try out these alternatives in an accepting atmosphere. Practitioners must be aware of forces within clients' environment and the clients themselves that oppose sex-role change, and must be patient with the gradual nature of such changes. It is crucial for practitioners to have a thorough understanding of sex-role influences upon individuals, and of their own sex-role values.

In some respects, the literature displays a somewhat curious blend of new and more traditional perspectives on sex roles. The awareness of the possibility and desirability of alternatives to traditional sex typing is obvious. Contrary to traditional perspectives, there is also an assumption that individuals can make significant changes in their sex-role identities, attitudes, and behaviors in adulthood. However, the literature maintains the overriding emphasis on between-sex differences characteristic of more traditional perspectives. It is implicitly assumed that socialization processes have sharply dichotomized the sexes, with members of each sex sharing a constellation of characteristics and problems unique from the other sex. The sex-role problems generally discussed are those of the traditional sex-typed person (with little attention to nonsex-typed or cross-sex-typed persons).

This dichotomization of the sexes and focus upon sex-typed individuals may be for simplicity's sake, stressing modal problems each sex faces as a result of the most powerful trends in sex-role socialization. That is, the new "stereotyping" of the sexes' problems implied in the counseling literature may reflect a desire to emphasize what are seen to be the most prevalent, and negative, aspects of sex roles. This desire is quite different from a lack of awareness or concern with the individual differences and secondary trends resulting in between-sex similarities and within-sex differences in sex-role related problems.

This emphasis upon between-sex differences and traditional sex-role identities may also be a sign of the more general uncertainty in recent sex-role literature about the importance of sex (gender) as a causative factor in behavior. Sex-role literature in general, and counseling literature in particular explicitly recognize that variations in sex-role related characteristics cannot be explained by biological sex alone, and that in some cases within-sex differences may be more meaningful than between-sex differences. Yet, experts also recognize that the presence of sex differences in behavior should not be underestimated. A balance between overstressing and ignoring sex differences in light of sex-role related differences *within* each sex is difficult to strike.

The literature on counseling men/women could be supplemented by models that recognize the possibility of similarities as well as differences among women and men, a range of problems beyond those associated with a traditional sex-role identity, and particular problems that an individual may face as a function of his/her personal identity, attitudes, behaviors, and environmental demands. A preliminary statement along these lines will be provided at the end of this chapter.

OTHER APPLICATIONS OF ANDROGYNY

This section discusses several diverse ways in which the concept of androgyny has been used in ways other than in the typical counseling situations described earlier. Some professionals in businesses and education have also adopted the concept of androgyny in their work. Examples of these applications in nontherapeutic settings are described in this section. Some practitioners who explicitly utilize the concept of androgyny in their work have used androgyny measures to evaluate the effectiveness of their efforts. Some of these studies are also summarized in this section. Finally, an interesting variant of sex-role counseling is counseling for gender identity or behavior disturbance. Whether the process and goals of this counseling focus are in opposition to the philosophy of androgyny will be briefly discussed.

Applications to Nontherapeutic Settings

The androgyny concept has been attractive in other areas to professionals, who recognize the importance of combining instrumental and expressive orientations and skills in leaders. In a training and development journal, Sargent (1979) outlined the skills each sex needs to develop a more androgynous combination, and stressed the value of the full range of masculine and feminine behaviors to problem-solving in business. Borland (1980), in a book on leadership for women, spoke of the development of androgynous leaders as "not only desirable but necessary for today's world" (p. 6). The lack of androgyny has meant that there are untapped resources in members of both sexes.

Androgyny has also been seen as an alternative to traditional sex-role stereotyping in schools. Remer and Ross (1982) recommend that school counselors should conduct classroom activities and lead the educational staff in self-assessment and planned changes to move them away from sexist educational practices. According to Remer and Ross, this process would move the schools toward androgyny.

Perhaps the most ambitious and successful effort to operationalize the concept is through the DICEL Project (Developing Interpersonal Competencies in Educational Leadership, Nancy Evers, Director) developed through grant funds from the Women's Educational Equity Act Program. The project was designed to increase the interpersonal competence of women aspiring to or holding educational leadership positions, thus improving their potential for leader effectiveness. Four areas of interpersonal competence were addressed: androgyny, assertion, power, and leadership. For each area a competency-based prototypic training module was developed for use in preservice and inservice learning experience. Each module consisted of: (a) an instructor's manual including detailed competencies, associated teaching/learning activities, suggested evaluation procedures, assessment tools, guidelines for implementing the module in workshops and graduate courses, and suggestions for use of the second module component; and (b) a color videotape, for use as resource material for the competencies.

In the androgyny module, attention was focused on helping future women leaders to become aware of and to practice the blending of masculine and feminine characteristics and behaviors in situationally appropriate conditions.

This integration was seen as personally and professionally beneficial to administrators. The module incorporated a didactic unit on the concept of androgyny; assessment of personal androgyny and its consequences; skill-building in traditional masculine (e.g., problem-solving) and feminine (e.g., facilitation) skills; and discussion of how these sets of skills can be used singly or together to create an androgynous leadership style. The DICEL materials were intended to be used flexibly by the instructor in a variety of learning experiences, although prototype courses and workshops are outlined in the module. Obviously, the focus in the DICEL project is upon developing or expanding an androgynous behavior repertoire rather than upon personality trait androgyny. (More information about the project and directions for ordering one or several modules is available.[2])

Research on Applications of Androgyny

Berzins (1979) has suggested that if androgyny as a model of mental health is adopted, androgyny measures can be used as counseling outcome measures to determine if change in this direction has taken place. Few researchers have done this, or what is probably more accurate, few professionals have publicly reported the androgyny data relating to the success of their interventions. Vedovato and Vaughter (1980) and Bennett and Grossner (1981) used the BSRI as a pre-post measure for their psychology of women courses attended by both sexes. In both studies there was significant shift toward androgynous scoring for women, effected largely by a change in Masculinity scale scores. No similar movement was found for men. The presence of some significant change in scores of comparison groups, however, makes the meaningfulness of the results difficult to interpret. Kahn (1982) found no posttest only differences in BSRI scores for classes focusing on awareness of sex role stereotyping when compared to a more traditional personality development class. Ridley, Lamke, Avery, and Harrell (1982) noted changes only in feminine scores after a communication skills workshop held for dating couples.

As noted previously, Gulanick et al. (1979) developed a group incorporating consciousness-raising and behavioral rehearsal techniques to help feminine women to become more androgynous. Women participated in a program "aimed at fostering androgyny," which included discussion of assertion, self-confidence, sex-role stereotypes, and their relevance to androgyny. Differences in BSRI scores that appeared at follow-up were attributed to changes in masculinity. O'Neil, Ohlde, Barke, Gelwick, and Garfield (1980) used the BSRI as one measure of changes in college women resulting from a four-week workshop on sex-role factors in career planning. These women, compared to control groups, described themselves as more masculine after the experience.

[2]Contact: Dr. Nancy Evers, Director, DICEL Project, College of Education, M.L. 02, University of Cincinnati, Cincinnati, OH 45221, Phone: (513) 475-5913.

No significant changes in feminine or neutral self-descriptors were noted.

This brief sampling of research suggests that changes in masculinity and femininity scores as a result of educational programs and counseling are not large, if present at all. It is not clear whether these modest successes are explained best by methodological problems that beset many outcome studies in the psychological literature (cf. Garfield & Bergin, 1978), the content of the experiences, the unsuitability of using present masculinity/femininity measures for assessing short-term changes, or a combination of factors. It may also be inappropriate to use personality trait androgyny measures to assess targeted changes in sex-role attitudes or behaviors. Kahn (1982) does insist that her "subjective experience with the consciousness-raising treatment program indicated that it has a significant impact on the attitudes and behaviors of students who were exposed to it" (p. 982).

Counseling for Gender-Identity or Behavior Disturbances

An interesting sidelight to sex-role counseling is counseling/therapy for gender-identity or gender-behavior disturbances, diagnosed most frequently in young boys. Rekers, Bentler, Rosen, and Lovaas (1977) defined *gender identity* disturbances as a condition in which the boy has assumed the sex-role identity of a girl, expressing wishes or beliefs about actually being female while engaging in female stereotypic behaviors. In *gender behavior* disturbance, feminine behaviors are manifested without having a female core identity. In diagnosing disturbances in either area, a number of indicators are reviewed: personal identity statements, cross dressing, cross-gender play, type of parent-child relationships, parental attitudes about the role behaviors, physical appearance, and relation to other signs of psychopathology (Rosen, Rekers, & Friar, 1977). Serious adjustment problems are likely to ensue. The boys often dislike interacting with their male peers, fear school because of rejection and scapegoating, and have problems forming close interpersonal relationships. They are often shy, detached, and defensive, with low self-esteem. These boys are believed to be at risk for transvestism (in behavior-disturbed boys) or transsexualism (identity-disturbed) in adulthood, and are also at risk for depression and suicide (Rekers et al., 1977).

Treatment is focused on teaching traditionally masculine sex-role behaviors. Biological bases for some sex-related distinctions are learned, and negative social reactions to violating certain distinctions are emphasized. Behavior modification procedures, social learning curricula, instruction in athletics and boys' games, parent-child counseling, and use of male models are all employed to reinforce masculine sex-typed behaviors and eliminate the compulsively feminine ones (Marlowe, 1979; Rekers, Rosen, Lovaas, & Bentler, 1978).

It appears as if these therapeutic activities are diametrically opposed to those of androgyny, where engaging in behavior traditionally reserved for the other sex is encouraged. Rekers and colleagues emphasize that these boys are *not* behaving androgynously, but instead display a rigid, compulsive adherence to feminine behaviors. They are grossly inhibited and anxious about performing masculine behaviors, regardless of their situational appropriateness. The degree of maladjustment suffered by the boys presumably mandates intervention. The intent is to alter the ratio of masculine to feminine behaviors, with a goal of greater sex-role flexibility through less self-concept confusion and an expanded behavior repertoire (cf. Rekers, 1977; Rekers et al., 1977; Rekers et al., 1978).

The potential for abuse of such a therapy is obvious. The blending of characteristics that androgyny connotes, however, would logically suggest that extremes of other-sex as well as of same-sex typical behaviors may need to be modulated. A statement from Rekers et al. (1978) echoes sentiments of many practitioners working toward androgyny: "What is needed is greater tolerance by society in general when it comes to accepting people as persons despite their range of sex-role behaviors, and greater tolerance by individuals for cross-gender flexibility (i.e., androgyny) in their own sex-role behavior" (p. 135).

SUMMARY

As a new model of healthy psychological functioning, psychological androgyny has become popular with mental health practitioners convinced of the negative ramifications of traditional sex roles for men and women. Both sexes suffer from the failure to blend instrumental/agentic and expressive/communal characteristics and skills. In general, men's problems are characterized as frequently involving issues of emotional expressiveness and power, whereas women's problems often center around passivity and dependency. Many practitioners working with sex-role issues support goals of increasing the options for the sexes and alleviating the negative consequences of sex-role socialization.

Counseling for androgyny has generally been discussed in the context of one sex's particular role-related problems. The literature on counseling men has focused upon specific recommendations for goal formulation and interviewing styles. For women, more attention has been given to essential modification of the philosophy and attitudes in counseling. For both sexes, counseling for androgyny involves "resocialization" where clients are encouraged to consider and experiment with sex-role alternatives within a safe environment. In this process, practitioners must have a thorough understanding of the impact of sex roles upon individuals, and of their own sex-role attitudes. Potential applications of the androgyny concept to business and educational settings are beginning to be explored.

CONCEPTUAL AND VALUES ISSUES
IN SEX-ROLE CHANGE

As noted in the first chapter, changes in perspective in the study of sex roles as exemplified by the androgyny literature are concurrent with changes occurring over recent years. The trend in views of sex roles is away from simplicity toward complexity: away from dichotomous sex roles identified with biological sex towards recognition of multiple sex role alternatives, individual difference, and determinants of behavior.

Practitioners encounter an increasing number of individuals coping with the pain of sex-role discordance: finding themselves in situations or facing life options that comfortable traditional standards simply do not equip them to handle. To use Bardwick's (1979) evocative term, these clients lost their "existential anchors" stabilizing them in a rapidly changing world. Practitioners attracted by the sex-role options for their clients afforded by androgyny face acute conceptual and pragmatic issues. What aspects of androgyny can be reasonably encouraged through short-term interventions? Does counseling for androgyny require adding, deleting, or creating behaviors, or a combination? Is it possible to encourage androgynous functioning within just one realm of functioning (for example, in attitudes but not traits)? Is androgyny an appropriate goal for everyone?

Professionals need to consider what broader sex-role changes might be best for individuals in the future, how individuals might be expected to respond to sex-role change, and some values issues inherent in sex-role interventions.

These issues will be discussed in this section. At the end of the chapter, a model for sex-role counseling will be proposed that suggests a way to conceptualize sex-role problems and associated goals for counseling individuals of both sexes.

Variations of Future Sex-Role Changes

The most fundamental value underlying androgyny is that traditional sex-based prescriptions for personality traits, attitudes, and behaviors are limiting to individuals. The evolutionary process jarring loose these traditions is not likely either to stop or to reverse itself irrevocably. The eventual form these changes will take is uncertain, but it is clear that changes are likely to occur in a number of directions.

In its simplest form, the goal of sex-role change is psychological and social equality of the sexes. Rossi (1976) noted that several models of eventual sex equality are possible. In the pluralist model, the presence of sex-related differences would be perpetuated and even valued for the diversity they provide (also can be aptly labeled the "vive la différence" model). In the assimilation model, the minority group is gradually absorbed into the more powerful group, losing its unique qualities. The hybrid model effects a blending of the groups through a process of mutual change. All types of changes can be discussed in terms of androgyny, for somewhat different reasons.

The pluralist model is perhaps most attractive to those who emphasize hypothetical biological factors in the emergence of sex-related differences, and those who are afraid that androgyny connotes erasing of individual differences entirely. Thus Wesley and Wesley (1977) recommend "group androgyny" as a way of recognizing the existence of masculine and feminine characteristics within each sex as healthy for the group at large. Both masculine and feminine men (and women) supposedly would be equally valued.

As Rossi explained, the pluralist model often maintains segregation. The lip service given to the value of heterogeneity is accompanied by very real distinctions in terms of power and privileges. The appealingly democratic notion behind the pluralist model of sex-role change overlooks the differential valuing of masculinity and femininity in today's society. The chance that increased tolerance for a range of characteristics would be accompanied by an equal valuing of all appears unlikely indeed.

In the assimilation model, women would increasingly adopt the characteristics of men (except biologically, of course). The vision of the new woman is a masculine one: ambitious, career-oriented, assertive, logical. Research to date has indicated the superior social utility, self-esteem, and adjustment value masculinity confers over femininity.

Yet, masculine sex typing for all is not an ideal. Bardwick (1979) succinctly labeled the devaluing of feminine qualities in favor of masculine ones as a form of sexism. Women trying to assimilate themselves in the masculine ideal are pushed into an equally narrow range of experiences, which does nothing to erase women's feelings of insecurity and low self-esteem. And, men have nothing to gain from the assimilation strategy. In Bardwick's words, "the lives of too many men signal that, for society's sake, women must not subscribe to the sexist assumption that a work preoccupied life is intrinsically more worthy and gratifying than the complex of role commitments that increasingly characterizes women's lives" (p. 57). The assimilation model is not an androgynous vision of sex-role change, but an *androcentric* one. What has been rewarded in the past—masculine characteristics—would explicitly become the ideal for all. The devaluation of femininity would become explicit.

Our society's dichotomous view of the sexes suggests that such a uniform adoption of one of the polarities would not remain long. Without a recognition that a *range* of characteristics is in fact desirable, the end result may well be a new definition of the "other," providing new distinctions that discriminate the most-valued from the lesser-valued group.

The hybrid model recognizes the importance of change in *both* sexes. Individuals who are willing to express both instrumental and expressive characteristics, and are unwilling to use sex-based standards as prescriptive guides for behavior are needed. Bardwick recommended *human* (as opposed to masculine) goals for the sex-role revolution: an increased range of feelings and experiences for everyone, an increased commitment to others and to a sense of community, a heightened feeling of responsibility for one's own life. Major changes in how home life as well as work are sex-segregated will have to occur, with changes in roles in both domains for each sex (cf. Pleck, 1977).

The hybrid model actually implies two types or levels of sex-role change. Garnets and Pleck (1979) distinguished between two components of positive sex-role change: changes in sex-role ideals and norms, permitting a broader range of sex-role related characteristics among individuals; and a reduction in sex-role salience, which would reduce the linking of characteristics with sex (gender). The latter is a long-term goal that would eliminate the occurrence of sex-role strain. Both changes in attitudes about sex roles and in the pervasive tendency to categorize the world in sex-related terms are needed.

Changes in sex-role ideals and norms would reduce or eliminate pressure placed upon persons to conform to a restrictive sex-based standard of behavior. However, as Bem (1981a) argued, standards that permit the sexes to be both masculine and feminine maintain artificial sex distinctions that continue to organize society and our perceptions of ourselves. In Bem's words, "human behaviors and society should cease to have gender" (p. 363). Bem thus perceives androgyny as an intermediate step, with the final goal for society to reduce sex-role salience (Garnets and Pleck, 1979), to become aschematic with respect to gender (Bem, 1981a), or to facilitate sex-role transcendence in individuals (Rebecca, Hefner, & Oleshansky, 1976).

The hybrid model promises the greatest latitude in characteristics and roles for men and women, and is probably the most palatable model to professionals who value both masculinity and femininity. It is also the only model that presents a range of positive options for both sexes, with elimination of sex as a descriptive criterion dichotomizing human behavior. To accomplish this model, more is required than simply lifting the old prescriptions and proscriptions at the individual level. Changes at the cultural, ideological, and institutional levels are also important (Kaplan & Bean, 1976).

To summarize, various models of sex equality recommend somewhat contrasting patterns of characteristics among the sexes as ideal. The pluralist model would maintain and equally value present sex-related differences for the diversity these differences provide. The assimilation model predicts that women become more masculine to blend into the dominant group (men) more smoothly. The hybrid model recognizes the need for two types of sex-role changes: changes in sex-role ideals and norms applicable to both sexes, and a reduction in sex-role salience. The latter model is probably most compatible with the philosophy of sex roles underlying the concept of androgyny, but will require extensive changes at the individual and social levels.

As Sargent (1977) pointed out, personal change is an arduous although necessary route for broad, social changes in sex roles, since the goal of the revolution is fuller actualization on the individual level. The movement toward androgyny in roles and behavior is likely to be a slow, painful one. Factors at the individual level, as well as institutional inertia, may be expected to retard the changes many professionals view as desirable and inevitable.

Personal Resistance to Sex-Role Change

By its very nature the sex-role system is resistant to change. This is true on the individual as well as the systemic level. Collier and Williams (1981) suggested that sex-role maintenance is enforced on the individual level, so that in some respects it is in a person's own best interests to resolve role conflict in line with society's standards. A sense of agreement between one's sex-role stereotypes and personal identity can lend a sense of security that is replaced by anxiety, ambivalence, and loss of self-esteem when sex-role changes begin to occur (Bardwick, 1979; Money & Tucker, 1975).

As social changes occur, people frequently return to old values with a fervor, or embrace the new values unquestioningly. Individuals are also inventive in their ability to reduce an internal sense of dissonance between personal standards for behavior and their perceptions of their own behavior. Individuals who do not perceive themselves as matching their abstract conceptions of being a man or woman may judge personal masculinity/femininity only on the basis of the positive characteristics they do possess. They can preserve a sense of self-worth by disposing of personally perceived sex-role shortcomings through relabeling, denial, or dismissal. The difficulty of efforts to reconcile all the diverse sex-role beliefs and demands into cognitively consistent, global self-concepts may help to explain why proposed changes in sex roles elicit strong fears and resentment (Spence & Helmreich, 1978).

When sex-role norms and personal behavior no longer agree because of personal change, violation of others' expectations may provoke rejection by them. From childhood on, sex-atypical behavior generally does not receive the same response as sex-traditional behavior. Deviations may be especially disconcerting when they involve close relationships with others. When a marriage partner behaves in sex-atypical ways, both partners may feel anxious and may attempt to deal with the anxiety by symbolic concessions affirming each partner's masculinity or femininity (Bardwick, 1979). Scanzoni (1977) recognized how sex-role changes in marriage require the couple to make decisions and bargain around issues that they never had to consider before. The situation can become especially sensitive if the sex-role change had an impact on how the person is willing to negotiate (as in women becoming more assertive).

Few couples welcome new opportunities for painful negotiations in areas that threaten their personal sense of identity.

Professionals may advocate the desirability of changes in both sexes toward a blurring of traditional distinctions, but many men as individuals do not agree. Research suggests that men are more likely to describe ideal persons in ways differing by sex than women are (Gilbert, Deutsch, & Strahan, 1978; McPherson & Spetrino, 1983; Silvern & Ryan, 1983). Men are also less likely to view androgynous other-sex persons as ideal than women are (Kimlicka, Wakefield, & Goad, 1982). Traditional men are particularly unlikely to view masculinity as ideal for women (Silvern & Ryan, 1983). Orlofsky (1982) suggested that there may be more of a discrepancy for men between what they say they want in a woman and what they would actually prefer in a dating partner than there is for women. In short, men as a group appear to be more interested than women in preserving the sex-role status quo. Women who desire to become less traditionally sex-typed may feel conflicted as a result of perceiving that many if not most men prefer them to be traditionally feminine (Orlofsky, 1982). Some women may choose not to make changes in themselves to avoid rejection or painful confrontations. Despite these reasons for women's reluctance, Skovholt and Hansen (1980) labeled current sex-role changes as far more lopsided than the desirable synthesis, because women are incorporating significantly more nontraditional attitudes and behaviors than men.

This trend favoring women's change is predictable, for a number of reasons. Masculinity still offers greater advantages than femininity (see Chapter 3). Men who define themselves primarily in terms of what women are *not* may see changes as heralding more competitors with no new options for themselves (Skovholt, 1978). Men who perceive changes in sex roles as promising only reverse sex discrimination and increased competition, more domestic responsibilities, heightened sexual demands, and uncertainties about previously predictable etiquette are not likely to welcome sex-role change in their own lives. And, as evident in the literature on counseling men, it is not easy to convince many men of the value of expressivity, emotionality, and nurturance. Silvern and Ryan's (1983) research on sex-role ideals indicated that men are likely to value feminine characteristics much more for an ideal person than for an ideal man. Androgynous men were also likely to perceive greater differences between ideal men and women than were androgynous women. Thus, sex-role changes for men in the direction of androgyny may entail greater personal conflict than for women.

The benefits of sex-role changes away from traditional patterns may appear to be obvious to professionals. However, many individuals, especially men, are likely to resist making such changes. Sex-role changes require individuals to reevaluate central aspects of themselves, and changes may be perceived negatively by others. Individuals do not opt to make painful changes in their lives unless the status quo is unacceptable in some essential respects. Many of these persons enter counseling to cope with these sex-role changes and the anxieties they incur. The professionals they encounter should be aware of some values issues inherent in the sex-role options commonly endorsed as an outcome for counseling.

Androgyny as a Value

The range of sex-role options that practitioners value now is more varied than before. Probably few professionals share Odenwald's (1965) fear that "we are raising a race of less masculine men and less feminine women, and we are in danger, if this trend continues, of developing a population of neutrals. . . . This development is the source of many great social evils—sexual promiscuity, juvenile delinquency, homosexuality, and others" (p. 3). Odenwald's dire (and almost humorous) prediction graphically depicts the sex-role values of an earlier age. As noted previously in the chapter, practitioners are increasingly aware of the negative personal and interpersonal consequences restrictive sex-traditional standards have imposed on men and women. Sex-role standards for professionals and lay persons alike are now characterized by change, and for many by a new ideal of psychological androgyny. Yet, this ideal is no less rooted in sex-role values than were traditional sex-role ideals.

As an ideal, androgyny represents a willingness to abandon traditional sex-role prescriptions for a more flexible, situation-appropriate mode of behaving, which can incorporate either or both masculine and feminine attributes. Foxley (1979) asserted that professionals who ignore the potential of androgyny are doing their clients a disservice by implicitly supporting the value of traditional sex stereotypes.

The ideal of androgyny has its own ideological overtones, evident in how its virtues have been extolled far beyond what empirical data would allow (Gilbert, 1981). As preandrogyny masculinity-femininity research well illustrated, ideology can inhibit understanding in psychology when it is not recognized. Aware of this problem, Lenney (1979a) accused androgyny researchers of "value ossification": perceiving research questions, designs, and data only as their own sex-role values would allow.

The dangers of values ossification apply to practitioners as well. The concept of androgyny has been widely accepted by practitioners not because they were convinced of its importance by the weight of empirical literature supporting it. Instead, the concept represents a particular values stance about sex roles many practitioners find congenial. Practitioners may be guilty of shortsightedness in what sex-role alternatives they see as viable for their clients, if they simply replace traditional sex typing with androgyny as the new ideal for their clients.

Psychological androgyny may not be problem-free. As noted in Chapter 3, androgyny may have been overidealized: it may incur its own negative consequences for a variety of reasons. Nor is it a panacea for troubled clients. Movement away from sex-traditional characteristics and the frequently stabilizing norms supporting them can provide additional anxiety in clients, as it does for nonclients. Some clients with poorly defined identities may in fact require the boundaries provided by traditional sex-role stereotypes (Lerner, 1978).

It would also be an oversimplification to conclude that nonsex-stereotyped behavior patterns are invariably most desirable. Research summarized in Chapter 3 suggests that depending upon the situation and persons involved, sex-role identities and behaviors labeled as sex-typed may be more adaptive and functional for some individuals. These benefits may vary as a function of life stage or circumstances (cf. Feldman et al., 1981). Identical behaviors may also provide very different payoffs for men and women. And, depending upon an individual's perceptions of a situation, what others may perceive as less adaptive may be perceived by the individual as most likely to lead to positive outcomes (Lenney, 1979b). What is or is not "adaptive" sex-role behavior must be judged in light of the individual's perceptions, the situation, and the short and long-term consequences following from the behavior.

From a more philosophical perspective, Sampson (1977) questioned the present cultural ethos of self-contained individualism as expressed in the ideal of psychological androgyny. For Sampson, the equating of androgyny with good health reflects our society's current emphasis on wholeness of functions within a person, a perspective that puts the entire burden for maintenance and change upon the individual. Other models of interdependence and community are possible that recognize that good health can come from an effective coordination of characteristics and functions among persons.

In my perspective, practitioners can and should be opposed to the many subtle and overt sex-discriminatory practices in our society. The most desirable alternative to traditional sex-role prescriptions may be what Knefelkamp, Widick, and Stroad (1976) defined as the highest stage of sex-role identity formation: evolving a personal meaningful identity in the face of many possible valid options through recognizing and blending together diverse themes in oneself. In this task, the practitioner's role is to facilitate clients' self-exploration and, to paraphrase Knefelkamp et al., to assist clients in finding, experiencing, and committing themselves to their own "balance points."

The "androgyny is ideal" equation is problematic where it fails to recognize that psychological adjustment cannot be simply prescribed as possession of certain specified attributes. However, it *is* consistent with the philosophy of androgyny to state that the enforced dichotomization of personality traits, life roles, behaviors, and so on by sex is undesirable. A range of positive personality characteristics and behavior should be recognized as appropriate for individuals regardless of sex, and instrumental and expressive characteristics are valuable for all individuals. Changes in sex-role ideals and norms, and a reduction of sex-role salience would facilitate individuals' attempts to find their own balance points. This perspective recognizes the desirability of sex-role changes, towards enhancing individual adaptability and choice and away from determinations based on biological sex alone.

This perspective also suggests that androgyny in and of itself may not serve as a useful goal in counseling. Androgyny represents turning away from traditional sex roles toward less sex-dichotomized characteristics and options for men and women. Describing what clients are moving *towards* requires more specificity than the general concept of androgyny presently provides.

Previous chapters of this book indicated that androgyny is a multidimensional concept, which can refer to traits, cognitive processing styles, sex-role attitudes, and so on. Many of the implications of these various definitions of androgyny for an individual's behavior have also not yet been clarified. In this respect, use of the term to define an outcome of counseling can be more confusing that it is descriptive. Instead, practitioners should attempt to specify what types of sex-role changes their individual clients could benefit from making. For example, positive sex-role change for one client may require working through an internal conflict between his or her sex-role ideal and less traditional lifestyle, where for another client it involves acquiring and practicing some other-sex traditional behaviors. A movement toward specificity would aid discussion of sex-role issues considerably in counseling, and would help to generate new conceptualizations and interventions for work with clients. This perspective emphasizes the complexity of sex roles, and the unique problems individuals may face in working through these issues.

A MODEL FOR SEX-ROLE INTERVENTIONS

The diversity of conceptualizations about androgyny inhibits the development of more sophisticated definitions and hypothesis testing to some extent. Syntheses of these diverse conceptualizations will help to point out areas requiring revision and further exploration. This preliminary statement based on the sex-role literature reviewed in this book is an invitation for others to do likewise.

Definitions of Sex Roles

The study of sex roles requires analysis at the individual, personal interaction, and societal levels. In general, sex roles refer to the organizing social/cognitive principles prescribing and regulating the behavior of the sexes. Individuals develop their sense of personal identity as a man or woman by learning and integrating these principles. Sex roles involve a number of discrete but interrelated dimensions: personality traits more typical of or desirable for each sex; learned behaviors and habits; attitudes and associated sanctions concerning desirable behaviors; values; explanations or attributions for personal and others' behaviors; and so on. Sex roles are stable over time and among individuals, but not immutable; learned similarly by members of one sex, but subject to an individual's personal learning history. Whereas sex is biological and (for the most practical purposes) innately dichotomous, sex roles are overlapping and are taught formally or informally.

Sex roles correspond to two dimensions used to describe central personality traits and tasks to be performed in society: the agentic/instrumental and communal/expressive. The needs for goal-directed action, assertion, autonomy (agency/instrumentality) and for interdependence, cooperation, emotional awareness (communion/expressiveness) are present in everyone to some degree and represent equally valid components of social interaction. Traditionally, men's characteristics and activities have largely been linked to the agentic/instrumental and women's to the communal/expressive (masculine and feminine), a tendency consistent across societies. What has differed across societies is the manner in which the sexes have been expected to carry out their prescribed functions, and to what degree they have been permitted to express the "other side" of their natures. Many mental health practitioners now regard a congenial balance between the two dimensions to be desirable.

Sex roles are inherently conservative, although their prescriptions for behavior are not always clear-cut. They have a strong impact in essential arenas of human relationships: family, friendships, work, religion, politics. At their most efficient, sex roles provide easy answers for questions of behavior appropriateness through dichotomous thinking patterns: male or female, us and them. This easy compartmentalization provides limited comfort at times because answers based on sex are sometimes simplistic, inappropriate for the person, or simply unavailable.

Individual Differences in Sex Roles

Individuals may be predisposed from birth to assume and express characteristics associated with one dimension more comfortably. It is popularly believed that men as a group naturally find the masculine and women the feminine to be more comfortable. This "preference" is difficult to separate from the effects of powerful sex-socialization processes set into motion at birth. Individuals do largely acquire feminine and masculine characteristics through observational learning and attempts to understand the sex-role distinctions they observe around them. This learning is facilitated and enforced through a system of socially based sanctions externally applied and then internalized by an individual.

An individual's sex-role identity and behavior are likely to be somewhat unique as a result of his or her personal learning history. Members of a given sociocultural group usually understand in a fairly consistent manner general outlines of what a man or women should be and do, commonly labeled as sex-role standards. As a result of their own experiences, however, individuals may differ in their conceptions of:

1. To what situations they believe the general sex-role standards should apply;
2. What are the positive and negative outcomes of conformity, and whether these outcomes are personally important to them;
3. In what specific manner these standards should be applied; and even
4. Whether these rules are to be regarded as personally meaningful at all.

Consequently, variability among individual's sex-role characteristics is likely to be complex and subtle. Interestingly, individuals are often unaware that others may perceive sex-role related behavior differently, that there may be behavioral options different from the sex-traditional choices made in a given situation, and that there may be little that is inherent that requires the sexes to behave in markedly different ways (with the exception of biological reproduction).

Frequently, aspects of individuals' sex-role characteristics are internally consistent. For example, many men are predominantly masculine in traits, work preferences, modes of interaction, and so on. People may perform behaviors consistent with traditional sex-role standards for a variety of reasons. For example, these behaviors may be the most familiar as a result of past experiences; they are consistent with self-perceptions (and self-perceptions are also made to be consistent with behavior); they may be more compatible with personal (trait) predispositions; they are low-risk ways to obtain positive social approval and avoid negative reactions. The same reasons may account for nontraditional behaviors. However, complete consistency *within* a person's own sex-role characteristics and across situations is probably rare. For example, a woman with strong feminine traits may be a successful businesswoman, a nurturant mother, and simultaneously dominant with her co-workers and emotionally yielding with her partner. She may or may not perceive these characteristics to be contradictory and may or may not feel engaging in any of these particular aspects to be a strain or inappropriate. Whether or not a given person is comfortable with his or her sex-role identity and behavior is potentially attributable to a variety of factors.

Sex-role Adjustment

In previous years, sex-role adjustment denoted conformity to and satisfaction with the dichotomous set of characteristics and functions prescribed separately for women and men. Significant aspects of traditional sex-role standards have become increasingly obsolescent. This obsolescence is a pervasive cause of sex-role related discomfort in individuals. Rapid technological and sociocultural changes have required behaviors for which many individuals are unprepared and which are inconsistent with traditional sex-role standards. Work has increasingly become sedentary, intellectual, and interdependent rather than requiring physical labor, autonomy, and aggressiveness on the part of men. More women work and for longer periods of time outside the home. As family size decreases and lifespan increases, women spend more years in activities other than child care. Men may find themselves custodial parents and women childless. With mobility and superior communications, alternative lifestyles are better publicized.

Behavior change has preceded normative change for many, leading to confusion, dissonance between behaviors and attitudes, and a sense of personal incongruity. Many persons have lost their "existential anchors" (Bardwick, 1979) and feel anxious and unsettled in light of conflicting demands and expectations. In addition, many individuals in the past have found traditional sex-role expectations to be unsatisfying to some degree. That is, recently identified anxieties and dissatisfactions are not only attributable to sociocultural changes, but are also an inevitable component of a restrictive sex-role system.

In today's society, comfortable sex-role adjustment requires engaging in a minimum of personally satisfying, socially approved same-sex behaviors and fulfilling needs associated with both complementary dimensions (i.e., being both masculine and feminine to some degree) in a manner which: (a) minimizes personally salient negative social sanctions and maximizes positive sanctions; and (b) preserves an internally consistent self-concept. One important component of this definition is recognition of others' reactions to the individual as anticipated and actually experienced by the person. As with many norms, variability from the sex-role mean is tolerated within certain limits. Criteria for minimal sex-role conformity can vary, ranging from superficial aspects of sex roles (e.g., men should not wear dresses) to carefully defined life patterns (e.g., women should be full-time homemakers). Some minimal conformity appears to be necessary to avoid severe censure; for example, young men who wear dresses are not likely to be tolerated cheerfully by most of society. Individuals differ in how motivated they are to avoid this censure. Some individuals may and do choose to ignore these minimal standards with varying consequences in terms of how they and others subsequently view themselves.

Achieving a personally comfortable degree of conformity is easiest to accomplish when societal sex-role standards and sanctions are explicit and relevant for daily behavioral demands, when sex-role standards are flexible enough to permit some individual differences (especially in tolerating various blends of masculine and feminine characteristics), and when an individual's traits and learning history are compatible with the broader social standards. It does *not* follow automatically that more conformity to same-sex standards indicates better adjustment. Research has outlined the cost of overly strong adherence to these prescriptions.

The second major component of the definition of sex-role adjustment refers to intrapersonal consistency. Sex-role identity is a central element in individuals' conceptions of themselves. Therefore, an absence of self-perceived dissonance among one's sex-role related personality traits, attitudes, and behaviors is basic to intrapersonal adjustment. Categories of sex-role related variables especially pertinent to individual functioning are:

1. *Self-perceptions*: masculine and feminine personality characteristics, which a person views as self-descriptive. People are generally consistent in their self-descriptions over time, although changes can occur.
2. *Attitudes/standards*: perceptions of desirable behavior for the sexes in general and for oneself in terms of masculinity and femininity. These perceptions overlap, but are not necessarily identical.
3. *Behavioral repertoire*: the potential for and actual performance of behaviors traditionally linked to one or the other sex. There is an important distinction between those behaviors and skills a person actually possesses and those he or she is willing to use in various settings. Actual performance is strongly affected by a person's perceptions of environmental demands and rewards.
4. *Environmental demands and rewards/costs*: socially based requirements for behavior often accompanied by rewards and costs depending upon adherence to them. These environmental influences can be generalized or situation-specific. Individuals are expected to understand and adhere to these expectations, even through the expectations may not be clearly stated and in fact may be unfamiliar to the person. The various contexts of a person's life (e.g., work, family, social contacts) may present conflicting sets of standards and rewards.

It can be hypothesized that at any given point of time consistency among an individual's masculine and feminine self-attributions, sex-role attitudes, environmental demands and accompanying rewards and costs, and behavioral repertoire available for dealing with current situations is needed for a comfortable sense of self as a woman or man. This sense of self is the essence of sex-role adjustment. In this sense, sex-role "adjustment" denotes an *absence of conflict* among a number of interrelated elements within a person rather than simple conformity to a particular set of sex-role requirements. Adjustment is individually determined and takes into account environmental expectations and rewards. Some individuals more than others seem to be attuned to the influence of sex roles and may be more sensitive to perceived inconsistencies as a result.

For a given person, sex-role adjustment is not static and can vary as a function of a number of personal and social factors. With age, changes in family constellation or career, economic fluctuations, and so on, what may have been satisfying sex-role behavior at one time may become less adaptive. What an individual regards as appropriate behavior may not elicit the expected (and desired) positive reactions from others. An individual may be required to engage in certain behaviors which he or she may later view as extremely discrepant with past sex-role performance or self-concept. Examination of personal values may uncover inconsistencies among them or between essential life values and certain sex-role attitudes or behaviors. An individual may find prescriptions for behavior in a certain setting compelling enough to stifle personal expression of the complementary dimension (as when a newly-hired ambitious male corporate manager discovers his colleagues to ridicule his interest in child care). Regardless of the cause of the disjunctions among such perceptions, expectations, and reactions, many individuals today face recurring dilemmas of how to reconcile conflicting elements to maintain a comfortable sense of self.

Individuals who successfully manage complex sex-role requirements, contradictions, and changes are likely to exhibit the following characteristics:

1. Valuing themselves based on agreement of self-perceptions and personal conceptions of what are desirable characteristics independent of sex, instead of exclusively upon sex-based standards.
2. A willingness to trust perceptions of themselves and of the environment, and reliance upon personal values in making major decisions rather than upon simplistic sex-based guidelines.
3. Possession of self-concepts flexible enough to accommodate a range of feminine and masculine personality characteristics without feelings of dissonance (e.g., a person can see oneself as interdependent and assertive, sensitive and dominant).
4. Related to 3, possession of self-concepts that are stable yet can assimilate new sex-role relevant information about themselves (e.g., a young man who can be pleased to discover previously unrecognized nurturing abilities or a capacity for leadership).
5. Possession of a behavior repertoire including masculine (agentic/instrumental) and feminine (communal/expressive) skills.
6. An ability to tolerate sex-role ambiguity in interpersonal situations (does not need to know "what a woman or a man should do" in order to determine desirable alternatives).
7. An ability to assess new situations and select sex-role related behaviors likely to earn personally valued positive reinforcements without relinquishing or devaluing other personal behaviors or preferences.

These persons may be labeled "androgynous" in a number of sex-role spheres, or perhaps more simply defined as persons who are *not* rigidly sex-typed.

Varieties of Sex-role Distress

No one is immune from distress engendered by sex-role related disjunctions between personal characteristics, attitudes, and behavior and the environment in which he or she is embedded. In some cases, sex-role difficulties can be a symptom, byproduct, or exacerbating factor in more generalized problems of personal functioning. This broader syndrome may require primary attention by a professional. In other cases, problems that prompt individuals to seek professional help may be meaningfully interpreted in sex-role related terminology, which can suggest specific modes of therapeutic intervention.

Examples of such problems associated with sex-role distress include the following:

1. Overconformity to restrictive sex-role standards. Overlearning the traditional role for one's sex too well can have a variety of negative consequences. These consequences include overly rigid self-perceptions and attitudes, failure to develop adaptive behavior skills, and hypersensitivity to sex-role cues to determine personal behavior and life decisions. The extensive effects of this overly restrictive sex-role learning are exemplified in more specific problem descriptions below.

2. Dissonance between self-perceptions and personal sex-role standards for behavior. An individual may perceive inconsistencies among some subset of self-perceptions of characteristics and behavior, and associated sex-role related attitudes. Anxiety and guilt may result, depending upon the importance the person places on conforming to sex-role standards and the degree to which nonconformance is perceived. For example, women who believe that motherhood should be a woman's primary responsibility may feel dissonance if they also perceive themselves to be ambitious and career-oriented. This type of disjunction between personal self-concept, perceptions of desirable same-sex behavior, and social approval or disapproval of personal ideals and behavior produces a special type of dissonance called sex-role strain (Garnets & Pleck, 1979). Individuals may also perceive inconsistencies between their personal characteristics and others' standards. Especially when the other persons are important to the individual, these perceived inconsistencies may cause feelings of self-doubt, insecurity, and interpersonal stress.

3. Disjunctions between personal sex-role standards and present environmental/life stage demands. Familiar standards for behavior may prove to be inadequate, inappropriate, or obsolete guides for dealing with current situations. These changes in standards have occurred on a societal basis as

previously noted. On a personal level, a man who has defined men's role primarily in terms of career might find himself at a loss when he suddenly gains total custody of his small children (witness the recent movie *Kramer vs. Kramer*). Such disjunctions may cause feelings of anger, confusion, anxiety, and self-alienation.

4. Possession of an inadequate behavioral repertoire to cope with present environmental/life stage demands. The stress from the disjunctions described above multiply if the person has never learned the skills needed to deal productively with the new demands. Widowers lacking domestic skills may suffer serious strain in coping with their life situations beyond their emotional loss.

5. Inhibition of behavioral skills because of sex-role standards. Individuals who possess some behavioral skills may not use them for fear of appearing "unmasculine" or "unfeminine." For example, a woman with good decision-making or analytic skills may choose not to display them in mixed-sex settings, because she expects that her companions may not appreciate such skills in women. This inhibition can eliminate some potential pleasure and rewards for her in the interactions.

6. Ambiguity about appropriate behavior and possible consequences in an upcoming situation. To maintain the perception of personal control, individuals need to be able to anticipate and assess new situations, and select behaviors likely to earn personally valued rewards. Especially when an individual anticipates undesirable consequences as a result of sex-role related attitudes and behavior, intense anxiety may accompany the implied questioning of oneself as a man or woman. For example, the first male nursing student may feel considerable anxiety about how he as a "man" should behave in the female-dominated setting, how others will expect him to behave, and the reactions of others to him. For some individuals in similar situations, this anxious apprehension of future events may be chronic and contribute to burnout.

7. Coping with actual externally imposed sanctions incurred. On a systemic basis, ascription of devalued characteristics and consequent imposition of negative sanctions on the basis of sex is sexism. The frustrations and pain suffered by individuals because of sexism need no further amplification here. Individuals whose personality characteristics and behavior are perceived as nontraditional frequently must cope with negative responses of others. Men who are full-time homemakers/parents commonly experience these responses. This is also true of individuals countering more liberal standards in certain situations. A woman professional who chooses to become a full-time homemaker/parent may confront open consternation from her co-workers.

In other cases, anticipating but failing to receive rewards for conforming to prevailing sex-role standards can cause resentment and frustration. Women who choose to be emotionally subservient to the needs of their husbands may not get the affection and security they view as their reward. Men who become "workaholics" to provide a high income for their families may feel unappreciated and even betrayed if their singlemindedness creates conflict with their wives or children.

8. Conflicts ensuing from overly rigid attitudes about others. Interpersonal conflicts in a variety of arenas can arise from imposing strict expectations upon others (e.g. "real men never walk away from a fight"; "real women should be happy to stay at home with their children").

Individuals facing the problems listed above may need to reorient central perceptions of themselves and others, learn new behaviors, develop interpersonal coping strategies, and work through often dimly perceived emotional and attitudinal conflicts. As Goodman (1979) poignantly illustrates, many individuals weather this process alone through self-examination, confrontations, and life transitions. Others require counseling.

Goals in Sex-role Counseling

The issues outlined above characterize a wide range of clients requesting psychological services: anxiety and guilt, distress from not conforming to social norms and personal standards, inflexible self-concepts, cognitive dissonance, interpersonal/relationship conflicts, lack of social rewards or presence of punishment when no behavioral alternatives are seen, or inadequate behavioral repertoires. However, these problems may also be explicitly tied to sex roles.

Sex-role counseling works toward general goals common in psychological practice, for example: (a) to help individuals to recognize and capitalize upon their own unique strengths and potential; (b) to help them make choices which are maximally adaptive in their own lives; (c) to remedy skills deficits; and (d) to encourage positive and flexible self-concepts.

The implicit goal is to help a person work toward the positive characteristics listed earlier: a flexible, stable self-concept that can assimilate both masculine and feminine characteristics; an ability to determine adaptive, personally satisfying behaviors without resorting to dichotomous, traditional sex roles as a necessary guide; an ability and willingness to engage in masculine and feminine-typed behaviors as environmental demands and personal evaluations recommend; a reliance on self-assessment and values in making major life decisions rather than homogeneous sex-based standards. The type of changes an individual needs to make in counseling is predicated upon careful analysis of his or her problems. The goals should enhance a person's ability to cope with similar dilemmas in the future. In this context "androgyny" as a generic therapeutic goal carries little meaning, because goals are tailored to the client's own situation, values, and potential.

Examples of Therapeutic Interventions

The reframing of sex-role problems above should suggest strategies already familiar to practitioners. Specific interventions may include the following:

1. Behavioral skills training (e.g., in assertive or expressive/communication skills). Modeling and shaping procedures are examples of strategies suitable in remedying skills deficits or inhibitions. These may be useful in moderating extreme sex-role characteristics in frequency, intensity, or situation-appropriateness; in adding to restrictive sex-traditional response repertoires; or in encouraging persons to develop uniquely personal blends of masculine and feminine characteristics.

2. Career or life planning. Individuals may benefit from examining personal values, interests, abilities, responsibilities, and goals with full awareness of sex-role pressures. An emphasis on values clarification is especially pertinent here.

3. Cognitive interventions, including cognitive restructuring, reattribution, and cognitive dissonance focuses. Examples of problems that are especially appropriate for cognitive interventions include individuals' sex-role relevant distorted views of themselves and others, attributions of causes for events that prevent their perceptions of self-control or are unnecessarily punitive to others, and feelings of dissonance among one's personality characteristics, attitudes, and behavior.

4. Couples counseling. Sex-role issues can cause serious strain in intimate relationships, heterosexual and homosexual alike. Working with the couple as a unit may be essential in resolving conflicts for the individuals involved.

5. Working through polarities or dichotomies in a person. Many individuals find it difficult to reconcile masculine and feminine tendencies in themselves, especially if these tendencies appear to be contradictory in nature (e.g., nurturing and aggressive tendencies). Gestalt techniques that focus on integrating the polarities (e.g., the empty-chair technique) can be helpful here.

6. Consciousness-raising (C-R) groups. C-R groups can be invaluable in assisting individuals within a supportive atmosphere to become aware of sex-role demands and sanctions placed upon them and of potential options for growth.

7. Self-management techniques. Individuals may find it helpful to identify personally salient social reinforcements and to determine satisfying ways to obtain them through explicit management of their own sex-role relevant behaviors with others.

8. Expressive therapy approaches. Permission to explore previously denied or painful conflictual feelings about oneself as a man or woman with a skilled practitioner may be essential to gain greater self-acceptance and to evolve more satisfying roles. Understanding and acceptance from the practitioner can be particularly therapeutic for clients whose personal identity and behaviors lead to disapproval of others.

Both men and women suffer from sex-role concerns, for reasons which may be common to everyone, endemic to their sex, or idiosyncratic. The impact of their sex-based experiences and their personal perceptions and values needs to be carefully considered. Counseling for sex-role change requires clear comprehension of the impact of sex roles on an individual's functioning. This appreciation can help clients work at times within and at times beyond the sex-role system which so powerfully structures our interactions with others and feelings about ourselves. The goals are flexible adaptation to changing circumstances and positive valuing of oneself perhaps simultaneously in light of and in spite of personal masculinity and femininity. Such counseling is not value-free. Because not all sex-role options are equally acceptable in a sex-typed society, practitioners need to help clients consider the possible consequences of their changes, to themselves and to others.

The interventions described above focus upon potential adaptive changes within the client. However, sex-role change as described here does *not* mean that individuals must learn to surrender themselves to a new sex-based ethic, as was previously required for sex-role adjustment. Instead, all individuals must learn to cope productively, on an ongoing basis, with the multitude of expectations and options confronting the sexes today. The need for real change may indeed lie in the restrictive and punitive perceptions and attitudes of others. What may be most therapeutic for a client is an opportunity to ventilate feelings, check out personal perceptions, explore possibilities for coping, and strengthen self-acceptance. Sociopolitical awareness, assertion of legal rights, and working productively toward social reform can also be therapeutic.

SUMMARY

A framework for sex-role counseling was proposed based upon the multidimensionality of, and individual differences in sex roles. In today's sex-typed society, comfortable sex-role adjustment generally requires engaging in a minimum of personally satisfying, socially approved same-sex behaviors and fulfilling needs associated with both masculine and feminine dimensions in a manner that minimizes personally salient, negative social sanctions and maximizes positive sanctions, and preserves an internally consistent self-concept. This definition recognizes the importance of others' reactions to the individual as anticipated and as experienced, and of intrapersonal consistency among self-perceptions, attitudes, behaviors, and environmental demands and rewards. Sex-role "adjustment" denotes an absence of conflict within a person rather than simple conformity to a particular set of sex-role requirements.

Both androgyny (or lack of rigid sex typing) and sex-role distress can be defined in terms of these self-perceptions, attitudes, behaviors, and environmental influences. Goals of sex-role counseling include helping a person to develop a flexible, stable self-concept that can incorporate both masculine and feminine characteristics; an ability to choose adaptive, personally satisfying behaviors without relying upon dichotomous sex-based prescriptions; an ability and willingness to perform masculine and feminine behaviors as the situation and personal assessment recommend; a reliance upon self-assessment and values in making life decisions. The particular goals and counseling interventions for a client depend upon careful analysis of the nature of her or his problems in sex-role related terms. Individuals frequently need to reorient central perceptions of themselves and others, work through emotional and attitudinal conflicts, learn new behaviors, and develop interpersonal coping strategies. The particular goals and counseling interventions appropriate for a given client need to be determined through careful analysis of her or his problems in sex-role terms.

This model for sex-role counseling recognizes the types of problems individuals face in a society that structures its socialization, expectations, and rewards for individuals along sex-differentiated lines. The model recognizes that although people may experience similar problems, there are important individual differences in the type, extent, and ways of coping with these problems. If the sex typing in society changes to lessen sex differentiations and sex-role salience, then the sex-role related problems of individuals should also change.

BIBLIOGRAPHY

This is a partial listing of the studies reviewed in preparation of this book by general topic area. It is extensive but not meant to be exhaustive, and there is some overlapping among categories. The purpose of the listing is to provide interested readers with a good starting point for their own review of the literature.

Achievement/Fear of Success

Alagna, 1982; Brewer & Blum, 1979; Cano, Solomon, & Holmes, 1984; Doherty, 1979; Gackenback, Heretick, & Alexander, 1979; Gayton, Havu, Barnes, Ozmon, & Bassett, 1978; Helmreich, Spence, Beane, Lucker, & Matthews, 1980; Jacobsen, 1979; Major, 1979; Marshall & Wijting, 1980; Olds & Shaver, 1980; Olejnik, Tompkins, & Hein-buck, 1982; Orlofsky, 1981a; Pasquella, Mednick, & Murray, 1981; Spence & Helmreich, 1978; Welch & Huston, 1982.

Adjustment (Global Measures)

Adams & Sherer, 1982; Bassoff & Glass, 1982; Burchardt & Serbin, 1982; DeGregorio & Carver, 1980; Erdwins, Small, & Gross, 1980; Hinrichsen, Follansbee, & Ganellen, 1981; Hoffman & Fidell, 1979; Logan & Kaschak, 1980; Lubinski, Tellegen, & Butcher, 1981; Orlofsky & Windle, 1978; Silvern & Ryan, 1979; Taylor & Hall, 1982; Thomas & Reznikoff, 1984; Wells, 1980; Whitley, 1983.

Anxiety/Fear/Worry/Stress

Babl, 1979; Carsrud & Carsrud, 1979; Erdwins, Small, & Gross, 1980; Holahan & Spence, 1980; Jordan-Viola, Fassberg, & Viola, 1976; Krasnoff, 1981; Shaw, 1982.

Assertiveness/Social Competency/Loneliness

Avery, 1982; Berg & Peplau, 1982; Campbell, Steffen, & Langmeyer, 1981; Gayton, Havu, Baird, & Ozman, 1983; Kelly, O'Brien, & Hosford, 1981; Lohr & Nix, 1982; Nix, Lohr, & Stauffacher, 1980; Wheeler, Reis, & Nezlek, 1983.

Attitudes About Sex Roles

Atkinson & Huston, 1984; Baucom & Sanders, 1978; Bem, 1977; Bridges, 1978; Colker & Widom, 1980; Hansen, 1982; Heilbrun, 1976; Hogan, 1977; Jones, Chernovetz, & Hansson, 1978; Jordan-Viola, Fassberg, & Viola, 1976; Minnigerode,

1976; Orlofsky, 1981b; Orlofsky, Aslin, & Ginsburg, 1977; Spence & Helmreich, 1979c; Spence, Helmreich, & Stapp, 1975.

Attractiveness/Attraction

Andersen & Bem, 1981; Antill, 1983; Bankart & Wittenbraker, 1980; Bridges, 1981; Cash & Smith, 1982; Kimlicka, Wakefield, & Goad, 1982; Kulik & Harackiewicz, 1979; Lamke & Bell, 1982; Major, Carnevale, & Deaux, 1981; Orlofsky, 1982.

Career Choice

Arkin & Johnson, 1980; Berzins, Welling, & Wetter, 1978; Clarey & Sanford, 1982; Doherty, 1979; Harren & Biscardi, 1980; Harren, Kass, Tinsley, & Moreland, 1979; Kanter & Ellerbusch, 1980; Long, 1982; Marshall & Wijting, 1980; Moreland, Harren, Krimsky-Montague, & Tinsley, 1979; Motowidlo, 1982; Piel, 1977; Spence & Helmreich, 1978; Tinsley, Kass, Moreland, & Harren, 1983; Tyer & Erdwins, 1979; Vandever, 1978; Waddell, 1983; Welch, 1979; Williams & McCullers, 1982; Williams & Miller, 1983; Wolfe & Betz, 1981; Yanico, 1981, 1982; Yanico & Hardin, 1981; Yanico, Hardin, & McLaughlin, 1978.

Career/Family Roles

Allgeier, 1975; Atkinson & Huston, 1984; Berzins, Welling, & Wetter, 1978; DeFronzo & Boudreau, 1977; Doherty, 1979; Falbo, Graham, & Gryskiewicz, 1978; Farmer & Fyans, 1983; Gaddy, Glass, & Arnkoff, 1983; Hoffman & Fidell, 1979; Holahan & Gilbert, 1979; Piel, 1977; Pursell, Banikiotes, & Sebastian, 1981; Rotheram & Weiner, 1983; Spence & Helmreich, 1978; Waddell, 1983; Williams & McCullers, 1983.

Cognitive Processing

Andersen & Bem, 1981; Bem, 1981a; Hollinger, 1984; Lippa, 1977; Markus, Crane, Bernstein, & Siladi, 1982; Mills, 1983; Mills & Tyrrell, 1983; Neimeyer, Banikiotes, & Merluzzi, 1981; Tunnell, 1981; Wolff & Taylor, 1979.

Conflict Management/Leadership Behaviors

Astley & Downey, 1980; Baxter & Shepherd, 1978; Hamby, 1978; Inderlied & Powell, 1979.

Developmental Variables

Amstey & Whitbourne, 1981; Block, 1973; Feldman, Biringen, & Nash, 1981; Heilbrun, 1976; Orlofsky, 1977; Schiff & Koopman, 1978.

Diagnostic Category Differences

Depression. Baucom, 1983; Baucom & Danker-Brown, 1979; Berzins, Welling, & Wetter, 1978; Golding & Singer, 1983; Holahan & Spence, 1980.

Neurosis. Berzins, Welling, & Wetter, 1978; Jones, Chernovetz, & Hansson, 1978; LaTorre, Endman, & Gossman, 1976.

Psychosomatic Problems. Hoffman & Fidell, 1979; Nix & Lohr, 1981; Olds & Shaver, 1980.

Schizophrenia. Berzins, Welling, & Wetter, 1978; LaTorre, Endman, & Gossman, 1976.

Substance Abuse (especially Alcohol). Beckman, 1978; Berzins, Welling, & Wetter, 1978; Davis, Pursell, & Burnham, 1979; Jones, Chernovetz, & Hansson, 1978; Kleinke & Hinrichs, 1983; Kondo, Powell, & Penick, 1978; Penick, Powell, & Read, 1984; Powell, Penick, & Read, 1980.

Familial (especially Parental) Variables

DeFronzo & Boudreau, 1979; Hansson, Chernovetz, & Jones, 1977; Heilbrun, 1978; Heilbrun & Thompson, 1977; Kelly & Worell, 1976; Kirkpatrick, 1979; Lamke, Bell, & Murphy, 1980; Pursell, Banikiotes, & Sebastian, 1981; Russell, 1978; Shaw & Rodriguez, 1981; Spence & Helmreich, 1978.

Flexibility

Babladelis, 1978; Bem, 1975, 1977; Bem & Lenney, 1976; Bem, Martyna, & Watson, 1976; Heilbrun & Pitman, 1979; Helmreich, Spence, & Holahan, 1979; LaFrance & Carmen, 1980; Orlofsky & Windle, 1978.

Locus of Control

Bem, 1977; Berzins, Welling, & Wetter, 1978; Brehony & Geller, 1981; Evanoski & Maher, 1979; Johnson & Black, 1981; Jones, Chernovetz, & Hansson, 1978; Minnigerode, 1976.

Self-disclosure/Intimacy

Banikiotes, Kubinski, & Pursell, 1981; Bem, 1977; Berg & Peplau, 1982; Bridges, 1978; Fischer & Narus, 1981b; Lombardo & Lavine, 1981; Narus & Fischer, 1982; Stokes, Child, & Fuehrer, 1981.

Self-esteem

Antill & Cunningham, 1979; Bem, 1977; Berzins, Welling, & Wetter, 1978; Colker & Widom, 1980; DeFronzo & Boudreau, 1979; Evanoski & Maher, 1979; Flaherty & Dusek, 1980; Gauthier & Kjervik, 1982; Heilbrun, 1981a, 1981b; Hinrichsen, Follansbee, & Ganellen, 1981; Hoffman & Fidell, 1979; Jones, Chernovetz, & Hansson, 1978; Kelly & Worell, 1977; Kimlicka, Cross, & Tarnai, 1983; Lamke, 1982; O'Connor, Mann, & Bardwick, 1978; Orlofsky, 1977; Schiff & Koopman, 1978; Spence & Helmreich, 1979c; Spence, Helmreich, & Stapp, 1975; Wetter, 1975; Wiggins & Holzmuller, 1978.

Sexual Behavior

Attitudes and Experiences. Allgeier, 1976, 1981; Allgeier & Fogel, 1978; Evans, 1984; Garcia, 1982; Jones, Chernovetz, & Hansson, 1978; Kenrick, Stringfield, Wagenhals, Dahl, & Ransdell, 1980; Kimlicka, Cross, & Tarnai, 1983.

Homosexual/Heterosexual Groups. Bernard, 1982; Bernard & Epstein, 1978a, 1978b; Berzins, Welling, & Wetter, 1978; Cardell, Finn, & Marecek, 1981; Heilbrun, 1976; Heilbrun & Thompson, 1977; Kweskin & Cook, 1982; Spence & Helmreich, 1978.

REFERENCES

Abrahams, B., Feldman, S. S., & Nash, S. C. (1978). Sex role self-concept and sex role attitudes: Enduring personality characteristics or adaptations to changing life situations? *Developmental Psychology*, **14**, 393–400.

Adams, C. H., & Sherer, M. (1982). Sex-role orientation and psychological adjustment: Comparison of MMPI profiles among college women and housewives. *Journal of Personality Assessment*, **46**, 607–613.

Alagna, S. W. (1982). Sex role identity, peer evaluation of competition, and the responses of women and men in a competitive situation. *Journal of Personality and Social Psychology*, **43**, 546–554.

Allgeier, E. R. (1975). Beyond sowing and growing: The relationship of sex typing to socialization, family plans, and future orientation. *Journal of Applied Social Psychology*, **5**, 217–226.

Allgeier, E. R. (1976, May). *Heterosexuality and sex-typing*. Paper presented at the annual meeting of the Midwestern Psychological Association, Chicago.

Allgeier, E. R. (1981). The influence of androgynous identification on heterosexual relations. *Sex Roles*, **7**, 321–330.

Allgeier, E. R., & Fogel, A. F. (1978). Coital position and sex roles: Responses to cross-sex behaviors in bed. *Journal of Consulting and Clinical Psychology*, **46**, 588–589.

American Psychological Association. (1975). Report of the task force on sex bias and sex-role stereotyping in psychotherapeutic practice. *American Psychologist*, **30**, 1169–1175.

Amstey, F. H., & Whitbourne, S. K. (1981). Continuing education, identity, sex role, and psychosocial development in adult women. *Sex Roles*, **7**, 49–58.

Andersen, S. M., & Bem, S. L. (1981). Sex typing and androgyny in dyadic interaction: Individual differences in responsiveness to physical attractiveness. *Journal of Personality and Social Psychology*, **41**, 74–86.

Antill, J. K. (1983). Sex role complementarity versus similarity in married couples. *Journal of Personality and Social Psychology*, **45**, 145–155.

Antill, J. K., & Cunningham, J. D. (1979). Self-esteem as a function of masculinity in both sexes. *Journal of Consulting and Clinical Psychology*, **47**, 783–785.

Arkin, R. M., & Johnson, K. S. (1980). Effects of increased occupational participation by women on androgynous and nonandrogynous individuals' ratings of occupational attractiveness. *Sex Roles*, **6**, 593–605.

Astley, S. L., & Downey, R. G. (1980). Sex role consequences: Depends on the point of view. *Journal of College Student Personnel*, **21**, 419–426.

Atkinson, J., & Huston, T. L. (1984). Sex role orientation and division of labor early in marriage. *Journal of Personality and Social Psychology*, **46**, 330–345.

Avery, A. W. (1982). Escaping loneliness in adolescence: The case for androgyny. *Journal of Youth and Adolescence*, **11**, 451–459.

Babl, J. D. (1979). Compensatory masculine responding as a function of sex role. *Journal of Consulting and Clinical Psychology*, **47**, 252–257.

Babladelis, G. (1978). Sex-role concepts and flexibility on measures of thinking, feeling, and behaving. *Psychological Reports*, **42**, 99–105.

Bakan, D. (1966). *The duality of human existence*. Chicago: Rand McNally.

Baker, S. (1980, April). *Counseling for androgyny*. Paper presented at the annual meeting of the American Educational Research Association, Boston.

Bandura, A. (1969). Social-learning theory of identificatory processes. In D. A. Goslin (Ed.), *Handbook of Socialization Theory and Research*. Chicago: Rand McNally.

Banikiotes, P. G., Kubinski, J. A., & Pursell, S. A. (1981). Sex role orientation, self-disclosure, and gender-related perceptions. *Journal of Counseling Psychology*, **28**, 140–146.

Banikiotes, P. G., & Merluzzi, T. V. (1981). Impact of counselor gender and counselor sex role orientation on perceived counselor characteristics. *Journal of Counseling Psychology*, **28**, 342–348.

Bankart, C. P., & Wittenbraker, J. E. (1980). Sex-role orientation of perceivers and targets as variables in the person perception process. *Psychological Record*, **30**, 143–153.

Bardwick, J. (1979). *In transition*. New York: Holt, Rinehart and Winston.

Baruch, G., Barnett, R., & Rivers, C. (1983). *Life prints: New patterns of love and work for today's women*. New York: McGraw-Hill.

Basow, S. A. (1980). *Sex role stereotypes: Traditions and alternatives*. Monterey, CA: Brooks/Cole.

Bassoff, E. S., & Glass, G. V. (1982). The relationship between sex roles and mental health: A meta-analysis of twenty-six studies. *Counseling Psychologist*, **10**, 105–112.

Baucom, D. H. (1976). Independent masculinity and femininity scales on the California Psychological Inventory. *Journal of Consulting and Clinical Psychology*, **44**, 876.

Baucom , D. H. (1980). Independent CPI masculinity and femininity scales: Psychological correlates and a sex-role typology. *Journal of Personality Assessment*, **44**, 262–271.

Baucom, D. H. (1983). Sex role identity and the decision to regain control among women: A learned helplessness investigation. *Journal of Personality and Social Psychology*, **44**, 334–343.

Baucom, D. H., & Danker-Brown, P. (1979). Influence of sex roles on the development of learned helplessness. *Journal of Consulting and Clinical Psychology*, **47**, 928–936.

Baucom, D. H., & Sanders, B. S. (1978). Masculinity and femininity as factors in feminism. *Journal of Personality Assessment*, **42**, 378–384.

Baxter, L. A., & Shepherd, T. L. (1978). Sex-role identity, sex of other, and affective relationship as determinants of interpersonal conflict-management styles. *Sex Roles*, **4**, 813–825.

Bear, S., Berger, M., & Wright, L. (1979). Even cowboys sing the blues: Difficulties experienced by men trying to adopt nontraditional sex roles and how clinicians can be helpful to them. *Sex Roles*, **5**, 191–198.

Beckman, L. J. (1978). Sex-role conflict in alcoholic women: Myth or reality. *Journal of Abnormal Psychology*, **87**, 408–417.

Bem, S. L. (1974). The measurement of psychological androgyny. *Journal of Consulting and Clinical Psychology*, **42**, 155–162.

Bem, S. L. (1975). Sex role adaptability: One consequence of psychological androgyny. *Journal of Personality and Social Psychology*, **31**, 634–643.

Bem, S. L. (1976). Probing the promise of androgyny. In A. G. Kaplan & J. P. Bean (Eds.), *Beyond sex-role stereotypes: Readings toward a psychology of androgyny*. Boston: Little, Brown and Company.

Bem, S. L. (1977). On the utility of alternative procedures for assessing psychological androgyny. *Journal of Consulting and Clinical Psychology*, **45**, 196–205.

Bem, S. L. (1979). Theory and measurement of androgyny: A reply to the Pedhazur-Tetenbaum and Locksley-Colten critiques. *Journal of Personality and Social Psychology*, **37**, 1047–1054.

Bem, S. L. (1981a). Gender schema theory: A cognitive account of sex typing. *Psychological Review*, **88**, 354–364.

Bem, S. L. (1981b). The BSRI and gender schema theory: A reply to Spence and Helmreich. *Psychological Review*, **88**, 369–371.

Bem, S. L. (1982). Gender schema theory and self-schema theory compared: A comment on Markus, Crane, Bernstein, and Siladi's "Self-Schemas and Gender." *Journal of Personality and Social Psychology*, **43**, 1192–1194.

Bem, S. L., & Lenney, E. (1976). Sex-typing and the avoidance of cross-sex behavior. *Journal of Personality and Social Psychology*, **33**, 48–54.

Bem, S. L., Martyna, W., & Watson, C. (1976). Sex typing and androgyny: Further explorations of the expressive domain. *Journal of Personality and Social Psychology*, **34**, 1016–1023.

Bennett, B. W., & Grossner, G. S. (1981). Movement toward androgyny in college females through experiential education. *Journal of Psychology*, **107**, 177–183.

Berg, J. H., & Peplau, L. A. (1982). Loneliness: The relation of self-disclosure and androgyny. *Personality and Social Psychology Bulletin*, **8**, 624–630.

Berger, M., & Wright, L. (1980). Divided allegiance: Men, work, and family life. In T. M. Skovholt, P. G. Schauble, and R. Davis (Eds.), *Counseling men*. Monterey, CA: Brooks/Cole.

Bernard, L. C. (1980). Multivariate analysis of new sex role formulations and personality. *Journal of Personality and Social Psychology*, **38**, 323–336.

Bernard, L. C. (1981). The multidimensional aspects of masculinity-femininity. *Journal of Personality and Social Psychology*, **41**, 797–802.

Bernard, L. C. (1982). Sex-role factor identification and sexual preference of men. *Journal of Personality Assessment*, **46**, 292–299.

Bernard, L. C., & Epstein, D. J. (1978a). Androgyny scores of matched homosexual and heterosexual males. *Journal of Homosexuality*, **4**, 169–178.

Bernard, L. C., & Epstein, D. J. (1978b). Sex role conformity in homosexual and heterosexual males. *Journal of Personality Assessment*, **42**, 505–511.

Berzins, J. I. (1979). Discussion: Androgyny, personality theory, and psychotherapy. *Psychology of Women Quarterly*, **3**, 248–254.

Berzins, J. I., Welling, M. A., & Wetter, R. E. (1976). *Androgynous vs. traditional sex roles and the interpersonal behavior circle*. Paper presented at the annual meeting of the American Psychological Association, Washington, DC.

Berzins, J. I., Welling, M. A., & Wetter, R. E. (1978). A new measure of psychological androgyny based on the Personality Research Form. *Journal of Consulting and Clinical Psychology*, **46**, 126–138.

Betz, N. E., & Bander, R. S. (1980). Relationship of MMPI and CPI Fe scales to fourfold sex role classifications. *Journal of Personality and Social Psychology*, **39**, 1245–1248.

Biaggio, M. K., & Nielsen, E. C. (1976). Anxiety correlates of sex-role identity. *Journal of Clinical Psychology*, **32**, 619–623.

Block, J., Von der Lippe, A., & Block, J. H. (1973). Sex-role and socialization patterns: Some personality concomitants and environmental antecedents. *Journal of Consulting and Clinical Psychology*, **41**, 321–341.

Block, J. H. (1973). Conceptions of sex role: Some cross-cultural and longitudinal perspectives. *American Psychologist*, **28**, 515–526.

Block, J. H. (1976). Issues, problems, and pitfalls in assessing sex differences: A critical review of *The Psychology of Sex Differences*. *Merrill-Palmer Quarterly*, **22**, 283–308.

Borlana, L. (1980). *Moving up! Women and Leadership*. Amacom, NY: Hart.

Brehony, K. A., & Geller, E. S. (1981). Relationships between psychological androgyny, social conformity, and perceived locus of control. *Psychology of Women Quarterly*, **6**, 205–217.

Brewer, M. B., & Blum, M. W. (1979). Sex-role androgyny and patterns of causal attribution for academic achievement. *Sex Roles*, **5**, 783–795.

Bridges, J. S. (1978). Correlates of sex role and attitudes toward women. *Psychological Reports*, **43**, 1279–1282.

Bridges, J. S. (1981). Sex-typed may be beautiful but androgynous is good. *Psychological Reports*, **48**, 267–272.

Brodsky, A. M. (1977). Therapeutic aspects of consciousness-raising groups. In E. I. Rawlings & D. K. Carter (Eds.), *Psychotherapy for women: Treatment toward equality*. Springfield, IL: Charles C. Thomas.

Brodsky, A. M., & Hare-Mustin, R. T. (Eds.). (1980). *Women and psychotherapy: An assessment of research and practice*. NY: Guilford Press.

Brodzinsky, D. M., Barnet, K., & Aiello, J. R. (1981). Sex of subject and gender identity as factors in humor appreciation. *Sex Roles*, **7**, 561–573.

Bronfenbrenner, U. (1960). Freudian theories of identification and their derivatives. *Child Development*, **31**, 15–40.

Broverman, I. K., Broverman, D. M., Clarkson, F. E., Rosenkrantz, P. S., & Vogel, S. R. (1970). Sex-role stereotypes and clinical judgments of mental health. *Journal of Consulting and Clinical Psychology*, **34**, 1–7.

Broverman, I. K., Vogel, R. S., Broverman, D. M., Clarkson, F. E., & Rosenkrantz, P. S. (1972). Sex-role stereotypes: A current appraisal. *Journal of Social Issues*, **28**, 59–78.

Brown, D. G. (1957). Masculinity-femininity development in children. *Journal of Consulting Psychology*, **21**, 197–202.

Bruch, M. (1978). Holland's typology applied to client-counselor interaction: Implications for counseling with men. *Counseling Psychologist*, **7**, 26–32.

Bryan, L., Coleman, M., & Ganong, L. (1981). Geometric mean as a continuous measure of androgyny. *Psychological Reports*, **48**, 691–694.

Burchardt, C. J., & Serbin, L. A. (1982). Psychological androgyny and personality adjustment in college and psychiatric populations. *Sex Roles*, **8**, 835–851.

Campbell, M., Steffen, J. J., & Langmeyer, D. (1981). Psychological androgyny and social competence. *Psychological Reports*, **48**, 611–614.

Cano, L., Solomon, S., & Holmes, D. S. (1984). Fear of success: The influence of sex, sex-role identity, and components of masculinity. *Sex Roles*, **10**, 341–346.

Cardell, M., Finn, S., & Marecek, J. (1981). Sex-role identity, sex-role behavior, and satisfaction in heterosexual, lesbian, and gay male couples. *Psychology of Women Quarterly*, **5**, 488–494.

Carlson, N. L. (1981). Male client-female therapist. *Personnel and Guidance Journal*, **60**, 228–231.

Carlson, R. (1971). Sex differences in ego functioning. *Journal of Consulting and Clinical Psychology*, **37**, 267–277.

Carlson, R. (1972). Understanding women: Implications for personality theory and research. *Journal of Social Issues*, **28**, 17–32.

Carsrud, A. L., & Carsrud, K. B. (1979). The relationship of sex role and levels of defensiveness to self-reports of fear and anxiety. *Journal of Clinical Psychology*, **35**, 573–575.

Cash, T. F., & Smith, E. (1982). Physical attractiveness and personality among American college students. *Journal of Psychology*, **111**, 183–191.

Chesler, P. (1972). *Women and madness*. New York: Avon.

Clarey, J. H., & Sanford, A. (1982). Female career preference and androgyny. *Vocational Guidance Quarterly*, **30**, 258–264.

Clark-Stedman, M., & Wolleat, P. L. (1979). A nonsexist group-counseling intervention: Moving toward androgyny. *School Counselor*, **27**, 110–118.

Colker, R., & Widom, C. S. (1980). Correlates of female athletic participation: Masculinity, femininity, self-esteem, and attitudes toward women. *Sex Roles*, **6**, 47–58.

Collier, B. J., & Williams, L. N. (1981). Towards a bilateral model of sexism. *Human Relations*, **34**, 127–139.

Collins, M., Waters, C. W., & Waters, L. K. (1979). Factor analysis of sex-typed items from the Bem Sex-Role Inventory: A replication. *Psychological Reports*, **44**, 517–518.

Colwill, N. L., & Lips, H. M. (1978). Masculinity, femininity, and androgyny: What have you done for us lately? In H. M. Lips & N. L. Colwill (Eds.), *The psychology of sex differences*. Englewood Cliffs, NJ: Prentice-Hall.

Constantinople, A. (1973). Masculinity-femininity: An exception to a famous dictum? *Psychological Bulletin*, **80**, 389–407.

Cosentino, F., & Heilbrun, A. B. (1964). Anxiety correlates of sex-role identity in college students. *Psychological Reports*, **14**, 729–730.

Crane, M., & Markus, H. (1982). Gender identity: The benefits of a self-schema approach. *Journal of Personality and Social Psychology*, **43**, 1195–1197.

Crites, J. O., & Fitzgerald, L. F. (1980). The competent male. In T. M. Skovholt, P. G. Schauble, & R. Davis (Eds.), *Counseling men*. Monterey, CA: Brooks/Cole.

Croteau, J. M., & Burda, P. C. (1983). Structured group programming on men's roles: A creative approach to change. *Personnel and Guidance Journal*, **62**, 243–245.

Davis, W. E., Pursell, S. A., & Burnham, R. A. (1979). Alcoholism, sex-role orientation, and psychological distress. *Journal of Clinical Psychology*, **35**, 209–212.

DeBeauvoir, S. (1977). The second sex. In J. English (Ed.), *Sex equality*. Englewood Cliffs, NJ: Prentice-Hall. (Originally published, 1952).

DeFronzo, J., & Boudreau, F. (1977). An alternative procedure for assessing effects of psychological androgyny. *Psychological Reports*, **41**, 1059–1062.

DeFronzo, J., & Boudreau, F. (1979). Further research into antecedents and correlates of androgyny. *Psychological Reports*, **44**, 23–29.

DeGregorio, E., & Carver, C. S. (1980). Type A behavior pattern, sex role orientation, and psychological adjustment. *Journal of Personality and Social Psychology*, **39**, 286–293.

Deutsch, C. J., & Gilbert, L. A. (1976). Sex role stereotypes: Effect on perceptions of self and others and on personal adjustment. *Journal of Counseling Psychology*, **23**, 373–379.

Division 17 of the American Psychological Association. (1979). Principles concerning the counseling and therapy of women: Preamble. *Counseling Psychologist*, **8**, 21.

Doherty, P. H. (1979). *Psychological sex typing, dimensions of achievement motivation, and educational, career, and family plans of single, traditional-age, female college seniors*. Unpublished doctoral dissertation, University of Iowa, Iowa City.

Downing, N. E. (1979). Theoretical and operational conceptualizations of psychological androgyny: Implications for measurement. *Psychology of Women Quarterly*, **3**, 284–292.

Downing, N. (1981, March). *Counseling men: Issues for female counselors.* Paper presented at the annual convention of the American College Personnel Association, Cincinnati, OH.

Edwards, A. L., & Ashworth, C. D. (1977). A replication study of item selection for the Bem Sex-Role Inventory. *Applied Psychological Measurement, 1,* 501–508.

Edwards, K. J., & Norcross, B. N. (1980). A comparison of two sex-role androgyny measures in a study of sex-role identity for incarcerated delinquent and non-delinquent females. *Sex Roles, 6,* 859–870.

Engel, I. M. (1966). A factor-analytic study of items from five masculinity-femininity tests. *Journal of Consulting Psychology, 30,* 565.

Erdwins, C., Small, A., & Gross, R. (1980). The relationship of sex role to self-concept. *Journal of Clinical Psychology, 36,* 111–115.

Evanoski, P. J., & Maher, T. J. (1979, September). *Masculinity, femininity, and psychological well-being.* Paper presented at the annual meeting of the American Psychological Association, New York.

Evans, R. G. (1984). Hostility and sex guilt: Perceptions of self and others as a function of gender and sex-role orientation. *Sex Roles, 10,* 207–215.

Falbo, T. (1977). Relationships between sex, sex role, and social influence. *Psychology of Women Quarterly, 2,* 62–72.

Falbo, T., Graham, J. S., & Gryskiewicz, S. S. (1978). Sex roles and fertility in college women. *Sex Roles, 4,* 845–851.

Farmer, H. S. (1976). What inhibits achievement and career motivation in women? *Counseling Psychologist, 6,* 12–15.

Farmer, H. S., & Fyans, L. J. (1983). Married women's achievement and career motivation: The influence of some environmental and psychological variables. *Psychology of Women Quarterly, 7,* 358–372.

Feldman, S. S., Biringen, Z. C., & Nash, S. C. (1981). Fluctuations of sex-related self-attributions as a function of stage of family life cycle. *Developmental Psychology, 17,* 24–35.

Feldstein, J. C. (1979). Effects of counselor sex and sex role and client sex on clients' perceptions and self-disclosure in a counseling analogue study. *Journal of Counseling Psychology, 26,* 437.

Feldstein, J. C. (1982). Counselor and client sex pairing: The effects of counseling problem and counselor sex role orientation. *Journal of Counseling Psychology, 29,* 418–420.

Fidell, L. S. (1981). Sex differences in psychotropic drug use. *Professional Psychology, 12,* 156–162.

Fischer, J. L., & Narus, L. R. (1981a). Sex role development in late adolescence and adulthood. *Sex Roles, 7,* 97–106.

Fischer, J. L., & Narus, L. R. (1981b). Sex roles and intimacy in same sex and other sex relationships. In C. Safilios-Rothschild (Ed.)., *Relationships* (Special issue of *Psychology of Women Quarterly*). New York: Human Sciences Press.

Fisher, S., & Greenberg, R. P. (1979). Masculinity-femininity and response to somatic discomfort. *Sex Roles, 5,* 483–493.

Fitzgerald, L. F., & Crites, J. O. (1979). Career counseling for women. *Counseling Psychologist, 8,* 33.

Flaherty, J. F., & Dusek, J. B. (1980). An investigation of the relationship between psychological androgyny and components of self-concept. *Journal of Personality and Social Psychology, 38,* 984–992.

Forisha, B. L. (1978). *Sex roles and personal awareness.* Morristown, NJ: General Learning Press.

Foxley, C. H. (1979). *Nonsexist counseling.* Dubuque, IA: Kendall-Hunt.

Franks, V. (1979). Gender and psychotherapy. In E. S. Gomberg & V. Franks (Eds.), *Gender and disordered behavior: Sex differences in psychopathology.* New York: Brunner/Mazel.

Gackenbach, J. I., Heretick, D. M. L., & Alexander, D. (1979). The effects of unipolar sex-role identities and situational determinants on components of fear of success. *Journal of Vocational Behavior, 15,* 347–366.

Gaddy, C. D., Glass, C. R., & Arnkoff, D. B. (1983). Career involvement of women in dual-career families: The influence of sex-role identity. *Journal of Counseling Psychology, 30,* 388–394.

Garcia, L. T. (1982). Sex-role orientation and stereotypes about male-female sexuality. *Sex Roles, 8,* 863–876.

Garfield, S. L., & Bergin, A. E. (1978). *Handbook of psychotherapy and behavior change* (2nd ed.). New York: John Wiley.

Garnets, L., & Pleck, J. H. (1979). Sex role identity, androgyny, and sex role transcendence: A sex role strain analysis. *Psychology of Women Quarterly, 3,* 270–283.

Gaudreau, P. (1977). Factor analysis of the Bem Sex-Role Inventory. *Journal of Consulting and Clinical Psychology, 45,* 299–302.

Gauthier, J., & Kjervik, D. (1982). Sex-role identity and self-esteem in female graduate nursing students. *Sex Roles, 8,* 45–55.

Gayton, W. F., Havu, G., Baird, J. G., & Ozman, K. (1983). Psychological androgyny and assertiveness in females. *Psychological Reports, 52,* 283–285.

Gayton, W. F., Havu, G., Barnes, S., Ozman, K. L., & Bassett, J. S. (1978). Psychological androgyny and fear of success. *Psychological Reports, 42,* 757–758.

Gayton, W. F., Havu, G. F., Ozman, K. L., & Tavormina, J. (1977). A comparison of the Bem Sex Role Inventory and the PRF ANDRO scale. *Journal of Personality Assessment, 41,* 619–621.

Gelwick, B. P., & Heppner, P. P. (1981). Men's lives: Toward a proactive sex role intervention for men and women. *Journal of College Student Personnel, 22,* 559–560.

Gilbert, L. A. (1981). Toward mental health: The benefits of psychological androgyny. *Professional Psychology, 12,* 29–38.

Gilbert, L. A., Deutsch, C. J., & Strahan, R. F. (1978). Feminine and masculine dimensions of the typical, desirable, and ideal woman and man. *Sex Roles, 4,* 767–778.

Gilligan, C. (1982). *In a different voice.* Cambridge, Mass.: Harvard University Press.

Goldberg, H. (1979). *The new male.* New York: William Morrow.

Golding, J. M., & Singer, J. L. (1983). Patterns of inner experience: Daydreaming styles, depressive moods, and sex roles. *Journal of Personality and Social Psychology, 45,* 663–675.

Goodman, E. (1979). *Turning points.* New York: Fawcett Crest.

Gough, H. G. (1957). *Manual for the California Psychological Inventory.* Palo Alto, CA: Consulting Psychologists Press.

Gough, H. G., & Heilbrun, A. B. (1965). *Manual for the Adjective Check List and the Need Scales for the ACL.* Palo Alto, CA: Consulting Psychologists Press.

Gould, M., & Kern-Daniels, R. (1977). Toward a sociological theory of gender and sex. *American Sociologist, 12,* 182–189.

Gove, W. R. (1979). Sex differences in the epidemiology of mental disorder: Evidence and explanations. In E. S. Gomberg & V. Franks (Eds.), *Gender and disordered behavior: Sex differences in psychopathology.* New York: Brunner/Mazel.

Gove, W. R., & Tudor, J. F. (1973). Adult sex roles and mental illness. *American Journal of Sociology, 78,* 812–835.

Gross, R., Batlis, N., Small, A., & Erdwins, C. (1979). Factor structure of the Bem Sex-Role Inventory and the Personal Attributes Questionnaire. *Journal of Consulting and Clinical Psychology*, **47**, 1122–1124.

Gulanick, N. A., Howard, G. S., & Moreland, J. (1979). Evaluation of a group program designed to increase androgyny in feminine women. *Sex Roles*, **5**, 811–827.

Hall, J. A., & Halberstadt, A. G. (1980). Masculinity and femininity in children: Development of the Children's Personal Attributes Questionnaire. *Developmental Psychology*, **16**, 270–280.

Hall, J. A., & Halberstadt, A. G. (1981). Sex roles and nonverbal communication skills. *Sex Roles*, **7**, 273–287.

Hall, S. M., & Havassy, B. (1981). The obese woman: Causes, correlates, and treatment. *Professional Psychology*, **12**, 163–170.

Hamby, R. (1978). Effects of gender and sex-role on tension and satisfaction in small groups. *Psychological Reports*, **42**, 403–410.

Hansen, G. L. (1982). Androgyny, sex-role orientation, and homosexism. *Journal of Psychology*, **112**, 39–45.

Hansson, R. O., Chernovetz, M. E., & Jones, W. H. (1977). Maternal employment and androgyny. *Psychology of Women Quarterly*, **2**, 76–78.

Harackiewicz, J. M., & DePaulo, B. M. (1982). Accuracy of person perception: A component analysis according to Cronbach. *Personality and Social Psychology Bulletin*, **8**, 247–256.

Harmon, L. W. (1977). Career counseling for women. In E. I. Rawlings & D. K. Carter (Eds.), *Psychotherapy for women: Treatment toward equality*. Springfield, IL: Charles C. Thomas.

Harren, V. A., & Biscardi, D. L. (1980). Sex roles and cognitive styles as predictors of Holland typologies. *Journal of Vocational Behavior*, **17**, 231–241.

Harren, V. A., Kass, R. A., Tinsley, H. E. A., & Moreland, J. R. (1979). Influence of gender, sex-role attitudes, and cognitive complexity on gender-dominant career choices. *Journal of Counseling Psychology*, **26**, 227–234.

Harrington, D. M., & Andersen, S. M. (1981). Creativity, masculinity, femininity, and three models of psychological androgyny. *Journal of Personality and Social Psychology*, **41**, 744–757.

Harris, T. L., & Schwab, R. (1979). Personality characteristics of androgynous and sex-typed females. *Journal of Personality Assessment*, **43**, 614–616.

Harrison, J. (1978). Warning: The male sex role may be dangerous to your health. *Journal of Social Issues*, **34**, 65–85.

Hatzenbuehler, L. C., & Joe, V. C. (1981). Stress and androgyny: A preliminary study. *Psychological Reports*, **48**, 327–332.

Hefner, R., Rebecca, M., & Oleshansky, B. (1975). Development of sex-role transcendence. *Human Development*, **18**, 143–158.

Heilbrun, A. B. (1968). Sex role, instrumental-expressive behavior, and psychopathology in females. *Journal of Abnormal Psychology*, **73**, 131–136.

Heilbrun, A. B. (1976). Measurement of masculine and feminine sex role identities as independent dimensions. *Journal of Consulting and Clinical Psychology*, **44**, 183–190.

Heilbrun, A. B. (1978). An exploration of antecedents and attributes of androgynous and undifferentiated sex roles. *Journal of Genetic Psychology*, **132**, 97–107.

Heilbrun, A. B. (1981a). Gender differences in the functional linkage between androgyny, social cognition, and competence. *Journal of Personality and Social Psychology*, **41**, 1106–1118.

Heilbrun, A. B. (1981b). *Human sex-role behavior*. New York: Pergamon.

Heilbrun, A. B. (1984). Sex-based models of androgyny: A further cognitive elaboration of competence difference. *Journal of Personality and Social Psychology*, **46**, 216–229.

Heilbrun, A. B., & Pitman, D. (1979). Testing some basic assumptions about psychological androgyny. *Journal of Genetic Psychology*, **135**, 175–188.

Heilbrun, A. B., & Schwartz, H. L. (1982). Sex-gender differences in level of androgyny. *Sex Roles*, **8**, 201–214.

Heilbrun, A. B., & Thompson, N. L. (1977). Sex-role identity and male and female homosexuality. *Sex Roles*, **3**, 65–79.

Heilbrun, C. G. (1973). *Toward a recognition of androgyny*. New York: Alfred A. Knopf.

Helmreich, R. L., Spence, J. T., Beane, W. E., Lucker, G. W., & Matthews, K. A. (1980). Making it in academic psychology: Demographic and personality correlates of attainment. *Journal of Personality and Social Psychology*, **39**, 896–908.

Helmreich, R. L., Spence, J. T., & Holahan, C. K. (1979). Psychological androgyny and sex role flexibility: A test of two hypotheses. *Journal of Personality and Social Psychology*, **37**, 1631–1644.

Helmreich, R. L., Spence, J. T., & Wilhelm, J. A. (1981). A psychometric analysis of the Personal Attributes Questionnaire. *Sex Roles*, **7**, 1097–1108.

Heppner, P. P. (1981). Counseling men in groups. *Personnel and Guidance Journal*, **60**, 249–252.

Heppner, P. P. (1983). Structured group activities for counseling men in groups. *Journal of College Student Personnel*, **24**, 275–277.

Herman, J. (1981). Father-daughter incest. *Professional Psychology*, **12**, 76–80.

Highlen, A. S., & Russell, B. (1980). Effects of counselor gender and counselor and client sex role on females' counselor preference. *Journal of Counseling Psychology*, **27**, 157–165.

Hinrichsen, J. J., Follansbee, D. J., & Ganellen, R. (1981). Sex-role related differences in self-concept and mental health. *Journal of Personality Assessment*, **45**, 584–599.

Hinrichsen, J. J., & Stone, L. (1978). Effects of three conditions of administration on Bem Sex Role Inventory scores. *Journal of Personality Assessment*, **42**, 512.

Hoferek, M. J. (1982). Sex-role prescriptions and attitudes of physical educators. *Sex Roles*, **8**, 83–98.

Hoffman, D. M., & Fidell, L. S. (1979). Characteristics of androgynous, undifferentiated, masculine, and feminine middle class women. *Sex Roles*, **5**, 765–781.

Hoffman, L. W. (1977). Changes in family roles, socialization, and sex differences. *American Psychologist*, **32**, 644–657.

Hogan, H. W. (1977). The measurement of psychological androgyny: An extended replication. *Journal of Clinical Psychology*, **33**, 1009–1013.

Hogan, H. W. (1979). German and American responses to the Bem Sex Role Inventory. *Journal of Social Psychology*, **109**, 141–142.

Holahan, C. K., & Gilbert, L. A. (1979). Interrole conflict for working women: Careers versus jobs. *Journal of Applied Psychology*, **64**, 86–90.

Holahan, C. K., & Spence, J. T. (1980). Desirable and undesirable masculine and feminine traits in counseling clients and unselected students. *Journal of Consulting and Clinical Psychology*, **48**, 300–302.

Hollinger, C. L. (1984). The impact of gender schematic processing on the Self-Directed Search responses of gifted and talented female adolescents. *Journal of Vocational Behavior*, **24**, 15–27.

Hoppe, C. M. (1979). Interpersonal aggression as a function of subject's sex, subject's sex-role identification, opponent's sex, and degree of provocation. *Journal of Personality*, **47**, 317–329.

Huston, A. C. (1983). Sex-typing. In P. H. Mussen (Ed.), *Handbook of child psychology* (4th ed., Vol. 4). New York: John Wiley.

Hyde, J. S., & Phillis, D. E. (1979). Androgyny across the life span. *Developmental Psychology*, **15**, 334–336.

Inderlied, S. D., & Powell, G. (1979). Sex-role identity and leadership style: Different labels for the same concept? *Sex Roles*, **5**, 613–625.

Jackson, D. N. (1967). *Personality Research Form Manual*. Goshen, NY: Research Psychologists Press.

Jacobson, S. F. (1979, September). *Another look at sex-role identity and women's achievement motivation*. Paper presented at the annual meeting of the American Psychological Association, New York.

Jaggar, A. (1977). On sexual equality. In J. English (Ed.), *Sex equality*. Englewood Cliffs, NJ: Prentice-Hall.

Jakubowski, P. A. (1977a). Assertive behavior and clinical problems of women. In E. I. Rawlings & D. K. Carter (Eds.), *Psychotherapy for women: Treatment toward equality*. Springfield, IL: Charles C. Thomas.

Jakubowski, P. A. (1977b). Self-assertion training procedures for women. In E. I. Rawlings & D. K. Carter (Eds.), *Psychotherapy for women: Treatment toward equality*. Springfield, IL: Charles C. Thomas.

Johnson, S. J., & Black, K. N. (1981). The relationship between sex-role identity and beliefs in personal control. *Sex Roles*, **7**, 425–431.

Jones, W. H., Chernovetz, M. E., & Hansson, R. O. (1978). The enigma of androgyny: Differential implications for males and females? *Journal of Consulting and Clinical Psychology*, **46**, 298–313.

Jordan-Viola, E., Fassberg, S., & Viola, M. T. (1976). Feminism, androgyny, and anxiety. *Journal of Consulting and Clinical Psychology*, **44**, 870–871.

Kagan, J. (1964). Acquisition and significance of sex typing and sex-role identity. In M. L. Hoffman & L. W. Hoffman (Eds.), *Review of child development research* (Vol. 1). New York: Russell Sage Foundation.

Kahn, S. E. (1982). Sex-role attitudes: Who should raise consciousness? *Sex Roles*, **8**, 977–985.

Kahn, S. E., & Greenberg, L. S. (1980). Expanding sex-role definitions by self-discovery. *Personnel and Guidance Journal*, **59**, 220–225.

Kalin, R. (1979). Method for scoring androgyny as a continuous variable. *Psychological Reports*, **44**, 1205–1206.

Kanter, J. E., & Ellerbusch, R. C. (1980). Androgyny and occupational choice. *Psychological Reports*, **47**, 1289–1290.

Kaplan, A. G. (1976). Androgyny as a model of mental health for women: From theory to therapy. In A. G. Kaplan & J. P. Bean (Eds.), *Beyond sex-role stereotypes: Readings toward a psychology of androgyny*. Boston: Little, Brown and Company.

Kaplan, A. G. (1979). Clarifying the concept of androgyny: Implications for therapy. *Psychology of Women Quarterly*, **3**, 223–230.

Kaplan, A. G., & Bean, J. P. (Eds.). (1976). *Beyond sex-role stereotypes: Readings toward a psychology of androgyny*. Boston: Little, Brown.

Kaplan, A. G., & Sedney, M. A. (1980). *Psychology and sex roles: An androgynous perspective*. Boston: Little, Brown.

Kelly, J. A., Caudill, M. S., Hathorn, S., & O'Brien, C. G. (1977). Socially undesirable sex-correlated characteristics: Implications for androgyny and adjustment. *Journal of Consulting and Clinical Psychology*, **45**, 1185–1186.

Kelly, J. A., Furman, W., & Young, V. (1978). Problems associated with the typological measurement of sex roles and androgyny. *Journal of Consulting and Clinical Psychology*, **46**, 1574–1576.

Kelly, J. A., O'Brien, G. G., & Hosford, R. (1981). Sex roles and social skills consider-ations for interpersonal adjustment. *Psychology of Women Quarterly*, 5, 758–765.

Kelly, J. A., & Worell, L. (1976). Parent behaviors related to masculine, feminine, and androgynous sex role orientations. *Journal of Consulting and Clinical Psychology*, 44, 843–851.

Kelly, J. A., & Worell, J. (1977). New formulations of sex roles and androgyny: A critical review. *Journal of Consulting and Clinical Psychology*, 45, 1101–1115.

Kenrick, D. T., Stringfield, D. O., Wagenhals, W. L., Dahl, R. H., & Ransdell, H. J. (1980). Sex differences, androgyny, and approach responses to erotica: A new varia-tion on the old volunteer problem. *Journal of Personality and Social Psychology*, 38, 517–524.

Kenworthy, J. A. (1979). Androgyny in psychotherapy: But will it sell in Peoria? *Psychology of Women Quarterly*, 3, 231–240.

Kimlicka, T., Cross, H., & Tarnai, J. (1983). A comparison of androgynous, feminine, masculine, and undifferentiated women on self-esteem, body satisfaction, and sex-ual satisfaction. *Psychology of Women Quarterly*, 7, 291–294.

Kimlicka, T. M., Wakefield, J. M., & Goad, N. A. (1982). Sex roles for ideal opposite sexed persons for college males and females. *Journal of Personality Assessment*, 46, 519–521.

Kirkpatrick, S. W. (1979). Sex-role classification of adolescents: Relationship to actual and perceived parental types. *Journal of Genetic Psychology*, 135, 237–244.

Klein, H. M., & Willerman, L. (1979). Psychological masculinity and femininity and typical and maximal dominance expression in women. *Journal of Personality and Social Psychology*, 37, 2059–2070.

Kleinke, C. L., & Hinrichs, C. A. (1983). College adjustment problems and attitudes toward drinking reported by feminine, androgynous, and masculine college women. *Psychology of Women Quarterly*, 7, 373–382.

Knefelkamp, L. L., Widick, C. C., & Stroad, B. (1976). Cognitive-developmental theory; A guide to counseling women. *Counseling Psychologist*, 6, 15–19.

Kohlberg, L. (1966). A cognitive-developmental analysis of children's sex-role concepts and attitudes. In E. E. Maccoby (Ed.), *The development of sex differences*. Stan-ford, CA: Stanford University Press.

Kondo, C. Y., Powell, B. J., & Penick, E. C. (1978). Clinical correlates of the PRF androgyny scale in an alcoholic population. *Journal of Personality Assessment*, 42, 611–612.

Korabik, K. (1982). Sex-role orientation and impressions: A comparison of differing genders and sex roles. *Personality and Social Psychology Bulletin*, 8, 25–30.

Krasnoff, A. G. (1981). The sex difference in self-assessed fears. *Sex Roles*, 7, 19–23.

Kulik, J. A., & Harackiewicz, J. (1979). Opposite-sex interpersonal attraction as a function of the sex roles of the perceiver and the perceived. *Sex Roles*, 5, 443–452.

Kweskin, S. L., & Cook, A. S. (1982). Heterosexual and homosexual mothers' self-described sex-role behavior and ideal sex-role behavior in children. *Sex Roles*, 8, 967–975.

LaFrance, M., & Carmen, B. (1980). The nonverbal display of psychological androg-yny. *Journal of Personality and Social Psychology*, 38, 36–49.

Lamke, L. K. (1982). Adjustment and sex-role orientation in adolescence. *Journal of Youth and Adolescence*, 11, 257–259.

Lamke, L. K., Bell, N. J., & Murphy, C. (1980). Sibling constellation and androgynous sex role development. *Journal of Psychology*, 105, 139–144.

LaTorre, R. A., Endman, M., & Gossman, I. (1976). Androgyny and need achieve-ment in male and female psychiatric inpatients. *Journal of Clinical Psychology*, 32, 233–235.

Laws, J. L., & Schwartz, P. (1977). *Sexual scripts: The social construction of female sexuality*. Hinsdale, IL: The Pryden Press.

Lee, A. G. (1982). Psychological androgyny and social desirability. *Journal of Personality Assessment*, **46**, 147–152.

Lee, A. G., & Scheurer, V. L. (1983). Psychological androgyny and aspects of self-image in women and men. *Sex Roles*, **9**, 289–306.

Lee, P. C., & Stewart, R. S. (Eds.). (1976). *Sex differences: Cultural and developmental dimensions*. New York: Urizen Books.

Lenney, E. (1979a). Androgyny: Some audacious assertions toward its coming of age. *Sex Roles*, **5**, 703–719.

Lenney, E. (1979b). Concluding comments on androgyny: Some intimations of its mature development. *Sex Roles*, **5**, 829–840.

Lerner, H. E. (1978). Adaptive and pathogenic aspects of sex-role stereotypes: Implications for parenting and psychotherapy. *American Journal of Psychiatry*, **135**, 48–52.

Lester, D. (1979). Sex differences in suicidal behavior. In E. S. Gomberg & V. Franks (Eds.), *Gender and disordered behavior: Sex differences in psychopathology*. New York: Brunner/Mazel.

Levy, S. M. (1981). The aging woman: Developmental issues and mental health needs. *Professional Psychology*, **12**, 92–102.

Lewis, M., & Weinraub, M. (1979). Origins of early sex-role development. *Sex Roles*, **5**, 135–153.

Lewis, R. A. (1980). Emotional intimacy among men. In T. M. Skovholt, P. G. Schauble, & R. Davis (Eds.), *Counseling men*. Monterey, CA: Brooks/Cole.

Lindeman, R. H., Merenda, P. F., & Gold, R. Z. (1980). *Introduction to bivariate and multivariate analysis*. Glenview, IL: Scott, Foresman & Company.

Lippa, R. (1977). Androgyny, sex-typing, and the perception of masculinity-femininity in handwritings. *Journal of Research in Personality*, **11**, 21–37.

Lippa, R., & Beauvais, C. (1983). Gender jeopardy: The effects of gender, assessed femininity and masculinity, and false success/failure feedback on performance in an experimental quiz game. *Journal of Personality and Social Psychology*, **44**, 344–353.

Locksley, A., & Colten, M. E. (1979). Psychological androgyny: A case of mistaken identity? *Journal of Personality and Social Psychology*, **37**, 1017–1031.

Logan, D. D., & Kaschak, E. (1980). The relationship of sex, sex role, and mental health. *Psychology of Women Quarterly*, **4**, 573–580.

Lohr, J. M., & Nix, J. (1982). Relationship of assertiveness and the short form of the Bem Sex-Role Inventory: A replication. *Psychological Reports*, **50**, 114.

Lombardo, J. P., & Lavine, L. O. (1981). Sex-role stereotyping and patterns of self-disclosure. *Sex Roles*, **7**, 403–411.

Long, V. O. (1982). Ending the perpetuation of sex-role stereotypes in our schools: A possible consequence of psychological androgyny. *Psychology in the Schools*, **19**, 250–254.

Lorr, M., & Diorio, M. (1978). Analysis and abbreviation of Bem's Sex-Role Inventory. *Psychological Reports*, **43**, 879–882.

Lorr, M., & Manning, T. T. (1978). Personality correlates of the sex role types. *Journal of Clinical Psychology*, **34**, 884–888.

Lubinski, D. (1983). The androgyny dimension: A comment on Stokes, Childs, and Fuehrer. *Journal of Counseling Psychology*, **30**, 130–133.

Lubinski, D., Tellegen, A., & Butcher, J. N. (1981). The relationship between androgyny and subjective indicators of well-being. *Journal of Personality and Social Psychology*, **40**, 722–730.

Lubinski, D., Tellegen, A., & Butcher, J. N. (1983). Masculinity, femininity, and androgyny viewed and assessed as distinct concepts. *Journal of Personality and Social Psychology*, **44**, 428–439.

Lunneborg, P. W. (1972). Dimensionality of MF. *Journal of Clinical Psychology*, **28**, 313–317.

Maccoby, E. E., & Jacklin, C. N. (1974). *The psychology of sex differences*. Stanford, CA: Stanford University Press.

Major, B. (1979). Sex-role orientation and fear of success: Clarifying an unclear relationship. *Sex Roles*, **5**, 63–70.

Major, B., Carnevale, P. J. D., & Deaux, K. (1981). A different perspective on androgyny: Evaluations of masculine and feminine personality characteristics. *Journal of Personality and Social Psychology*, **41**, 988–1001.

Maloney, P., Wilkof, J., & Dambrot, F. (1981). Androgyny across two cultures: United States and Israel. *Journal of Cross-Cultural Psychology*, **12**, 95–102.

Marecek, J. (1979). Social change, positive mental health, and psychological androgyny. *Psychology of Women Quarterly*, **3**, 241–247.

Marecek, J., & Kravetz, D. (1977). Women and mental health: A review of feminist change efforts. *Psychiatry*, **40**, 323–329.

Marino, T. M. (1979). Resensitizing men: A male perspective. *Personnel and Guidance Journal*, **58**, 102–105.

Markus, H. (1977). Self-schemata and processing information about the self. *Journal of Personality and Social Psychology*, **35**, 63–78.

Markus, H., Crane, M., Bernstein, S., & Siladi, M. (1982). Self-schemas and gender. *Journal of Personality and Social Psychology*, **42**, 38–50.

Marlowe, M. (1979). The assessment and treatment of gender-disturbed boys by guidance counselors. *Personnel and Guidance Journal*, **58**, 128–132.

Marshall, S. J., & Wijting, J. P. (1980). Relationships of achievement motivation and sex-role identity to college women's career orientation. *Journal of Vocational Behavior*, **16**, 299–311.

Marwit, S. J. (1981). Assessment of sex-role stereotyping among male and female psychologist practitioners. *Journal of Personality Assessment*, **45**, 593–599.

McPherson, K. S., & Spetrino, S. K. (1983). Androgyny and sex-typing: Differences in beliefs regarding gender polarity in ratings of ideal men and women. *Sex Roles*, **9**, 441–451.

Meinecke, C. E. (1981). Socialized to die younger? Hypermasculinity and men's health. *Personnel and Guidance Journal*, **60**, 241–245.

Meyerowitz, B. E. (1981). The impact of mastectomy on the lives of women. *Professional Psychology*, **12**, 118–127.

Millimet, C. R., & Votta, R. P. (1979). Acquiescence and the Bem Sex-Role Inventory. *Journal of Personality Assessment*, **43**, 164–165.

Mills, C. J. (1983). Sex-typing and self-schemata effects on memory and response latency. *Journal of Personality and Social Psychology*, **45**, 163–172.

Mills, C. J., & Bohannon, W. E. (1983). Personality, sex-role orientation, and psychological health in stereotypically masculine groups of males. *Sex Roles*, **9**, 1161–1169.

Mills, C. J., & Tyrrell, D. J. (1983). Sex-stereotypic encoding and release from proactive interference. *Journal of Personality and Social Psychology*, **45**, 772–781.

Minnigerode, F. A. (1976). Attitudes toward women, sex-role stereotyping and locus of control. *Psychological Reports*, **38**, 1301–1302.

Mischel, W. (1970). Sex-typing and socialization. In P. E. Mussen (Ed.), *Carmichael's manual of child psychology*, Vol. 2, 3rd ed. New York: Wiley.

Money, J., & Ehrhardt, A. (1972). *Man and woman, boy and girl*. Baltimore: Johns Hopkins University Press.

Money, J., & Tucker, P. (1975). *Sexual signatures*. Boston: Little, Brown and Company.

Moreland, J. (1980). Age and change in the adult male sex role. *Sex Roles*, **6**, 807–818.

Moreland, J. R., Harren, V. A., Krimsky-Montague, E., & Tinsley, H. E. A. (1979). Sex role self-concept and career decision making. *Journal of Counseling Psychology*, **26**, 329–336.

Motowidlo, S. J. (1982). Sex role orientation and behavior in a work setting. *Journal of Personality and Social Psychology*, **42**, 935–945.

Mussen, P. H. (1962). Long-term consequents of masculinity and interests in adolescence. *Journal of Consulting Psychology*, **26**, 435–440.

Mussen, P. H. (1969). Early sex-role development. In D. A. Goslin (Ed.), *Handbook of socialization theory and research*. Chicago: Rand McNally.

Myers, A. M., & Gonda, G. (1982). Empirical validation of the Bem Sex-Role Inventory. *Journal of Personality and Social Psychology*, **43**, 304–318.

Myers, A. M., & Lips, H. M. (1978). Participation in competitive amateur sports as a function of psychological androgyny. *Sex Roles*, **4**, 571–578.

Nadler, A., Maler, S., & Friedman, A. (1984). Effects of helper's sex, subjects' androgyny, and self-evaluation on males' and females' willingness to seek and receive help. *Sex Roles*, **10**, 327–339.

Narus, L. R., & Fischer, J. L. (1982). Strong but not silent: A re-examination of expressivity in the relationships of men. *Sex Roles*, **8**, 159–168.

Neimeyer, G. J., Banikiotes, P. G., & Merluzzi, T. V. (1981). Cognitive mediation of sex-role orientation. *Social Behavior and Personality*, **9**, 49–52.

Nettles, E. J., & Loevinger, J. (1983). Sex role expectations and ego level in relation to problem marriages. *Journal of Personality and Social Psychology*, **45**, 676–687.

Nix, J., & Lohr, J. M. (1981). Relationship between sex, sex-role characteristics and coronary-prone behavior in college students. *Psychological Reports*, **48**, 739–744.

Nix, J., Lohr, J. M., & Stauffacher, R. (1980). Relationship of sex, sex-role orientation and a self-report measure of assertiveness in college students. *Psychological Reports*, **47**, 1239–1244.

O'Connor, K., Mann, D. W., & Bardwick, J. M. (1978). Androgyny and self-esteem in the upper-middle class: A replication of Spence. *Journal of Consulting and Clinical Psychology*, **46**, 1168–1169.

Odenwald, R. P. (1965). *The disappearing sexes*. New York: Random House.

Olds, D. E., & Shaver, P. (1980). Masculinity, femininity, academic performance, and health: Further evidence concerning the androgyny controversy. *Journal of Personality*, **48**, 323–341.

Olds, L. (1981). *Fully human*. Englewood Cliffs, NJ: Prentice-Hall.

Olejnik, A. B., Tompkins, B., & Heinbuck, C. (1982). Sex differences, sex-role orientation, and reward allocations. *Sex Roles*, **8**, 711–719.

O'Neil, J. M. (1981a). Male sex role conflicts, sexism, and masculinity: Psychological implications for men, women, and the counseling psychologist. *Counseling Psychologist*, **9**, 61–80.

O'Neil, J. M. (1981b). Patterns of gender role conflict and strain: The fear of femininity in men's lives. *Personnel and Guidance Journal*, **60**, 203–210.

O'Neil, J. M., Ohlde, C., Barke, C., Gelwick, B. P., & Garfield, N. (1980). Research on a workshop to reduce the effects of sexism and sex role socialization on women's career planning. *Journal of Counseling Psychology*, **27**, 355–363.

Orlofsky, J. L. (1977). Sex-role orientation, identity formation and self-esteem in college men and women. *Sex Roles*, **3**, 561–575.

Orlofsky, J. L. (1981a). A comparison of projective and objective fear-of-success and sex-role orientation measures as predictors of women's performance on masculine and feminine tasks. *Sex Roles*, **7**, 999–1018.

Orlofsky, J. L. (1981b). Relationships between sex role attitudes and personality traits and the sex role behavior scale-1: A new measure of masculine and feminine role behaviors and interests. *Journal of Personality and Social Psychology*, **40**, 927–940.

Orlofsky, J. L. (1982). Psychological androgyny, sex-typing, and sex-role ideology as predictors of male-female interpersonal attraction. *Sex Roles*, **8**, 1057–1073.

Orlofsky, J. L., Aslin, A. L., & Ginsburg, S. D. (1977). Differential effectiveness of two classification procedures on the Bem Sex Role Inventory. *Journal of Personality Assessment*, **41**, 414–416.

Orlofsky, J. L., Ramsden, M. W., & Cohen, R. S. (1982). Development of the revised Sex-Role Behavior Scale. *Journal of Personality Assessment*, **46**, 632–638.

Orlofsky, J. L., & Windle, M. T. (1978). Sex-role orientation, behavioral adaptability and personal adjustment. *Sex Roles*, **4**, 801–811.

Osofsky, J. D., & Osofsky, H. J. (1972). Androgyny as a life style. *The Family Coordinator*, **21**, 411–418.

Parsons, J. E. (1980). Psychosexual neutrality: Is anatomy destiny? In J. E. Parsons (Ed.), *The psychobiology of sex differences and sex roles*. Washington, DC: Hemisphere Publishing Corporation.

Parsons, T., & Bales, R. F. (1953). *Family, socialization, and interaction process*. New York: Free Press.

Pasquella, M. J., Mednick, M. T. S., & Murray, S. R. (1981). Causal attributions for achievement outcomes: Sex-role identity, sex and outcome comparisons. *Psychology of Women Quarterly*, **5**, 586–590.

Pedhazur, E. J., & Tetenbaum, T. J. (1979). Bem Sex Role Inventory: A theoretical and methodological critique. *Journal of Personality and Social Psychology*, **37**, 996–1016.

Penick, E. C., Powell, B. J., & Read, M. R. (1984). Sex-role affiliation among male alcoholics. *Journal of Clinical Psychology*, **40**, 359–363.

Petersen, A. C. (1980). Biopsychosocial processes in the development of sex-related differences. In J. E. Parsons (Ed.), *The psychobiology of sex differences and sex roles*. Washington, DC: Hemisphere Publishing Corporation.

Piel, E. R. (1977). *Sex and careers: Relationships between sex typing and differences on career-related variables for men and women*. Unpublished doctoral dissertation, University of Iowa.

Piel, E. R. (1979, September). *Androgyny: The construct and its assessment*. Paper presented at the annual meeting of the American Psychological Association, New York.

Pleck, J. H. (1975). Masculinity-femininity: Current and alternative paradigms. *Sex Roles*, **1**, 161–178.

Pleck, J. H. (1977). The work-family role system. *Social Problems*, **24**, 417–427.

Powell, B. J., Penick, E. C., & Read, M. R. (1980). Psychological adjustment and sex-role affiliation in an alcoholic population. *Journal of Clinical Psychology*, **36**, 801–805.

Powell, G. N. (1979, September). *Factor of the BSRI revisited: A comprehensive study*. Paper presented at the annual meeting of the American Psychological Association, New York.

Puglisi, J. T. (1980). Equating the social desirability of Bem Sex-Role Inventory Masculinity and Femininity subscales. *Journal of Personality Assessment*, **44**, 272–276.

Pursell, S., Banikiotes, P. G., & Sebastian, R. J. (1981). Androgyny and the perception of marital roles. *Sex Roles*, **7**, 201–215.

Ratliff, E. S., & Conley, J. (1981). The structure of masculinity-femininity: Multidimensionality and gender differences. *Social Behavior and Personality*, 9, 41–47.

Rawlings, E. I., & Carter, D. K. (Eds.). (1977). *Psychotherapy for women: Treatment toward equality*. Springfield, IL: Charles C Thomas.

Rebecca, M., Hefner, R., & Oleshansky, B. (1976). A model of sex-role transcendence. *Journal of Social Issues*, 32, 197–206.

Rekers, G. A. (1977). Atypical gender development and psychosocial adjustment. *Journal of Applied Behavior Analysis*, 10, 559–571.

Rekers, G. A., Bentler, P. M., Rosen, A. C., & Lovaas, O. I. (1977). Child gender disturbances: A clinical rationale for intervention. *Psychotherapy: Theory, Research, and Practice*, 14, 2–11.

Rekers, G. A., Rosen, A. C., Lovaas, O. I., & Bentler, P. M. (1978). Sex-role stereotypy and professional intervention for childhood gender disturbances. *Professional Psychology*, 9, 127–136.

Remer, P., & Ross, E. (1982). The counselor's role in creating a school environment that fosters androgyny. *School Counselor*, 30, 4–14.

Richardson, M. S., Merrifield, P., & Jacobson, S. (1979, September). *A factor analytic study of the Bem Sex Role Inventory*. Paper presented at the annual meeting of the American Psychological Association, New York.

Richardson, M. S., Merrifield, P., Jacobsen, S., Evanoski, P., Hobish, T. T., & Goldstein, E. (1980). *The factor structure of the Bem Sex Role Inventory: A methodological inquiry and theoretical implications*. Unpublished paper, 1980.

Ridley, C. A., Lamke, L. K., Avery, A. W., & Harrell, J. E. (1982). The effects of interpersonal skills training on sex-role identity of premarital dating partners. *Journal of Research in Personality*, 16, 335–342.

Roe, M. D., & Prange, M. E. (1982). On quantifying the magnitude of sex-role endorsement. *Journal of Personality Assessment*, 46, 300–303.

Rosen, A. C., & Rekers, G. A. (1980). Toward a taxonomic framework for variables of sex and gender. *Genetic Psychology Monographs*, 102, 191–218.

Rosen, A. C., Rekers, G. A., & Friar, L. R. (1977). Theoretical and diagnostic issues in child gender disturbances. *Journal of Sex Research*, 13, 89–103.

Rosenkrantz, P. S. Vogel, S. R., Bee, H., Broverman, I. K., & Broverman, D. M. (1968). Sex role stereotypes and self-concepts in college students. *Journal of Consulting and Clinical Psychology*, 32, 287–295.

Rossi, A. (1976). Sex equality: The beginnings of ideology. In A. G. Kaplan & J. P. Bean (Eds.), *Beyond sex-role stereotypes: Readings toward a psychology of androgyny*. Boston: Little, Brown.

Rotheram, M. J., & Weiner, N. (1983). Androgyny, stress, and satisfaction: Dual-career and traditional relationships. *Sex Roles*, 9, 151–158.

Rotter, J. B. (1966). Generalized expectancies for internal versus external control of reinforcement. *Psychological Monographs*, 80, 609.

Rotter, N. G., & O'Connell, A. N. (1982). The relationships among sex-role orientation, cognitive complexity, and tolerance for ambiguity. *Sex Roles*, 8, 1209–1220.

Rowland, R. (1977). The Bem Sex-Role Inventory. *Australian Psychologist*, 12, 83–88.

Rowland, R. (1980). The Bem Sex-Role Inventory and its measurement of androgyny. *Australian Psychologist*, 15, 449–457.

Ruch, L. O. (1984). Dimensionality of the Bem Sex-Role Inventory: A multidimensional analysis. *Sex Roles*, 10, 99–117.

Russell, G. (1978). The father role and its relation to masculinity, femininity, and androgyny. *Child Development*, 49, 1174–1181.

Safilios-Rothschild, C. (Ed.). (1972). *Toward a sociology of women*. Lexington, MA: Xerox College Publishing.

Sampson, E. E. (1977). Psychology and the American ideal. *Journal of Personality and Social Psychology*, **35**, 767–782.

Sappenfield, B. R., & Harris, C. L. (1975). Self-reported masculinity-femininity as related to self-esteem. *Psychological Reports*, **37**, 669–670.

Sargent, A. G. (1977). *Beyond sex roles*. St. Paul, MN: West Publishing Company.

Sargent, A. G. (1979). Developing basic skills and knowledge. *Training and Development Journal*, **33**, 72–76.

Sassenrath, J. M., & Yonge, G. D. (1979). The Bem Sex-Role Inventory re-examined. *Psychological Reports*, **45**, 935–941.

Scanzoni, J. H. (1975). *Sex roles, life styles, and childbearing: Changing patterns in marriage and the family*. New York: The Free Press.

Scanzoni, J. (1977). Changing sex roles and emerging directions in family decision-making. *Journal of Consumer Research*, **4**, 185–188.

Scher, M. (1979). On counseling men. *Personnel and Guidance Journal*, **57**, 252–255.

Scher, M. (1981). Men in hiding: A challenge for the counselor. *Personnel and Guidance Journal*, **60**, 199–202.

Schiff, E., & Koopman, E. S. (1978). The relationship of women's sex-role identity to self-esteem and ego development. *Journal of Psychology*, **98**, 299–305.

Sedney, M. A. (1981). Comments on median split procedures for scoring androgyny measures. *Sex Roles*, **7**, 217–222.

Segal, M., & Richman, S. (1978). The Bem Sex-Role Inventory: A north-south comparison. *Psychological Reports*, **43**, 183–186.

Senneker, P., & Hendrick, C. (1983). Androgyny and helping behavior. *Journal of Personality and Social Psychology*, **45**, 916–925.

Shaw, J. S. (1982). Psychological androgyny and stressful life events. *Journal of Personality and Social Psychology*, **43**, 145–153.

Shaw, J. S., & Rodriguez, W. (1981). Birth order and sex-type. *Psychological Reports*, **48**, 387–390.

Sherman, J. A. (1976). Social values, femininity, and the development of female competence. *Journal of Social Issues*, **32**, 181–195.

Silvern, L. E., & Ryan, V. L. (1979). Self-rated adjustment and sex-typing on the Bem Sex-Role Inventory: Is masculinity the primary predictor of adjustment? *Sex Roles*, **5**, 739–763.

Silvern, L. E., & Ryan, V. L. (1983). A re-examination of masculine and feminine sex-role ideals and conflicts among ideals for the man, woman, and person. *Sex Roles*, **9**, 1223–1248.

Skovholt, T. M. (1978). Feminism and men's lives. *Counseling Psychologist*, **7**, 3–9.

Skovholt, T. M., & Hansen, A. (1980). Men's development: A perspective and some themes. In T. M. Skovholt, P. G. Schauble, & R. Davis (Eds.), *Counseling men*. Menlo Park, CA: Brooks-Cole.

Skovholt, T. M., & Morgan, J. I. (1981). Career development: An outline of issues for men. *Personnel and Guidance Journal*, **60**, 231–237.

Small, A. C., Erdwins, C., & Gross, R. B. (1979). A comparison of the Bem Sex-Role Inventory and the Heilbrun masculinity and femininity scales. *Journal of Personality Assessment*, **43**, 393–395.

Sobel, S. B., & Russo, N. F. (Eds.). (1981). Sex roles, equality, and mental health. *Professional Psychology*, **12**.

Spence, J. T. (1983). Comment on Lubinski, Tellegen, and Butcher's "Masculinity, Femininity, and Androgyny Viewed and Assessed as Distinct Concepts." *Journal of Personality and Social Psychology*, **44**, 440–446.

Spence, J. T., & Helmreich, R. L. (1978). *Masculinity and femininity: Their psychological dimensions, correlates, and antecedents*. Austin: University of Texas Press.

Spence, J. T., & Helmreich, R. L. (1979a). Comparison of masculine and feminine personality attributes and sex-role attitudes across age groups. *Developmental Psychology*, **15**, 583–584.

Spence, J. T., & Helmreich, R. L. (1979b). The many faces of androgyny: A reply to Locksley and Colten. *Journal of Personality and Social Psychology*, **37**, 1032–1046.

Spence, J. T., & Helmreich, R. L. (1979c). On assessing "androgyny." *Sex Roles*, **5**, 721–738.

Spence, J. T., & Helmreich, R. L. (1980). Masculine instrumentality and feminine expressiveness: Their relationships with sex role attitudes and behaviors. *Psychology of Women Quarterly*, **5**, 147–163.

Spence, J. T., & Helmreich, R. L. (1981). Androgyny versus gender schema: A comment on Bem's gender schema theory. *Psychological Review*, **88**, 365–368.

Spence, J. T., Helmreich, R. L., & Holahan, C. K. (1979). Negative and positive components of psychological masculinity and femininity and their relationships to self-reports of neurotic and acting out behaviors. *Journal of Personality and Social Psychology*, **37**, 1673–1682.

Spence, J. T., Helmreich, R., & Stapp, J. (1974). The Personal Attributes Questionnaire: A measure of sex role stereotypes and masculinity-femininity. *JSAS Catalog of Selected Documents in Psychology*, **4**, 43. (MS No. 617).

Spence, J. T., Helmreich, R., & Stapp, J. (1975). Ratings of self and peers on sex role attributes and their relation to self-esteem and conceptions of masculinity and femininity. *Journal of Personality and Social Psychology*, **32**, 29–39.

Spillman, B., Spillman, R., & Reinking, K. (1981). Leadership emergence: Dynamic analysis of the effects of sex and androgyny. *Small Group Behavior*, **12**, 139–157.

Stake, J. E., & Orlofsky, J. L. (1981). On the use of global and specific measures in assessing the self-esteem of males and females. *Sex Roles*, **7**, 653–661.

Stericker, A. B., & Kurdek, L. A. (1982). Dimensions and correlates of third through eighth graders' sex-role self-concepts. *Sex Roles*, **8**, 915–929.

Stokes, J., Childs, L., & Fuehrer, A. (1981). Gender and sex roles as predictors of self-disclosure. *Journal of Counseling Psychology*, **28**, 510–514.

Storms, M. E. (1979). Sex role identity and its relationships to sex role attributes and sex role stereotypes. *Journal of Personality and Social Psychology*, **37**, 1779–1789.

Strahan, R. F. (1975). Remarks on Bem's measurement of psychological androgyny: Alternative methods and a supplementary analysis. *Journal of Consulting and Clinical Psychology*, **43**, 568–571.

Taylor, D. (1981). Social desirability and the Bem Sex-Role Inventory. *Psychological Reports*, **48**, 503–506.

Taylor, M. C., & Hall, J. A. (1982). Psychological androgyny: Theories, methods, and conclusions. *Psychological Bulletin*, **92**, 347–366.

Thomas, D. A., & Reznikoff, M. (1984). Sex role orientation, personality structure, and adjustment in women. *Journal of Personality Assessment*, **48**, 28–36.

Tinsley, H. E. A., Kass, R. A., Moreland, J. R., & Harren, V. A. (1983). A longitudinal study of female college students' occupational decision making. *Vocational Guidance Quarterly*, **32**, 89–102.

Tittle, C. K. (1983). Studies of the effects of career interest inventories: Expanding outcome criteria to include women's experiences. *Journal of Vocational Behavior*, **22**, 148–158.

Toomer, J. E. (1980). Males in psychotherapy. In T. M. Skovholt, P. G. Schauble, & R. Davis (Eds.), *Counseling men*. Monterey, CA: Brooks-Cole.

Tunnell, G. (1981). Sex role and cognitive schemata: Person perception in feminine and androgynous women. *Journal of Personality and Social Psychology*, **40**, 1126–1136.

Tyer, Z. E., & Erdwins, C. J. (1979). Relationship of sex role to male- and female-dominated professions. *Psychological Reports*, **44**, 1134.

Tzuriel, D. (1984). Sex role typing and ego identity in Israeli, Oriental, and Western adolescents. *Journal of Personality and Social Psychology*, **46**, 440–457.

Unger, R. K. (1976). Male is greater than female: The socialization of status inequality. *Counseling Psychologist*, **6**, 2–9.

Unger, R. K. (1979). *Female and male: Psychological perspectives*. New York: Harper and Row.

Vandever, J. (1977). Sex typing and androgyny: An empirical study. *Psychological Reports*, **40**, 602.

Vandever, J. (1978). Nursing students: Stereotypically feminine. *Psychological Reports*, **43**, 10.

Vedovato, S., & Vaughter, R. M. (1980). Psychology of women courses changing sexist and sex-typed attitudes. *Psychology of Women Quarterly*, **4**, 587–590.

Vetter, L. (1973). Career counseling for women. *The Counseling Psychologist*, **4**, 54–66.

Volentine, S. Z. (1981). The assessment of masculinity and femininity: Scale 5 of the MMPI compared with the BSRI and the PAQ. *Journal of Clinical Psychology*, **37**, 367–374.

Wade, L. A., Wade, J. E., & Croteau, J. M. (1983). The man and the male: A creative outreach program on men's roles. *Journal of College Student Personnel*, **24**, 460–461.

Waddell, F. T. (1983). Factors affecting choice, satisfaction, and success in the female self-employed. *Journal of Vocational Behavior*, **23**, 294–304.

Wakefield, J. A., Sasek, J., Friedman, A. F., & Bowden, J. D. (1976). Androgyny and other measures of masculinity-femininity. *Journal of Consulting and Clinical Psychology*, **44**, 766–770.

Walker, L. E. (1981). Battered women: Sex roles and clinical issues. *Professional Psychology*, **12**, 81–91.

Walkup, H., & Abbott, R. D. (1978). Cross-validation of item selection on the Bem Sex Role Inventory. *Applied Psychological Measurement*, **2**, 63–71.

Washington, C. S. (1979). Men counseling men: Redefining the male machine. *Personnel and Guidance Journal*, **57**, 462–463.

Waters, C. W., Waters, L. K., & Pincus, S. (1977). Factor analysis of masculine and feminine sex-typed items from the Bem Sex-Role Inventory. *Psychological Reports*, **40**, 567–570.

Weissman, M. M., & Klerman, G. L. (1979). Sex differences and the epidemiology of depression. In E. S. Gomberg & V. Franks (Eds.), *Gender and disordered behavior: Sex differences in psychopathology*. New York: Brunner/Mazel.

Weitz, S. (1977). *Sex roles: Biological, psychological, and social foundations*. New York: Oxford University Press.

Welch, R. L. (1979). Androgyny and derived identity in married women with varying degrees of non-traditional role involvement. *Psychology of Women Quarterly*, **3**, 308–315.

Welch, R. L., & Huston, A. C. (1982). Effects of induced success/failure and attributions on the problem-solving behavior of psychologically androgynous and feminine women. *Journal of Personality*, **50**, 81–97.

Wells, K. (1980). Gender-role identity and psychological adjustment in adolescence. *Journal of Youth and Adolescence*, **9**, 59–73.

Wesley, F., & Wesley, C. (1977). *Sex-role psychology*. New York: Human Sciences Press.

Wetter, R. C. (1975, August). *Levels of self-esteem associated with four sex role categories.* Paper presented at the annual meeting of the American Psychological Association, Chicago.

Wheeler, L., Reis, H., & Nezlek, J. (1983). Loneliness, social interaction, and sex roles. *Journal of Personality and Social Psychology, 45,* 943–953.

Whetton, C., & Swindells, T. (1977). A factor analysis of the Bem Sex-Role Inventory. *Journal of Clinical Psychology, 33,* 150–153.

Whiteley, R. M. (1973). Women in groups. *The Counseling Psychologist, 4,* 27–43.

Whitley, B. E. (1983). Sex role orientation and self-esteem: A critical meta-analytic review. *Journal of Personality and Social Psychology, 44,* 765–785.

Wiggins, J. S., & Holzmuller, A. (1978). Psychological androgyny and interpersonal behavior. *Journal of Consulting and Clinical Psychology, 46,* 40–52.

Wiggins, J. S., & Holzmuller, A. (1981). Further evidence on androgyny and interpersonal flexibility. *Journal of Research in Personality, 15,* 67–80.

Williams, S. W., & McCullers, J. C. (1983). Personal factors related to typicalness of career and success in active professional women. *Psychology of Women Quarterly, 7,* 343–357.

Williams, J. M., & Miller, D. M. (1983). Sex-role orientation and athletic administration. *Sex Roles, 9,* 1137–1148.

Wilson, F. R. (1980, April). *If you say you're androgynous, how can I tell?* Paper presented at the annual meeting of the American Educational Research Association, Boston.

Wilson, F. R., & Cook, E. P. (1984). Concurrent validity of four androgyny instruments. *Sex Roles, 11,* 813–837.

Wolfe, L. K., & Betz, N. E. (1981). Traditionality of choice and sex-role identification as moderators of the congruence of occupational choice in college women. *Journal of Vocational Behavior, 18,* 43–55.

Wolff, L., & Taylor, S. E. (1979). Sex, sex-role identification, and awareness of sex-role stereotypes. *Journal of Personality, 47,* 177–184.

Worell, J. (1978). Sex roles and psychological well-being: Perspectives on methodology. *Journal of Consulting and Clinical Psychology, 46,* 777–791.

Worell, J. (1980). New directions in counseling women. *Personnel and Guidance Journal, 58,* 477–484.

Yager, G. G., & Baker, S. (1979, September). *Thoughts on androgyny for the counseling psychologist.* A paper presented at the annual meeting of the American Psychological Association, New York.

Yanico, B. J. (1981). Sex-role self-concept and attitudes related to occupational daydreams and future fantasies of college women. *Journal of Vocational Behavior, 19,* 290–301.

Yanico, B. J. (1982). Androgyny and occupational sex-stereotyping of college students. *Psychological Reports, 50,* 875–878.

Yanico, B. J., & Hardin, S. I. (1981). Sex-role self-concept and persistence in a traditional versus nontraditional college major for women. *Journal of Vocational Behavior, 18,* 219–227.

Yanico, B. J., Hardin, S. I., & McLaughlin, K. B. (1978). Androgyny and traditional versus nontraditional major choices among college freshmen. *Journal of Vocational Behavior, 12,* 261–269.

Yoder, J. D., Rice, R. W., Adams, J., Priest, R. F., & Prince, H. T. (1982). Reliability of the Attitudes toward Women Scale (AWS) and the Personal Attributes Questionnaire. *Sex Roles, 8,* 651–657.

Zuckerman, M., DeFrank, R. S., Spiegel, N. H., & Larrance, D. T. (1982). Masculinity-femininity and encoding of nonverbal cues. *Journal of Personality and Social Psychology, 42,* 548–556.

AUTHOR INDEX

Abbott, R. D., 49
Abrahams, B., 92
Adams, C. H., 94, 114, 189
Adams, J., 51
Aiello, J. R., 110
Alagna, S. W., 91, 94, 110, 189
Alexander, D., 102, 189
Allgeier, E. R., 192
American Psychological Association, 154
Amstey, F. H., 119, 190
Andersen, S. M., 22, 83, 85, 94, 99, 110, 190
Antill, J. K., 93, 94, 108, 190, 191
Arkin, R. M., 190
Arnkoff, D. B., 190
Ashworth, C. D., 49
Aslin, A. L., 59, 88, 100, 108, 190
Astley, S. L., 94, 190
Atkinson, J., 87, 109, 189, 190
Avery, A. W., 167, 189

Babl, J. D., 100, 115, 189
Babladelis, G., 81, 191
Baird, J. G., 189
Bakan, D., 4, 18, 22
Baker, S., 21, 24, 96, 155
Bales, R. F., 4
Bander, R. S., 53
Bandura, A., 8, 9
Banikiotes, P. G., 83, 99, 157, 190, 191
Bankart, C. P., 190
Bardwick, J., 7, 64, 108, 170, 171, 173, 180, 191
Barke, C., 167
Barnes, S., 94, 189
Barnet, K., 110
Barnett, R., 16
Baruch, G., 16
Basow, S. A., 3
Bassett, J. S., 94, 189
Bassoff, E. S., 54, 61, 94, 115, 116, 189
Batlis, N., 72

Baucom, D. H., 45, 46, 51, 52, 53, 63, 76, 94, 99, 100, 101, 102, 103, 110, 118, 189, 190
Baxter, L. A., 101, 190
Bean, J. P., 6, 17, 19, 156, 172
Beane, W. E., 189
Bear, S., 156, 158, 159
Beauvais, C., 87, 91, 111
Beckman, L. J., 94, 102, 117, 191
Bee, H., 4, 41
Bell, N. J., 109, 190
Bem, S. L., 3, 18, 20, 21, 22, 23, 25, 26, 27, 28, 31, 32, 40, 41, 49, 50, 51, 52, 53, 55, 57, 58, 60, 73, 79, 80, 82, 83, 84, 85, 93, 94, 97, 98, 99, 100, 101, 102, 103, 105, 108, 110, 114, 136, 138, 139, 151, 154, 172, 189, 190, 191
Bennett, B. W., 167
Bentler, P. M., 168
Berg, J. H., 189, 191
Berger, M., 156, 159
Bergin, A. E., 168
Bernard, L., 60, 75, 88, 96, 192
Bernstein, S., 26, 83, 99, 100, 101, 103, 138, 190
Berzins, J. I., 43, 44, 51, 52, 53, 63, 64, 66, 72, 73, 74, 88, 93, 94, 99, 100, 101, 102, 114, 117, 190, 191, 192
Betz, N. E., 53, 190
Biaggio, M. K., 115
Biringen, Z. C., 73, 140, 190
Biscardi, D. L., 93, 190
Black, K. N., 114, 191
Block, J., 111, 113
Block, J. H., 6, 18, 111, 113, 119, 190
Blum, M. W., 109, 189
Bohannon, W. E., 75, 89, 99
Borland, L., 166
Boudreau, F., 58, 93, 108, 109, 190, 191
Bowden, J. D., 75
Brehony, K. A., 101, 110, 114, 191
Brewer, M. B., 109, 189

SUBJECT INDEX

ABOUT THE AUTHOR

Ellen Piel Cook is coordinator and associate professor of Counselor Education at the University of Cincinnati. She received her Ph.D. in counseling psychology from the University of Iowa in 1977. Her major areas of interest are sex roles and career development.

Pergamon General Psychology Series

Editors: Arnold P. Goldstein, Syracuse University
Leonard Krasner, SUNY at Stony Brook